# COUNTERING THE FINANCING OF TERRORISM

Good Practices to Enhance Effectiveness

**Editor**
**CHADY EL KHOURY**

© 2023 International Monetary Fund
Cover design: IMF CSF Creative Solutions Division

**Cataloging-in-Publication Data**
**IMF Library**

Names: El Khoury, Chady, editor. | International Monetary Fund, publisher.
Title: Countering the financing of terrorism : good practices to enhance effectiveness / Editor Chady El Khoury.
Other titles: Good practices to enhance effectiveness.
Description: Washington, DC : International Monetary Fund, 2023. | Includes bibliographical references.
Identifiers:
    9798400204654   (paper)
    9798400208331   (ePub)
    9798400208447   (PDF)
Subjects: LCSH: Terrorism—Finance—Prevention. | Terrorism—Finance—International cooperation.
Classification: LCC HV6431.C6 2023

> **Disclaimer:** The views expressed in this book are those of the authors and do not necessarily represent the views of the IMF's Executive Directors, its management, or any of its members. The boundaries, colors, denominations, and any other information shown on the maps do not imply, on the part of the International Monetary Fund, any judgment on the legal status of any territory or any endorsement or acceptance of such boundaries. All information presented herein is accurate as of press date.

Recommended citation: El Khoury, Chady, ed. 2023. *Countering the Financing of Terrorism: Good Practices to Enhance Effectiveness.* Washington, DC: International Monetary Fund.

ISBN: 9798400204654 (paper)
    9798400208331 (ePub)
    9798400208447 (PDF)

Please send orders to:
International Monetary Fund, Publication Services
P.O. Box 92780, Washington, D.C. 20090, U.S.A.
Tel.: (202) 623-7430 Fax: (202) 623-7201
E-mail: publications@imf.org
Internet: www.elibrary.imf.org
www.bookstore.imf.org

©International Monetary Fund. Not for Redistribution

# Contents

| | | |
|---|---|---|
| Foreword | | v |
| Preface | | vii |
| Acknowledgments | | ix |
| Authors | | xi |
| Abbreviations | | xv |
| Introduction | | xvii |
| 1 | Understanding Terrorist Financing Risk<br>*Steve Dawe* | 1 |
| 2 | The Role of the Private Sector in Detecting and Disrupting Terrorist Financing Activities<br>*Arz Murr, Terence Donovan, and Yee Man Yu* | 41 |
| 3 | The Production and Use of Financial Intelligence to Counter Terrorism and Terrorist Financing<br>*Sabrina Lando and Marilyne Landry* | 63 |
| 4 | Investigating, Prosecuting, and Sanctioning Terrorist Financiers<br>*Giuseppe Lombardo and Chady El Khoury* | 89 |
| 5 | Terrorism-Related Targeted Financial Sanctions<br>*Jay Purcell, Delphine Schantz, and Jacqueline Shire* | 113 |
| 6 | International Cooperation in Combating the Financing of Terrorism<br>*Kathleen Kao, Jean-Paul Laborde, Paul Riordan, Dermot Brauders, Hyung Keun Yoon, Miguel Angel Garcia, and Nedko Krumov* | 153 |
| Index | | 179 |

# Foreword

The need to tackle terrorist financing has been a priority for the international community for the last two decades. Terrorist attacks are a threat in many parts of the world and intensify in zones of conflict. Incidents of terrorism may undermine the stability of a country's economy and could bring losses for the economy, e.g., triggered by uncertainties and loss of confidence. Terrorism can also directly target key sectors of the economy, as did the attacks in New York City in 2001 and Paris in November 2015, which affected the financial markets, tourism, and the broader economy. Furthermore, a country's economic stability may be at risk of countermeasures (such as listing by the Financial Action Task Force) and economic sanctions (including multilateral and bilateral sanctions) for significant shortcomings in its framework for fighting money laundering and terrorist financing, leading to pressures on correspondent banking relationships.

Terrorism and terrorist financing activities are most acute in fragile and conflict-affected states, which are home to nearly 1 billion people. Fragility of institutions and conflicts in these countries could lead to the growth of terrorist groups without deterrence and to an increase in the risk of terrorist financing activities without detection. Furthermore, terrorist attacks could magnify the fragility of the state.

Since 2001, the IMF has been contributing significantly to global and domestic efforts to suppress the financing of terrorism. We do this in the context of our broader efforts to enhance the integrity of the international financial system and prevent the abuse of national financial systems and economies, including by helping our member countries improve their anti-money laundering and combating the financing of terrorism (AML/CFT) systems.

Many IMF member countries face challenges when it comes to improving the effective implementation of their CFT frameworks. The objective of this book is to provide guidance to policy makers and practitioners of IMF members—specially in fragile and conflicted-affected states at higher risk of terrorist and terrorism financing—by assisting them in identifying key challenges and good practices in strengthening the effectiveness of CFT frameworks. It includes six chapters focusing on (1) improving the understanding of terrorist financing risk, (2) the role of the private sector in detecting and disrupting terrorist financing activities, (3) the production and use of terrorist financing financial intelligence to counter terrorism and terrorist financing, (4) investigating, prosecuting, and sanctioning terrorist financiers, (5) terrorism-related targeted financial sanctions (TFS), and (6) international cooperation in combating the financing of terrorism.

Ultimately, this book aims to help our member countries strengthen their economies and the integrity of their financial sectors, and mitigate the inherent risks resulting from terrorism and terrorist financing. We hope it will be a useful tool for countries to strengthen the effectiveness of their counter terrorism financing frameworks.

Bo Li
*Deputy Managing Director*
*International Monetary Fund*

# Preface

The IMF has long recognized the relevance of countering terrorism financing for the institution's mandate, and is actively working to provide advice to IMF member countries on enhancing the effectiveness of their frameworks in this critical area.

Robust combating financing of terrorism (CFT) frameworks are critically important for reinforcing safeguards that deny terrorists access to the financial system and hinder their ability to plan and carry out terrorist acts. The Fund has supported member countries' efforts in this area in the context of its overall engagement on anti-money laundering and combating the financing of terrorism (AML/CFT).

In addition to contributing to the global dialogue and policy design of the AML/CFT standards—in close partnership with the Financial Action Task Force (FATF)—the Fund plays a unique role in these efforts as an integral part of its core functions related to surveillance, lending, and capacity development. First, AML/CFT and financial integrity issues are an integral part of the economic dialogue with members. For example, in 2020, it engaged with 108 of its members on AML/CFT issues as part of the "Article IV consultation" discussions held generally annually with members, including members publicly listed by the FATF as having weak AML/CFT systems.[1] When appropriate, AML/CFT discussions also take place in the context of Fund-supported financing programs, with reforms in these areas being part of program conditionality where critical for the success of the country's economic program. Second, the Fund helps members strengthen their AML/CFT frameworks through an extensive capacity development program. Since 2002, technical assistance and training have been provided to more than 80 member countries, with many of the projects focused exclusively on CFT issues. Finally, the Fund assesses members against the FATF standard, including in every Financial Sector Assessment Program,[2] to identify strengths and weaknesses as well as to recommend corrective measures to enhance the effectiveness of the relevant AML/CFT regimes. So far, more than 75 such AML/CFT assessments have been led by the Fund since 2001.

I am grateful to the donors of the AML/CFT Thematic Trust Fund for their generous contribution to the production of this book, all the external reviewers

---

[1] For more about publicly listed jurisdictions, please refer to the FATF website: https://www.fatf-gafi.org/en/countries/black-and-grey-lists.html

[2] Current Fund policy requires timely and accurate input of AML/CFT information into every FSAP. FSAPs are mandatory for jurisdictions with systemically important financial sectors as part of the Fund's bilateral surveillance under Article IV of the Fund's Articles of Agreement, and voluntary for all other jurisdictions. Inclusion of AML/CFT issues in the FSAP process is intended to enable staff to incorporate financial integrity issues into broader financial sector reform efforts.

and contributors who shared their experiences with us, and the outstanding staff of the Legal Department, who continue to make important contributions on these important issues.

The book has been developed in coordination with other international and regional organizations, including the United Nations Office of Counter-Terrorism (UNOCT), the United Nations Security Council Counter-Terrorism Committee Executive Directorate (CTED), the United Nations 1267 Monitoring Team, the Egmont Group of Financial Intelligence Units, International Criminal Police Organization (INTERPOL), and Europol. The book has also benefited from the review of colleagues from the FATF Secretariat. The useful comments of external reviewers are gratefully acknowledged.

We hope this book contributes to the global fight against terrorist financing.

Rhoda Weeks-Brown
*General Counsel and Director of the Legal Department*
*International Monetary Fund*

# Acknowledgments

Thanks are due to the many experts in combating the financing of terrorism (CFT) who helped to produce the book.

The editors gratefully acknowledge input from CFT practitioners during the CFT experts meeting on the use of financial intelligence to support CFT efforts, held in Austria, Vienna from February 28 to March 1, 2019. Other experts involved were Salah Abed (Judge, Supreme Judicial Council), Mohamed Ahmed (Chief of Staff, Nigerian FIU), Saad Aljebren (Head of AML/CFT Department, Saudi Arabian Monetary Authority), Abdullah Alosaimi (Compliance Supervisor, Saudi Arabian Monetary Authority), Kelli Andrews (former Chief of Staff, National Security Division, US Department of Justice), Joe Boustany (Chief Compliance Officer, IBL BANK Group (Lebanon)), John Carlson (Head of Unit, FATF), Philippe De Koster (Director, CTIF-CFI), Johan Du Yoit (Advocate, Institute for Security Studies, Pretoria), Neil Everitt (Policy Analyst, FATF Secretariat), Andrew Finkelman (Justice Attaché, United States Embassy in Paris), Oliver Gadney (United Nations Office against Drugs and Crime), Mohamed Jama (Permanent Secretary, Ministry of Internal Security of Somalia), Tom Keatinge (Director, Royal United Services Institute), Hiroko Mori (Advisor to Executive Director, IMF), Marie-Laurence Navarri (Prosecutor, Prosecuting Office), Karen Parkes (Liaison Officer, AUSTRAC), Cédric Perruchot (Head of EU AML Regulatory Affairs, BNP Paribas), Muhammad Randy Ramadhan (Head of Section, National Counter-Terrorism Agency of Republic of Indonesia), Jill Rose (Counsel, Department of Justice), Victor Josef Sambuaga (Deputy Director, National Counter-Terrorism Agency of Republic of Indonesia), Christian Sanabria (Head of Analytics, Colombian FIU), Udyahitani Secundaputeri (Staff Director, National Counter-Terrorism Agency of Republic of Indonesia), and Melissa Tullis (Programme Management Officer, UNODC).

A great thank you to Fadma Bouharchich (formerly Legal Expert, Banque de France), Neila Fathallah (Head of Unit, Tunisian FIU), Oliver Gardner (Programme Officer, UNODC), Michael Hertzberg (Assistant Director, Office of Terrorist Financing and Financial Crimes), Andrés Jiménez-Camargo (Financial Crime Consultant), Jody Myers (Chief Risk Officer, US International Development Finance Corporation), and Ivan Uvarov and other FATF secretariat staff who have generously contributed their advice and expertise as reviewers. Special thanks to Yohei Sakakibara (Fund intern in 2018, now with Ministry of Justice of Japan), who developed a database for court rulings on terrorist financing.

The book has benefited from inputs from both internal and external sources.[3] The book was drafted under the oversight of Nadim Kyriakos-Saad and direction of Chady El Khoury and with the assistance of their colleagues Steve Dawe, Arz Murr, Kathleen Kao, Jay Purcell (previously a financial sector expert in the Legal Department and currently working as a consultant) and external experts and consultants Sabrina Lando (former IMF staff), Giuseppe Lombardo (consultant), Marilyne Landry (consultant), Jean Paul Laborde (consultant), Delphine Schantz (previously with the United Nations Security Council Counter-Terrorism Committee Executive Directorate, currently with the United Nations Office on Drugs and Crime), and Jacqueline Shire (formerly United Nations Analytical Support and Sanctions Monitoring Team), Nedko Krumov and Henny Bakker (the Egmont Group of Financial Intelligence Units), Miguel Angel Garcia Sanchez (Europol/TFTP), Hyung Keun Yoon and Dermot Brauders, and Paul Riordan (INTERPOL).

The team wishes to thank IMF staff members Emmanuel Mathias, Richard Berkhout, Robin Sykes, Carlos Acosta, André Kahn, Alexander Malden, Santiago Texidor Mora, Kohei Noda and Mohammad Al Janahi who have also contributed as reviewers, and Rafaela Calomeni, Rosemary Fielden, Maria Rassokhina, Anna Strandquist, and Hanan Yazid for their support in the completion of this book. Thank you to the IMF Legal Department's Resource and Information Management Unit for their budgetary support; and the IMF's Communications Department, and in particular Lorraine Coffey, for their work in managing all the aspects of the production of this book.

Finally, none of this would have been possible without the support of the donors to Phase II and III of the IMF's AML/CFT Thematic Fund who funded this important project: Canada, France, Germany, Japan, Korea, Luxembourg, the Netherlands, Norway, Qatar, Saudi Arabia, Switzerland, and the United Kingdom.

The book was developed in coordination with other international and regional organizations including the United Nations Office of Counter-Terrorism (UNOCT), the United Nations Security Council Counter-Terrorism Committee Executive Directorate (CTED), the United Nations 1267 Monitoring Team, the Egmont Group of Financial Intelligence Units, INTERPOL, and Europol. It also benefited from the review of colleagues from the FATF Secretariat. The useful comments of external reviewers are gratefully acknowledged.

Chady El Khoury
*Editor*

---

[3] The views expressed in this book are those of the Fund's Legal Department and should not be attributed to the Executive Directors or the Management of the Fund.

# Authors

**Miguel Angel Garcia** is the Head of Analytical Project in the Terrorist Finance Tracking Program of Europol.

**Henny Bakker** is a Terrorist Financing Expert of the Netherlands' financial intelligence units (FIUs), representing the Egmont Group of FIUs.

**Dermot Brauders** is an Irish police officer seconded to the Counter-Terrorism Directorate of the International Criminal Police Organization (INTERPOL) since 2018. He has worked in law enforcement for 23 years, specializing in the investigation of economic crimes and terrorist financing offences for the past 14 years.

**Terence Donovan** is a Technical Assistance Advisor of the IMF. As a consultant since 2011, he provides strategic advice on effective risk-based measures to deter and detect financial crime. Recent experience includes designing strategies for effective implementation of risk-based AML/CFT preventive measures and risk measurement models; implementing effective AML/CFT supervision for financial institutions and nonfinancial sectors; and advising on beneficial ownership transparency. He has also guided countries in preparations for mutual evaluations. Donovan is a former staff member of the Central Bank of Ireland (1977–2001 and 2010) and the IMF (2002–2009).

**Stephen (Steve) Dawe** is Deputy Unit Chief of the Financial Integrity Group in the Legal Department of the IMF. Steve joined the IMF in September 2005. He works in the Financial Integrity Group (LEG) on issues related to Anti-Money Laundering/Countering the Financing of Terrorism (AML/CFT), focusing on ML and FT risk. For the previous 20 years, Steve worked for the Reserve Bank of New Zealand as a bank supervisor, financial sector and FDI regulator, and general counsel. He has worked on AML/CFT since 1993 including representing NZ and the IMF at the Financial Action Task Force (FATF). Within FATF, Steve has chaired working groups, served on its steering group, helped produce guidance on national ML/FT risk assessments, and was heavily involved in producing the 2013 FATF Methodology, particularly on effectiveness. He has led and participated in four FATF assessments, reviewed many others, and has trained FATF assessors. Steve has worked on AML/CFT issues for the IMF in relation to more than 50 countries. Steve is a lawyer and accountant with an LLB/BCA from Victoria University of Wellington.

**Chady El Khoury** is Deputy-Unit Chief of the Financial Integrity Group in the Legal Department of the IMF. His expertise includes AML/CFT, anti-corruption, and broader governance and integrity issues. Before joining the IMF in 2007, he worked at the financial intelligence unit (SIC) of the Lebanese Central Bank. He received his legal and finance education in Lebanon and France.

**Arz Murr** is a senior financial sector expert in the Legal Department of the International Monetary Fund. Arz joined the Financial Integrity Group in 2013 and is engaged in its anti-money laundering and combating financing of terrorism (AML/CFT) work streams. Before joining the IMF, Arz was a senior AML/CFT supervisor to financial and nonfinancial institutions in Lebanon for 10 years. At the FIU of Lebanon, Arz reviewed national legislation, regulations, and guidance on suppressing terrorist financing and helped prepare his country's risk assessment and those of Jordan and Saudi Arabia. Arz has implemented technical assistance and training in other Middle East and North Africa countries and helped the IMF deliver technical assistance since 2009.

**Kathleen Kao** is a Counsel of the Financial Integrity Group in the Legal Department of the IMF, specializing in AML/CFT, anti-corruption, and rule of law. Before that, she worked at the Organisation for Economic Co-operation and Development's Anti-Corruption Division and the Global Forum for Tax Transparency and earlier had focused on white collar and commercial litigation in private litigation. She has also worked in two United Nations war crimes tribunals.

**Nedko Krumov** is an Egmont Group Senior Officer with 15 years of AML/CFT experience, including working for the Egmont EUROPE II Regional Group. He was involved in drafting projects produced by the Information Exchange Working Group (IEWG) jointly with the FATF, the World Bank, the World Customs Organization, and the United Nations Office on Drugs and Crime (UNODC). Before joining the Egmont, Krumov was in the Financial Intelligence Directorate of Bulgaria's State Agency for National Security and for more than 10 years led its international cooperation efforts. He also coordinated Bulgaria's first National Risk Assessment and assessed mutual evaluation reports for Moldova, Bosnia and Herzegovina, and Slovenia. He is a former bureau member of the FATF-style regional body MONEYVAL and an information-exchange expert for the Council of Europe.

**Nadim Kyriakos-Saad** is Assistant General Counsel and co-Head of the Financial Integrity Group of the Legal Department at the International Monetary Fund. He is a member of the Legal Department's management team and is responsible for supervising its Financial Integrity Group in anti-money laundering and combating the financing of terrorism and related issues. Before joining the IMF, Nadim practiced law in Lebanon and Saudi Arabia.

**Jean-Paul Laborde** is a Roving Ambassador to the Parliamentary Assembly of the Mediterranean in charge of countering terrorism, organized crime, and promoting the rule of law. He is also a lawyer of the Toulouse Court of Appeal. Laborde has served among other roles as United Nations Senior Advisor on Crime Prevention and Criminal Justice in Vienna, Head of the Terrorism Prevention Branch, and then in New York as Special Advisor to the Under-Secretary General for Political Affairs, the Director of the Counter-Terrorism Implementation Task Force (CTITF) Office and chair of the CTITF. He was also Assistant Secretary General and Counter Terrorism Executive Director at the United Nations Security Council. Laborde has extensive experience as a prosecutor and judge in France and is Adjunct Professor and Director of the Center of Expertise on Counter Terrorism, holder of the Cyber Defense/Cyber Security Chair at the French Military Academy, and Adjunct Professor of International Criminal Law at the Catholic Institute of Higher Studies.

**Marilyne Landry** is President of Arcadia Advisory Services, a consulting firm that helps countries to establish or improve their AML/CFT frameworks. Landry's clients include the IMF, the World Bank, the Council of Europe, the Egmont Group and the French and German development agencies. Previously, she was a Financial Sector Expert in the Legal Department of the IMF, specializing in AML/CFT issues, and led technical assistance projects in Asia, Africa, Europe, and the Western Hemisphere. She has served the Canadian Federal government including its FIU.

**Dr. Giuseppe Lombardo** is an international strategic advisor with 20 years of public and private sector experience whose focus is on financial integrity and the control of money laundering, terrorist financing, corruption and organized crime. He is advising several countries on their National Risk Assessments and how to build effective, risk-based AML/CFT systems. Lombardo also works with international organizations including the Council of Europe, the IMF, the Organization for Security and Cooperation in Europe, and FATF-style regional bodies. He spent more than nine years in the Financial Integrity Group in the Legal Department of the IMF, where he assessed members' compliance with the FATF Recommendations. Before joining the IMF in 2004, he was a lawyer at Italy's FIU and a National Legal Expert for the European Commission for Justice and Home Affairs.

**Sabrina Lando** is an AML/CFT expert with experience in the conduct of assessments under the FATF Standards. She was formerly a member of the IMF's Financial Integrity Group, providing AML/CFT advice to member countries by contributing to financial integrity policy work and technical assistance projects. She has held diverse positions in other international organizations working on transnational threats and security cooperation.

**Jason (Jay) Purcell** is an AML/CFT consultant with a particular focus on targeted financial sanctions, risk-based supervision, and strengthening AML/CFT regimes in Africa. He was previously a Financial Sector Expert in the IMF's

Financial Integrity Group and a Senior Policy Advisor in the US Department of the Treasury's Office of Terrorist Financing and Financial Crimes. He has also worked at Georgetown University, the US Department of State, and the Atlantic Council of the United States.

**Paul Riordan** helped to form the Terrorist Financing Unit at INTERPOL and is currently a liaison officer between INTERPOL and the International Anti-Corruption Coordination Centre. He was seconded to INTERPOL in 2016 from New Scotland Yard's Counter Terrorist Command in London. After retiring from the Metropolitan Police Service as a Detective Inspector in 2018, he remained within INTERPOL. Riordan has led teams investigating offences of terrorism, terrorist financing, grand corruption, money laundering, cash seizures, and organized crime.

**Delphine Schantz** is the New York-based Representative of the UNODC Liaison Office at intergovernmental and interagency meetings held at the United Nations Headquarters. Until December 2020, she was Senior Legal Officer and Coordinator for terrorist financing-related issues within the Counter-Terrorism Committee Executive Directorate (CTED), where she was responsible for related policy responses and assessed member states' counter financing of terrorism frameworks for the Security Council Counter-Terrorism Committee.

**Jacqueline Shire** served as the Finance Expert of the ISIS-Al-Qaida-Taliban Monitoring Team at the United Nations from 2018 to June 2022. She was Director and Global Head of US Sanctions, Bank of Nova Scotia until 2018 and before that Director of the Global Financial Crimes Intelligence Division at Bank of Tokyo Mitsubishi. She was the US member of the United Nations Panel of Experts on Iran from 2010–2014. Shire began her career as a Foreign Affairs Officer at the United States Department of State where her work included nuclear nonproliferation and arms control.

**Hyung Keun Yoon** is a police officer of the Korean National Police Agency, seconded to INTERPOL in 2019. He has 20 years' experience in law enforcement including intelligence analysis, financial crimes investigation, and international cooperation for the last 15 years.

**Yee Man Yu** has been a consultant to the Legal Department of the IMF and Financial Market Integrity Unit of the World Bank since 2011, drafting AML/CFT legislation, developing technical assistance programs, and providing training. Before that, she was a senior policy advisor to the Dutch government.

# Abbreviations

| | |
|---|---|
| **AML/CFT** | Anti-Money Laundering/Combating the Financing of Terrorism |
| **AFCA** | Anti-Financial Crime Alliance |
| **AUSTRAC** | Australian Transaction Reports and Analysis Centre |
| **CDD** | Customer Due Diligence |
| **CICTE** | Inter-American Committee against Terrorism |
| **CJS** | Criminal Justice System |
| **CTED** | Counter-Terrorism Committee Executive Directorate |
| **DNFBP** | Designated Non-Financial Business and Profession |
| **DPMS** | Dealer in Precious Metals and Stones |
| **EFIPPP** | Europol Financial Intelligence Public Private Partnership |
| **EIO** | European Investigative Order |
| **EU** | European Union |
| **EUROJUST** | European Union Agency for Criminal Justice Cooperation |
| **EUROPOL** | European Union Agency for Law Enforcement Cooperation |
| **FATF** | Financial Action Task Force |
| **FI** | Financial Institution |
| **FDI** | Foreign Direct Investment |
| **FIU** | Financial Intelligence Unit |
| **FSRB** | FATF-Style Regional Body |
| **FTF** | Foreign Terrorist Fighter |
| **FTO** | Foreign Terrorist Organization |
| **GDP** | Gross Domestic Product |
| **IMF** | International Monetary Fund |
| **INTERPOL** | International Criminal Police Organization |
| **IO** | Immediate Outcome |
| **ISIL** | Islamic State of Iraq and the Levant |
| **JIG** | Joint Intelligence Group |
| **JMLIT** | Joint Money Laundering Intelligence Taskforce |
| **LEA** | Law Enforcement Agency |
| **ME** | Mutual Evaluation |
| **MER** | Mutual Evaluation Report |
| **ML** | Money Laundering |
| **MLA** | Mutual Legal Assistance |
| **MVTS** | Money or Value Transfer Service |
| **NCB** | INTERPOL National Central Bureau |
| **NRA** | National Risk Assessment |
| **R** | Recommendation |
| **RBA** | Risk-Based Approach |
| **SIENA** | Secure Information Exchange Network Application |
| **SLTD** | Stolen and Lost Travel Documents |

| | |
|---|---|
| **SRO** | Self-Regulatory Organization |
| **STR** | Suspicious Transaction Report |
| **TC** | Technical Compliance |
| **TCSP** | Trust or Company Service Provider |
| **TFS** | Targeted Financial Sanctions |
| **TFTP** | Terrorist Finance Tracking Program |
| **UN** | United Nations |
| **UNOCT** | United Nations Office of Counter-Terrorism |
| **UNODC** | United Nations Office on Drugs and Crime |
| **UNSCR** | United Nations Security Council Resolution |
| **UNTOC** | United Nations Convention against Transnational Organized Crime |
| **VA** | Virtual Asset |
| **VASP** | Virtual Asset Service Provider |

# Introduction

In the global effort to cut terrorism off from financing, particularly serious terrorist threats such as the Islamic State of Iraq and the Levant (ISIL)/Da'esh, Al-Qaida, and their affiliates, robust counter-terrorism financing frameworks reinforce the safeguards to deny terrorists access to the financial system and choke financial flows—large or small—that enable terrorists to inflict physical damage on people all over the world.

While the cost of conflict and violence is often a direct consequence of terrorist atrocities, their impacts can also threaten the stability of a jurisdiction's financial sector and broader economy, with enduring effects on the infrastructure, business activities, foreign investments, trade, tourism, and international financial flows. These immediate or direct costs can hardly be downplayed: experts estimate that from 2000 to 2018, terrorism cost the world economy around $855 billion (Bardwell, Harrison, and Iqbal 2021). Therefore, the financing of terrorism represents a risk to countries' monetary and financial stability and should be dealt with as a macro-critical issue for economies (Bardwell, Harrison, and Iqbal 2021). Terrorist acts can also disrupt supply and distribution chains, put upward pressure on commodity prices, and present cross-border and spillover effects to the global financial system. For financial institutions in particular, involvement with terrorist financing increases the perceived risk to depositors and investors, and so generates significant reputational risk (Masciandaro, Takats, and Unger 2007).

Terrorism and terrorist financing are very acute challenges in fragile and conflict-affected states and can produce profound shocks to the rule of law, the quality of institutions, and more broadly the role of the government. Domestically, when terrorism persists, the costs to regular business can also mount increasingly, as supply and distribution chains may suffer major disruptions. With the threat of terrorism, normal commercial and consumption activities require more time, extra security, and higher costs, reflecting the risks posed by imminent terrorist attacks (Gold 2004). In addition, countries or regions that depend heavily on tourism have been found to suffer significant economic losses from the persistent threat of terror.[4]

The fight against terrorist financing rests upon legitimate economic and public interests of jurisdictions, concerned not only with safeguarding the lives and

---

[4] Research has established that, for an additional terrorist attack per 1 million people in 18 western European countries, GDP per capita falls by 0.2 percent and the share of GDP directed to investment drops 0.33 percentage points. Among the 35 developing countries examined in Asia, for each additional transnational terrorist incident per one million inhabitants, the GDP per capita growth rate fell by 1.4 percent and government spending as a percentage of GDP increased by 1.6 percent.

fundamental rights of their societies, but also with the transparency and integrity of their financial systems and the stability of their economies.

Together, the IMF and international community have come a long way in building legal and institutional defenses against the financing of terrorism, and that progress can be built on to deal with remaining challenges. Some policy and operational questions are common to all countries: How could you assess and enhance the understanding of the terrorist financing risks that the country is facing? How, when interacting with their clients, could the private sector best contribute to conducting due diligence and detecting suspicious activities related to terrorist financing?

Further questions of common interest include: How can countries maximize the production and impact of financial intelligence related to terrorist financing to effectively investigate individual terrorists and terrorist organizations? How can investigators, prosecutors, and judges ensure the imposition of deterring sanctions against terrorist financiers? And how could information be exchanged across jurisdictions without impediments to allow effective action against terrorist financiers?

These issues interest policymakers, practitioners, and researchers alike. But satisfactory answers cannot emerge without first looking at common challenges and the good practices countries are developing to ensure their frameworks for combating the financing of terrorism (CFT) are effective in mitigating risks and in deterring terrorist financing.

The overarching task is to continue improving the effectiveness of CFT frameworks, whether by enhancing international cooperation and the exchange of information, bolstering the use of financial intelligence, better enabling the prosecution of terrorist financiers around the world, or effectively freezing terrorist assets.

This book identifies key challenges and good practices to achieve these objectives. Its chapters are structured to follow an intuitive sequence representing different pillars of a CFT framework. They can also be read in isolation, with only occasional need to cross reference between them.

## REFERENCES

Abadie, A., and J. Gardeazabal. 2008. "Terrorism and the World Economy" EconPapers: Terrorism and the World Economy (repec.org)

Bardwell, Harrison, and Mohib Iqbal. 2021. The Economic Impact of Terrorism from 2000 to 2018. *Peace Economics, Peace Science and Public Policy* 27 (2): 227–61. https://doi.org/10.1515/peps-2020-0031

Blomberg, S. B., and G. D. Hess. 2006. How Much Does Violence Tax Trade?: How Much Does Violence Tax Trade? on JSTOR

Gaibulloev, K., and T. Sandler. 2009. The Impact of Terrorism and Conflicts on Growth in Asia: The Impact of Terrorism and Conflicts on Growth in Asia by Khusrav Gaibulloev, Todd M. Sandler :: SSRN

Gold, David. 2004. *Economics of Terrorism.* Columbia International Affairs Online (CIAO). July, 2004: doc_10729_290_en.pdf (ethz.ch)

Masciandaro, D., Takats, E., and Unger, B. 2007. *Black Finance.* Cheltenham, UK, Northampton, MA, USA,. Black Finance (e-elgar.com)

# CHAPTER 1

# Understanding Terrorist Financing Risk

Steve Dawe

### CHAPTER IN BRIEF

*The Challenge*

Implementing a terrorist financing risk assessment is an integral component as countries seek to devise a customized framework for combating terrorist financing. The IMF's experience indicates, however, that countries (1) face increasing challenges in initiating a timely terrorist financing risk assessment and (2) often end up with ineffective mitigation measures.

*Why It Happens*

The IMF's experience reveals that countries tend to combine terrorist financing risk assessments with money laundering risk assessments. This approach often leads to ineffective results because the risk indicators between terrorist financing and money laundering (ML) differ—ML deals with the proceeds of crime, whereby terrorist financing may also include legitimate funds and small-scale activity in the informal sector (such as the provision of goods). This intrinsic disparity requires these tools to be assessed separately to achieve targeted and well-rounded results. An adequate terrorist financing risk assessment also demands a sound methodology and project management at an appropriate level of government to secure much-needed political support. Furthermore, the terrorist financing risk assessment is often conducted in parallel with the national risk assessment and shortly ahead of a mutual evaluation. This structure drives countries to (1) rush the assessment during a time when most country experts have limited capacity due to their mutual evaluation responsibilities and (2) often neglect to include critical stakeholders such as state security, customs, and border control in the assessment process.

*The Solution*

This chapter complements the Financial Action Task Force Terrorist Financing Risk Assessment Guidance and takes the further step of including the IMF's perspective and its on-the-ground country experiences. The chapter offers a detailed step-by-step guide to understanding terrorist financing risks within a particular jurisdiction and equips readers with answers to terrorist financing risk assessment-related questions, including: (1) how to conduct a terrorist financing risk assessment, (2) when to conduct it, (3) who should be involved, and (4) what needs to be included.

## BROAD THEMES AND STANDARDS FOR ACTION

> *Understanding risk is fundamental to combating terrorist financing. However, this first step is beyond the means of many jurisdictions and challenging for others. The IMF staff's experience in implementing a national risk assessment (NRA) methodology is significant for building a body of good practices and can be drawn upon to help overcome the challenges highlighted throughout this book.*

Countries face many challenges in understanding their terrorist financing risk. The Financial Action Task Force (FATF)—an intergovernmental body that sets the international standards for anti-money laundering/combating the financing of terrorism (AML/CFT) through its 40 Recommendations—identifies many of these challenges in the introduction to its *Terrorist Financing Risk Assessment Guidance* (FATF 2019a).[1]

Knowledge of the challenges featured in this chapter comes in large part from the experiences of the IMF staff in assisting member countries with terrorist financing risk assessments. It also leans on the FATF guide's qualitative analysis of how terrorist financing risk assessments have been evaluated in FATF assessments of countries' AML/CFT regimes in relation to Recommendation 1 (R.1) and Immediate Outcome 1 (IO.1). Consolidation of both experience and long-term analysis inform the good practices advocated for practitioners using this book. Five broad challenges are explored in this chapter:

1. Knowing how to conduct a terrorist financing risk assessment
2. Distinguishing between terrorism risk and terrorist financing risk
3. Assessing terrorist financing risks associated with other assets and the informal sector
4. Overcoming a lack of data and information for terrorist financing risk assessment
5. Determining how to disseminate the results of the terrorist financing risk assessment

The chapter summarizes the FATF standard for assessing terrorist financing risks and its implementation. Key challenges countries must tackle to implement the standard are also discussed, along with some good practices to overcome them. Box 1.1 presents a summary of the IMF staff's approach to assessing terrorist financing risks.

Applying traditional risk management concepts to CFT helps member countries understand and mitigate their terrorist financing risks. This helps a jurisdiction to design and implement appropriate and proportionate policy responses and allocate resources to mitigate risks, make and justify decisions about exempting or reducing

---

[1] The author contributed to this guidance.

obligations in relation to financial institutions and products in their AML/CFT system assessed as "low risk," and to improve their AML/CFT regimes. Good understanding and appropriate mitigation also help a country to comply with the FATF standards (FATF 2019b) and have a more effective AML/CFT regime.

Terrorism risk and terrorist financing risk are not the same. Terrorism risk relates to whether terrorist attacks occur. Terrorist financing risk is about exposure to terrorist funding activity. A country can be very exposed to terrorist financing risk without being at significant risk from terrorist attacks. This is because acts of terror often occur in jurisdictions other than where the funds that enabled them originated or transited.

---

### Box 1.1. Applying International Risk Management Standards to AML/CFT

**The IMF staff's terrorist financing risk management framework focuses on mitigating the risks that flow from terrorist financing that occurs.** Under this framework, an assessment of risk considers the likelihood of an event occurring and the consequences if it does occur. In determining likelihood, the framework examines the threat from the pool of assets that need processing and the vulnerabilities associated with a jurisdiction, its relevant regulated markets, and its AML/CFT controls. Assessment of consequences focuses on the social, economic, and political outcomes that result from terrorist financing risk events that occur.

**Applying risk management principles to the financing of terrorism is complex. This is due, in large part, to lack of data about past terrorist financing events.** Accordingly, terrorist financing risk assessment relies on a semi-qualitative risk-scoring system for key terrorist financing risk events, such as the following:

- Terrorist financing is attempted due to the coexistence of specific conditions.
    - Terrorist funds and other assets are available and need processing.
    - The terrorist financier can access products, services, assets, or other circumstances that they reckon can be abused to meet their needs.
- The perpetrator of the terrorist financing is not caught.
    - If it is attempted, terrorist financing will not be detected by the authorities, either directly or because of the efforts of businesses that must submit suspicious transaction reports (STRs).
    - If it is detected, terrorist financing will not be investigated by the authorities.
    - If investigated, the perpetrator will not be prosecuted.
    - If prosecuted, the perpetrator will not be convicted.
- The perpetrator of the terrorist financing is not sanctioned.
    - If convicted, the perpetrator will not be punished adequately.
    - If punished, the perpetrator will not be deprived of their assets.

**The relevance of any given consequence will vary depending on the objectives of a given risk management exercise.** The methodology focuses on the consequences of terrorist financing that is neither detected nor sanctioned.

Source: Author
Note: AML/CFT = anti-money laundering/combating the financing of terrorism.

Terrorist financing is a multifaceted and complex process that comprises raising, moving, and using funds and other assets. Fundraising comes from numerous sources, including legal and illegal, domestic and foreign, and it involves willing and unwilling actors. Moving funds and other assets can be done through the financial system, using underground and illegal financial channels, by smuggling, or through trade within or across jurisdictions. Using funds and other assets involves not only the direct funding of terrorist attacks but also the funding of preparatory and support activities. To understand terrorist financing risk, a jurisdiction must organize its assessment to examine all the facets and vulnerabilities terrorist financing seeks to exploit.

Assessing terrorist financing risk is further complicated by different views among jurisdictions about the classification of terrorist organizations. Common ground is typically only found in relation to organizations designated by the UN under relevant UN Security Council Resolutions (UNSCR) (legally binding on member states under Chapter 7 of the UN Charter), such as UNSCR 1267 (1999) and successor resolutions that cover Al-Qaida, the Taliban, and the Islamic State of Iraq and the Levant (ISIL/Da'esh). In comparison, UNSCR 1373 (2001) focuses on terrorists but leaves it up to member states to define who these terrorists are.

## Status of Implementation Worldwide

### *FATF Obligations Regarding Understanding Terrorist Financing Risk by Jurisdictions*

The FATF's Recommendation 1 (R.1) imposes the primary obligation on countries to understand their terrorist financing risks.[2] Specifically, it requires that they "*identify, assess and understand*" those risks, including by designating "*an authority or mechanism to coordinate actions to assess risk*" and to "*keep the assessments up to date*" (FATF 2012–2020).[3] Based on this assessment, jurisdictions are required to apply a risk-based approach to ensure that their measures to prevent or mitigate terrorist financing are commensurate with the risks identified.

Recommendation 8 obliges countries to identify nonprofit organizations (nonprofits) likely to be at risk from terrorist financing abuse so that the regulation and supervision of nonprofits to prevent terrorist financing abuse is risk-based.[4] This chapter does not discuss how to assess terrorist financing risks in nonprofits, but more details can be found in Chapter 5 of the FATF's 2019 guidance, which sets out how to prevent the misuse of nonprofits for terrorist financing while respecting their legitimate actions. The guidance puts the focus on identified risks rather than a one-size-fits-all approach that would spread resources too thin to mitigate any terrorist financing risks.[5]

---

[2] It also imposes obligations in relation to money laundering risks, but these are not discussed here.

[3] Accessed June 24, 2021.

[4] See Interpretative Note to R.8, specifically paragraph 6.

[5] FATF mutual evaluation reports have attributed low ratings to countries that imposed broad measures on nonprofit organizations (for example, assigning all nonprofits as designated nonfinancial businesses and professions [DNFBPs], without proper risk assessments). See, for example, the report for Uganda, which sets this out quite clearly.

## Country Effectiveness at Understanding Terrorist Financing Risk

The FATF Methodology is used to assess how well countries have discharged their R.1 obligations in three ways. First, technical compliance assessment against R.1 focuses on how well countries have identified and assessed their terrorist financing risks. Second, the effectiveness of their terrorist financing risk understanding is assessed under IO.1. Third, the effectiveness of a country's risk-based approach to mitigating terrorist financing is assessed across a number of other IOs.[6]

The FATF Methodology assessment results against R.1 and IO.1 are difficult to interpret when trying to determine how well countries understand terrorist financing risk because they combine results for terrorist financing and money laundering (ML). An unpublished qualitative study of completed AML/CFT mutual evaluations conducted by FATF indicates that 10–15 percent of countries had completed a specific terrorist financing risk assessment and nearly 20 percent were still producing their first assessment. That review found that for most completed NRAs, the terrorist financing component was too light and too general. Moreover, for countries perceived to have relatively low terrorist financing risk exposure, the NRAs focused more on assessing and combating ML risks while putting little effort into terrorist financing risks, presumably based on the blind assumption that such risks did not exist.

The Global FATF/FATF-Style Regional Body (FSRB) network has identified that performance needs to improve in relation to understanding terrorist financing risks. The introduction to FATF's 2019 guidance notes that "[terrorist financing] risk is often given limited attention in NRAs and is sometimes not differentiated from the risk of terrorism."

That guidance illustrates, mainly from qualitative analysis, that it is not appropriate to conclude that terrorist financing risk assessments are being carried out effectively across the global AML/CFT network even though ratings for R.1 and IO.1 may be higher than the ratings achieved across many other recommendations and IOs. Indeed, many mutual evaluation reports recommend that an assessed jurisdiction carry out more comprehensive analysis of their terrorist financing risks. Mutual evaluation reports have identified some common challenges, including not paying enough attention to cross-border terrorist financing risks (including to pass-through or transit funds or other assets), limited use of quantitative data, limited engagement with the private sector, and information on terrorist financing risk results disseminated to the private sector being too general.

The rest of this chapter describes such challenges and discusses the techniques officials can use to overcome them. Since some overlap in the suggested good practices is inevitable, cross-referencing is used to avoid duplication.

---

[6] This aspect is discussed in the rest of the chapters of this publication.

# HOW TO CONDUCT A TERRORIST FINANCING RISK ASSESSMENT

## Challenges

Many officials have conceded they do not know how to carry out a terrorist financing risk assessment. This is especially so if their country has no known terrorist financing cases or has not been directly exposed to terrorist attacks.

If officials do not know how to conduct a terrorist financing risk assessment, and either do not produce one or produce a suboptimal assessment, then they will not be able to mitigate their terrorist financing risks effectively. Authorities often struggle to know what sort of process or methodology to use, when to conduct an assessment, whether to consider terrorist financing risk separate from an assessment of ML risk, and who to involve in the terrorist financing risk assessment process.

## Good Practices

The IMF staff's experience highlights the following good practices that will help officials conduct a terrorist financing risk assessment: (1) using a logical, structured process involving multiple manageable stages agreed upon before the exercise starts; (2) using a robust methodology; (3) assessing the terrorist financing risks well in advance of and separately from any AML/CFT mutual evaluation; (4) putting separate focus on terrorist financing and ML risks; and (5) involving the right people—especially security/intelligence, customs/border, and anyone with expertise on activities in the informal sector.

## A Logical, Structured Terrorist Financing Risk Assessment Process

Generally, countries are advised to follow the FATF's *National ML and TF Risk Assessment* guidance note (FATF 2013)[7] and its 2019 guidance when designing their process. Key considerations for how to implement the process are discussed in Chapters 2 and 3 of the 2013 guidance. These chapters indicate that a country needs to have a clear agreement on purpose and scope, and a high-level commitment to the process. They outline considerations for planning and organizing the risk assessment, sources of information, and contributors to the risk assessment, whether to involve the private sector and other actors, the information and tools required, and the frequency and the manners in which to document the methodologies and the processes used. These matters are elaborated for terrorist financing in Chapter 2 of the 2019 guidance, while Chapter 5 discusses how to keep assessments up to date. That topic is not elaborated here since the more pressing issue

---

[7] The author was closely involved in its preparation, cochairing the project team that produced the guidance.

for most countries is their struggle to assess their terrorist financing risks, which must be addressed before they can even get to updating such efforts.

The IMF staff recommends that when implementing the principles in these two guidance documents, countries should assess terrorist financing risk using a logical plan with multiple practical and manageable stages. Assessing a country's terrorist financing risk exposure can appear daunting. Breaking it down into stages (the norm for major projects) makes a more systematic and robust outcome more likely. The process from the IMF staff's methodology illustrates some issues to bear in mind while organizing the assessment.

The IMF staff organizes the methodology around three stages: terrorist financing threat, vulnerability, and consequences.[8] It comprises eight phases of work:

1. Preparation
2. Threat data collection
3. Threat analysis
4. Vulnerability data collection
5. Vulnerability analysis
6. Consequence data collection
7. Consequence analysis (leading to risk findings)
8. Final drafting and review

The eight phases comprise 37 steps.[9] The main steps are summarized in Table 1.1. Readers are advised to study this table to appreciate the range of issues that need to be addressed when completing a terrorist financing risk assessment.

## A Robust Terrorist Financing Risk Assessment Methodology

Countries are advised to use an established risk methodology to assess their terrorist financing risks. They do so with the knowledge that no single right approach or methodology exists, and the goal is to find one that suits their circumstances. Some countries might be more focused on exposure in the formal financial sector, while others might target the informal sector. For others, the (un)availability of data might lead them to a methodology that relies more on qualitative information. However, each methodology needs to be founded on solid risk assessment concepts and principles (Figure 1.1); assess inherent risk and the effectiveness of controls to arrive at residual or net risk; and focus on all aspects of raising, moving, and using funds and other assets (while distinguishing between domestic and cross-border activities and those in the formal and informal sectors). To help illustrate these issues, the rest of this section describes the concepts and principles underpinning the IMF staff's methodology.

---

[8] These terms are defined in the IMF staff methodology and closely follow those set out in paragraph 15 of the FATF 2019 guidance.

[9] There are 48 steps if a joint assessment of money laundering and terrorist financing risks is undertaken.

**TABLE 1.1.**

### National Risk Assessment (NRA) Work Phases and Objectives

**Phase 1: Preparation[10]**
Form a NRA Committee.
Determine national AML/CFT objectives.
Establish the nature, scope, and purpose of the NRA and the context of the jurisdiction.
Agree on the project plan.
Agree on and understand the NRA methodology.
Agree on and understand the NRA process.
Map data availability in the jurisdiction.

**Phase 2: Threat Data Collection**
Obtain evidence of the magnitude of terrorist financing.
Collect publicly available information on the magnitude of terrorist financing.
Obtain authorities' perceptions of the threat.
Clean the threat data and load it into a terrorist financing Threat Data Collection and Analysis Tool.

**Phase 3: Threat Analysis**
Interpret the threat analysis.
Prepare for threat validation exercises.
Validate preliminary terrorist financing threat findings.
Draft and review the threat assessment.

**Phase 4: Vulnerability Data Collection**
Collect or update vulnerability data from public sources.
Obtain statistics related to vulnerability.
Obtain authorities' perceptions of vulnerability.
Obtain perceptions of vulnerability from main foreign counterparts.
Clean the vulnerability data and load it into risk analysis.

**Phase 5: Vulnerability Analysis**
Interpret the vulnerability analysis.
Prepare for vulnerability validation exercises.
Validate preliminary vulnerability findings.
Draft and review a vulnerability and likelihood assessment.

**Phase 6: Consequence Data Collection**
Obtain statistics for consequences indicators.
Obtain authorities' perceptions of consequence.
Clean the consequence data and load it into risk analysis.

**Phase 7: Consequence Analysis**
Interpret the consequence analysis.
Prepare for consequence validation exercises.
Validate preliminary consequence findings.
Draft and review the consequence assessment.

**Phase 8: Final Drafting and Review**
Combine threat, vulnerability, and consequence to decide on the level of terrorist financing risk.
Validate high-level preliminary NRA findings.
Draft and finalize NRA.
Deliver NRA.

Source: Author

---

[10] It is also assumed that the country will understand its existing legal framework on terrorist financing and targeted financial sanctions and its policy regarding terrorist organizations. These topics can often be handled by government agencies that might not necessarily be directly involved in conducting the NRA. These issues are directly relevant to the vulnerability component of the NRA, but understanding them also helps scope out the NRA.

### Figure 1.1. Likelihood in Terrorist Financing Risk Assessments

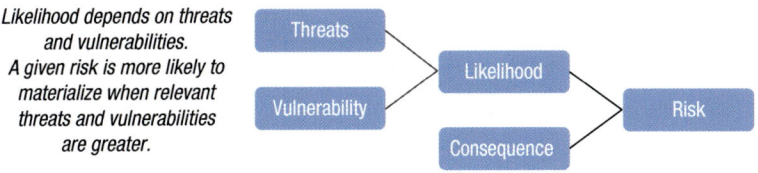

Likelihood depends on threats and vulnerabilities. A given risk is more likely to materialize when relevant threats and vulnerabilities are greater.

Source: Author.

## *Follow Risk Principles—Likelihood (Threat Exploiting Vulnerability) and Consequences*

The IMF staff's approach to understanding terrorist financing risks involves applying international risk management standards[11] to AML/CFT, with risk defined as a function of the likelihood of occurrence and the consequence (impact) of risk materializing.

The level of risk determined in risk analysis is commonly visualized with a risk chart, map, or matrix (Figure 1.2 displays a notional example of a risk heatmap), which illustrates the interplay of likelihood, consequence, and the level of risk. A risk chart, map, or matrix can also illustrate the effect of risk treatment (by plotting inherent risk (risk without controls) and residual or net risk (risk considering existing controls), where the impact of risk treatment represents the difference between inherent risk and residual or net risk).[12]

Drawing on international risk standards, a good assessment approach will involve the following aspects: being part of an overall risk management process; assessing risk in an agreed on context with agreed on objectives; identifying, analyzing, and evaluating risk; assessing risk as a function of likelihood and consequence; clearly specifying criteria for assessing whether the risk level is acceptable and for measuring likelihood and consequence; evaluating risk against criteria to determine whether it is acceptable (rather than aimed at eliminating the risks entirely); making decisions on how to mitigate unacceptable risks; and reassessing risks periodically (risk management is dynamic).

The risk assessment methodology must be directed to raising and processing funds and other assets that supply terrorists with the resources needed to carry out attacks, including resources to sustain terrorists and their organizations. Terrorist

---

[11] IMF staff's methodology draws heavily, though not exclusively, from standards promulgated in 2009 by the International Organization for Standardization (ISO): *ISO 31000: Risk Management—Principles and Guidelines* (ISO 2009a); *ISO 31010: Risk Management—Risk Assessment Techniques* (ISO 2009b); and *ISO Guide 73: Risk Management—Vocabulary* (ISO 2009c). For more information on these documents and on the ISO, see http://www.iso.org/.

[12] Risk treatment for terrorist financing risk includes the application of AML/CFT controls. The effectiveness of the controls needs to be determined in the assessment. The IMF staff's methodology scores the effectiveness of controls on a 1 to 7 scale, where 1 represents world best practice and 7 equals abysmal.

### Figure 1.2. Level of Risk Heatmap

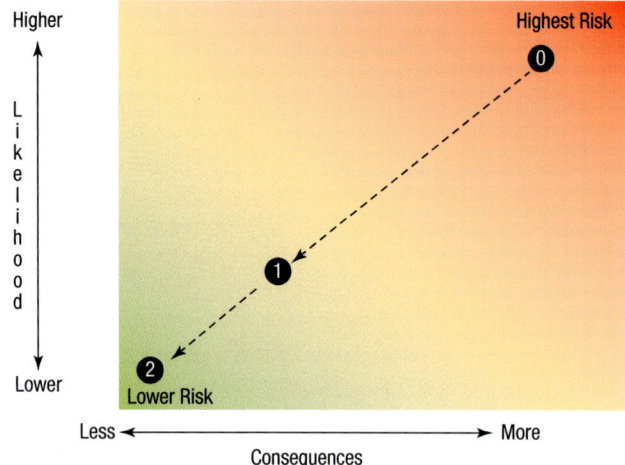

- ⓪ = inherent risk level
- ❶ = risk level with existing controls
- ⓪ to ❶ = effect of existing controls
- ❷ = risk level after additional or proposed steps taken to treat or mitigate risk
- ❶ to ❷ = effect of steps taken to treat or mitigate risk

Source: Author.
Note: Controls or steps taken to treat or mitigate risk can lower likelihood, consequences, or both.

financing involves the abuse of many of the same instrumentalities as ML[13] but differs in one key respect: funds and other assets can stem from both legal and illicit sources, whereas funds for ML are always of illicit origin (and the purpose is to make them appear as if they have been acquired legally).

In the IMF staff's methodology, the risk level is formally defined as the likelihood of successful terrorist financing events in a jurisdiction multiplied by the consequences of the events.[14] Likelihood is represented as a function (the coexistence) of the terrorist financing threat and vulnerability. Formally, $R_i$, a

---

[13] Money laundering may involve transactions in both the informal and formal sectors. Any provider of a product or service that can store or transfer value can itself be abused. Money laundering is, therefore, commonly associated with core financial sector businesses (that is, banks and deposit takers, and securities and insurance firms), other financial businesses (for example, money transfer agents), businesses and professions with links to the financial sector (such as lawyers and accountants), and others (like casinos and dealers in high-value assets).

[14] The focus of this risk assessment framework is national-level terrorist financing, not in firms or across different sectors. Whereas the components of risk between these levels does not change (risks are a function of likelihood and consequence in all cases), the evaluation criteria do change, not least given differing objectives.

jurisdiction's level of terrorist financing risk $i$, can be represented as $R_i = f[(t_i)(v_i)](c_i)$ with the following definitions:

- $t_i$, threat, in jurisdiction $i$, derives from the pool of assets for financing terrorism that need processing.
- $v_i$, vulnerability, represents the intrinsic properties of various features in jurisdiction $i$ that enable terrorist financing events.
- $f[(t_i)(v_i)]$ represents the likelihood that terrorist financing events will be successful in jurisdiction $i$.
- $c_i$ represents the consequences or outcomes that result from terrorist financing risk events occurring in jurisdiction $i$.

## Inherent Risk, Controls, and Net Risk

Good practice, based on principles of international risk standards, will first assess inherent risk, then determine the level of controls to measure the level of residual or net terrorist financing risk. That is, residual or net terrorist financing risk considers the effect of controls on the level of inherent risk. Controls are anything implemented to modify (usually intended to reduce) the inherent risk of terrorist financing. Controls therefore reduce inherent risk, but a lack of controls cannot increase it. Controls fall into two categories: (1) general controls and mitigants (such as general regulatory requirements); and (2) specific AML/CFT controls that implement the FATF Recommendations.

The NRA is orientated toward the generic objective of minimizing the amount of terrorist financing that occurs in a typical 12-month period.[15] Successful terrorist financing can refer to a single event or to a series of events that allows for successful terrorist financing over 12 months, either as part of a single scheme or a series of unrelated schemes, wherever the terrorist financing event takes place.

## Raise, Move, Use—Domestic and International—Formal and Informal

Terrorist financing threats mainly relate to the nature and scale of funds and other assets raised for use by terrorists that are in a jurisdiction in need of processing. Terrorist financing threats can be broken down into two components: (1) the nature and types of domestic fundraising and the funds and other assets generated; and (2) the funds and other assets raised outside the jurisdiction that likely move into the jurisdiction for further processing or use.

Thus, it is necessary to understand the key characteristics of the terrorist financing environment and its drivers and enablers.

---

[15] When the IMF staff's methodology is applied, an amount of $10 million a year in transactions related to terrorist funding is suggested as an upper reference point—based on analysis of published material on the cost of funding a substantial one-off terrorist incident and estimates of the annual operating costs of major terrorist organizations. The methodology involves assessing the likelihood of that amount being present in the subject jurisdiction in a 12-month period. The $10 million figure likely needs to be revised periodically as terrorist financing evolves around the globe.

Terrorist financing vulnerability encompasses the intrinsic properties in a product, service, distribution channel, customer base, institution, system, structure, or jurisdiction (including weaknesses in systems, controls, or measures) that enable terrorist financing abuse. Thus, assessing terrorist financing vulnerability involves examining factors associated with successful terrorist financing and generating vulnerability indicators for them. Since potential vulnerabilities are numerous, they need to be organized to reflect the terrorist financing stages they relate to, including distinguishing domestic from international activity. Generally, they can be described as follows:

- **Intrinsic properties**: Various features in the jurisdiction, such as financial services and products, levels of informality in various sectors, general levels of corruption, and other characteristics that could facilitate successful terrorist financing (such as through the existence of terrorist organizations), including features not altered by controls (such as geography, economy, currency, or political stability)
- **General controls and mitigants**: For example, non-AML/CFT supervision, tax scrutiny, registers of official information, and the effectiveness of law enforcement and the criminal justice system, among others
- **AML/CFT controls**: Specific measures called for by the FATF Recommendations, including any weaknesses in the AML/CFT systems and the adequacy of existing AML/CFT controls

The consequences of terrorist financing relate to outcomes that result when a terrorist financing risk event happens. Consequences can relate to cost, damage caused, or the significance of outcomes—either through enabling terrorist acts or through their effect on financial systems and institutions, as well as jurisdictions and their economies more generally.

The terrorist financing process generates two types of consequences: (1) those associated with carrying out the financing activity; and (2) those associated with the use of assets after they have been processed.

Thus, the consequences may at first involve short-term distortion of demand for products, services, or assets, including those in the financial sector,[16] as well as for informal remittance.

The consequences of using assets successfully processed by terrorist financing are terrorist attacks, which generate harmful effects that have broad, long-term social, economic, and political impacts and apply to citizens, businesses, communities, and national or international interests. The damage can impact jurisdictions where attacks take place, where victims of the attacks come from, or where the related funds and other assets were raised or transited. Longer-term consequences are of great importance when assessing terrorist financing risks. From a narrow IMF perspective, those of interest include impacts on the economy through reduced tourism and effects on correspondent banking relationships if countries earn poor reputations for facilitating or allowing terrorist financing to occur.

The purpose of consequence analysis is to help differentiate the risk level presented by diverse types of terrorist financing. It helps deepen understanding, allowing

---

[16] These are unlikely to be material for most financial systems.

authorities to prioritize the allocation of resources to mitigate risks. It is good practice for the risk methodology to explicitly require separate assessments of domestic and international terrorist financing activities, given that the consequences of terrorist financing often occur in other jurisdictions.

In some countries where the IMF staff helped authorities assess terrorist financing risk and the domestic risks were judged very low, it was noted that the transiting of terrorist financing funds represented higher risks, driven by higher consequences. Furthermore, while the consequences of funding terrorist attacks are horrific, it is important to distinguish the likely level of consequences from different types of terrorist financing activity. This helps differentiate the risks presented by diverse types of funding, although in practice, this may be difficult and involve speculation about the likelihood of different types of attacks. A practical approach may be to assume that the larger the amount of terrorist financing likely, the more sophisticated (and more severe) the consequences.

In conclusion, a good practice for assessing terrorist financing risks is to use a comprehensive and robust methodology that covers all aspects of raising, moving, and using funds and other assets in the formal and informal sectors, as well as domestically and internationally.

## *Assess Terrorist Financing Risk Separate from ML Risk*

It is good practice to assess (and thus understand) terrorist financing risk separately from ML risk. While ML and terrorist financing share some common attributes, their threats and consequences are sufficiently different to require assessing terrorist financing risk separately.[17]

The IMF staff's methodology illustrates some key differences countries need to consider when designing their assessment approach. It differentiates terrorist financing risk from ML risk in the following ways:

- The terrorist financing threat is analyzed separately and differently, and it overlaps with the ML threat only when terrorist funding comes from criminal activities.
- The vulnerability analysis shares some features but also deals with aspects that are unique to the financing of terrorism. Thus, assessment of terrorist financing risk involves the following:
  - It recognizes explicitly potential abuses of nonprofit organizations.
  - It focuses on customers and products, services, and delivery channels of regulated firms more likely to have elevated exposure. These are summarized in Box 1.2.[18] This activity is usually associated with moving terrorism funds and other assets. Generally, for the financial sector, terrorist financing

---

[17] A country can assess the risks of money laundering and terrorist financing in parallel and gain synergies from this. However, a separate formal assessment is needed on the level of terrorist financing risks.

[18] These were drawn from many sources, including typologies and reports from the FATF, which can be accessed at https://www.fatf-gafi.org/en/publications.html. While these are seen as more exposed to terrorist financing, types more generic to illicit activity are still relevant (and include, for example, complex and opaque corporate structures).

## Box 1.2. Vulnerability Indicators—Customers, Products, Services, and Delivery Channels

### Customers (including their beneficial owners):

- Dealers in precious metals, stones, or gems
- Cash-intensive businesses or owners of such businesses
- Charities or nonprofit organizations (including nonresidents)
- Dealers in antiquities and other items of cultural heritage
- Small businesses of a type that are known or suspected of offering informal remittance services
- Nonresident customers from countries or geographic areas with known terrorism or terrorist financing issues
- Resident customers operating in countries or geographic areas with terrorism or terrorist financing issues
- Customers doing business with regions or territories that share borders with territories controlled by terrorist organizations or where terrorist organizations operate
- Customers who transact with countries, jurisdictions, or territories that are known or suspected transit points for foreign terrorist fighters
- Customers who are, or who transact with, oil companies, brokers, and parts suppliers in territories controlled by terrorist organizations or where terrorist organizations operate
- Customers who are economic citizens where the background checks are not focused on terrorism links

### Products, services, delivery channels:

- Cash-based products
- Remittances
- Safekeeping and administration of cash
- Money (not foreign exchange) changing
- Dealing in precious metals and stones
- Trust or company service provider activity
- Soliciting donations or member contributions
- Lending through modest bank loans or other personal loans (if other lenders)
- Accounts that can be accessed and managed from foreign jurisdictions
- Credit cards and other means of payment that can be used in foreign countries
- Offering tourism and related services
- The buying and selling of domestic real estate to nonresidents
- Prepaid cards, e-money, e-purses, and the like
- Accounts of facilities denominated in foreign currencies
- Multiple branch networks
- ATM networks
- Virtual or remote access services
- Foreign branch networks
- International correspondent accounts
- Cross-border letters of credit

Source: Author.

favors liquid assets that can be moved rapidly (for example, cash withdrawals, ATM networks, wire transfers, and prepaid cards). Value has also been moved using other resources, such as precious metals.

- It emphasizes the effectiveness of controls directed more at CFT rather than at AML.[19] This includes giving more weight to record-keeping obligations of regulated firms (in recognition of the key role given to tracing finances back to their source during terrorism investigations).
- It includes targeted financial sanctions[20] related to terrorist financing in two ways: (1) as a tool for detecting the existence of funds to finance terrorism and identifying other assets; and (2) as a method for depriving terrorists of assets through temporary freezing measures.[21]

## Involve the Right People

Assessing terrorist financing risk only works if it involves the right stakeholders. They are often different from those assessing ML risk. Annex B of FATF's 2019 guidance lists potential agencies and the type of information they hold that might be useful for assessing terrorist financing risk. Compared with ML, terrorist financing risk assessment is likely to require more input from security and intelligence services, customs and immigration agencies, and regulators of nonprofit organizations. When assessing both types of risk together, countries need to be aware that if the officials involved work mostly on AML issues, they may not have much exposure to investigations into terrorism or terrorist financing. This blind spot could skew their appreciation of a country's terrorist financing risk.

It is good practice to ensure that security or intelligence services take central roles in assessing terrorist financing risks, especially regarding threats. Such services often have the best information or knowledge about terrorism or terrorist financing networks. However, in some cases, their full participation may be challenging. They may legitimately not want to share information about known or suspected terrorists or terrorist financing activity (especially relating to live investigations) or may not see the value in an exercise they may have already carried out themselves in a more private manner. Some challenges can be overcome by being transparent about how the assessment will be conducted, by involving these entities fully in the process, by giving assurances about how sensitive information will be used, by agreeing to share sanitized or general knowledge rather than

---

[19] In particular, FATF Recommendations 5, 6, 8, 14, 16, 19, and 36.

[20] From FATF R.6 and IO.10.

[21] FATF R.4 covers requirements that ultimately aim to deprive terrorists of funds permanently, through seizure and confiscation, usually based on a criminal procedure and punishment following a (attempted) terrorist crime (R.5). In contrast, R.6 covers targeted financial sanction requirements that on a temporary basis deprive designated terrorists and their supporters of access to assets as a preventive measure, with a view to freezing these assets for as long as is necessary (such as until the person stops their support for a terrorist organization).

details about specific terrorism or terrorist financing cases, and by giving these entities a role in clearing or approving the final risk assessment product(s).

It is also important to recognize that substantive benefits derive from involving the intelligence community in discussions about terrorist financing risk: the community can positively influence the outcome and potentially help avoid terrorist attacks. Not involving the intelligence community could lead to gaps in policy decisions if the terrorist financing risk assessment does not have intelligence inputs.

Anecdotal experience of the IMF staff in applying the NRA methodology exposed the perils of not integrating security or intelligence services with other agencies when assessing terrorist financing risks. Issues between the intelligence service and other key AML/CFT agencies meant no proper dialogue on terrorist financing occurred prior to the mutual evaluation on-site visit. As a result, the terrorist financing risk assessment was not completed, and agencies other than the intelligence service were largely unable to demonstrate proper understanding of terrorist financing risks or share useful terrorist financing information with the private sector. Not surprisingly, mitigation measures outside those of the intelligence service were not very effective by the time of the assessment.

A country's overall terrorist financing risk profile needs to be considered when determining which agency involvement is critical in assessing terrorist financing risks. A country that has had terrorist financing cases involving large sums moving through the financial sector will likely rely more on input from financial supervisors and data from its financial intelligence unit than a country where the risk profile is directed more toward cash, informality, and the smuggling of goods. The latter will likely rely more on input from intelligence, law enforcement, and customs agencies. For example, if the cash-based country put too much emphasis on analysis of suspicious transaction reports (STR) to drive terrorist financing risk assessment, the result would likely be skewed because STR data comes from a population base (the formal financial sector) where terrorist financing activity is unlikely to be happening. Such a country would most likely also need to assess risks associated with informality by involving experts on informality from its central bank, finance ministry, or treasury and couple their knowledge with military, security, or criminal intelligence sources.

Private sector involvement in terrorist financing risk assessment can also be good practice. Participants can share experiences about known or suspected situations where their businesses were exploited for terrorist financing, indicate potential terrorist financing vulnerabilities of products and services, and contribute more generally to brainstorming and discussing terrorist financing risks. However, sharing sensitive information with private sector participants can create issues. Accordingly, countries could limit the private sector to distinct parts of the assessment, or involve private sector representatives (for example, compliance officers) with proper security clearances who are able to have fruitful and substantial dialogue with the intelligence community.[22]

---

[22] In some countries, compliance officers would also help implement targeted financial freezing measures; for example, by searching business databases for persons or entities prior to designation, based on information shared by intelligence officials, to allow the businesses to freeze assets owned by such persons or entities within minutes of the designation order.

In one country where private sector representatives participated, they added value to terrorist financing risk discussions by providing immediate input on practical aspects of how certain products and services operated. This was especially useful to security and law enforcement agencies, and it helped clarify how certain products or services could be used for terrorist financing.

## Assess Risks Well Ahead of Mutual Evaluations

Countries are advised to assess their terrorist financing risks well in advance of, and separately from, any mutual evaluation. The primary motivation for conducting terrorist financing risk assessments should be to design mitigation strategies for identified risks, not to comply with R.1.

Countries trying to conduct a terrorist financing risk assessment close to a mutual evaluation are likely to have to deal with logistical challenges. Preparation for a mutual evaluation usually needs to start 18 to 24 months prior to the on-site visit of the evaluators. During that period, AML/CFT officials will be focused on compiling material to demonstrate the country's technical compliance with and effectiveness against the FATF standard. Requiring many of those same officials to get involved in a terrorist financing risk assessment exercise is probably not feasible—if they do get involved, one or perhaps both work streams may suffer. Moreover, once an on-site visit for the mutual evaluation is imminent, the time pressures on officials to respond to inquiries from assessors and to produce more material, in practice, make completing a proper terrorist financing risk assessment very challenging. Also, the time to agree formally on the written output from a risk assessment exercise likely takes longer than officials typically allow. Accordingly, it is likely not possible to complete the write-up of an assessment of terrorist financing risks during the intense period before an on-site visit for a mutual evaluation.

Assessing terrorist financing risks well in advance of a mutual evaluation also gives a country more time to begin mitigation efforts. R.1 is not just about assessing terrorist financing risks; it is also about taking measures to mitigate them. Furthermore, IO.1 assesses a jurisdiction's understanding of risk that percolates from having assessed terrorist financing risks, and the effectiveness of mitigation measures (with an impact on all other IOs). The earlier a country understands its terrorist financing risks, the more established its mitigation can be during the on-site mutual evaluation, and, more important, the better placed it can be to reduce the consequences of terrorist financing activity.

A good practice is to complete the terrorist financing risk assessment at least 18 months ahead of the on-site mutual evaluation. This provides time to begin implementing any new mitigation efforts identified during the risk assessment exercise.

In at least three countries where the IMF staff have assisted with an NRA, those countries did not complete the exercise prior to their on-site mutual evaluation because (1) they started too late; (2) the NRA exercise took longer than was anticipated (largely because key officials were drawn away to work on the mutual evaluation); or (3) both. In all three cases, the countries fared poorly for the technical compliance rating for R.1. (For criterion 1.1, they had not assessed their terrorist financing risk, and they were unable to show for criterion 1.5 that they were applying a risk-based approach to mitigate those risks.) They also had a poor effectiveness rating for IO.1. (The countries delivered mixed performances regarding their understanding of their terrorist financing risk, which is largely reflective of how far through the NRA exercise they were, and they had generally poor results concerning their ability to demonstrate that identified risks were being addressed or that the private sector was aware of the country's terrorist financing risks.)

In contrast, another country that started much earlier relative to its on-site mutual evaluation received good ratings for technical compliance and a substantial effectiveness rating for IO.1, largely because time was sufficient to ensure its CFT regime was dealing with terrorist financing risks ahead of the evaluation. Staff are also aware of other countries that the IMF has helped assess terrorist financing risks but have not yet had their mutual evaluation and are now implementing changes to their CFT system based on what they found through the NRA exercise.

# DISTINGUISHING TERRORISM RISK AND TERRORIST FINANCING RISK

## Challenges

Many officials believe their countries have no terrorist financing risks because they have no terrorism.[23] This suggests they fundamentally misunderstand the characteristics of terrorist financing risk.

If officials lack an understanding of terrorist financing risks, they are unlikely to be able to identify and assess their country's terrorist financing risk and take steps to mitigate them. The main issue here is interpreting no terrorism activity as meaning no terrorist financing risk and failing to appreciate their country's exposure to the different components of terrorist financing risk.

## Good Practices

From the IMF staff's experience, terrorism risk can be distinguished from terrorist financing risk through two good practices. First, help officials to understand that no terrorism does not mean no financing risk. Second, use a risk assessment methodology that defines terrorist financing activities comprehensively. This would include fundraising (from all potential sources and the types of assets involved), the movement of funds (domestic and international, formal and informal sectors, and intended recipients), and fund use (domestically for attacks, preparing for attacks, sustaining terrorists, and covering use by foreign terrorist fighters, or FTFs),[24] lone wolves, and all types of terrorists. Both good practices are explored next in detail.

---

[23] In some cases, terrorist attacks may be deliberately classified as other violent crimes for domestic political reasons.

[24] FTFs are defined by the UN as "individuals who travel to a State other than their State of residence or nationality for the purpose of the perpetration, planning or preparation of, or participation in, terrorist acts or the providing or receiving of terrorist training, including in connection with armed conflict."

## No, Terrorism Does Not Mean No Terrorist Financing Risk

Officials need to properly understand the difference between terrorism risk and terrorist financing risk. Terrorism risk is a country's exposure to terrorist attacks. Terrorist financing risk is a country's exposure to the raising, moving, or use of terrorist funds and other assets. While some overlap for use of funds and other assets may be apparent, a country can be exposed to financing risk without having experienced a terrorist attack. It is, therefore, wrong to assume that no terrorism exposure equates to no terrorist financing risk. Officials claiming a country has no known or suspected terrorism or terrorist financing would have to show, through qualitative or quantitative analysis, that their country meets the following criteria:

- Had no terrorism incidents (terrorist financing use)
- No terrorists or terrorist organizations (terrorist financing use)
- No residents or nationals who are FTFs (who raise, move, and use terrorist financing)
- No history of receiving or making any terrorism—or terrorist financing-related requests for mutual legal assistance, extradition, or administrative cooperation (raise, move, and use of terrorist financing—including countries transiting funds and other assets)
- Had not received any STRs (raised, moved, and to a lesser extent used—although such reports could be submitted after an attack and include countries where terrorist financing funds and other assets transit)[25]
- Never detected funds owned or controlled by designated entities under targeted financial sanctions for terrorist financing

It is also incorrect for officials in countries with domestic terrorism to ignore that funds and other assets raised in the country might be sent out for use in other countries.

## Assess Terrorist Financing Fundraising, Fund Movement, and Fund Use

A country must understand the nature of its exposure to fundraising, fund movement or transfer, and fund use if it is to understand terrorist financing risks properly. Its risk assessment process and methodology must cover these as separate and distinct terrorist financing risks.

### Terrorist Financing Fundraising

When assessing terrorist fundraising, authorities need to consider the likelihood of all potential sources for raising funds and other assets. They may also try to estimate the relative levels of funds and other assets each source can raise or otherwise try to rank them. Potential sources fall into the groups in Table 1.2.

---

[25] This could be a false indicator—no STRs might just signal that no activity has taken place in the regulated sector—but it cannot speak to whether terrorist financing activity has taken place outside of firms regulated for AML/CFT.

**TABLE 1.2.**

| Group | Subcategory |
|---|---|
| Willing donors | Individuals (including foreign terrorist fighters and lone wolves) |
| | Businesses |
| | Nonprofit organizations, charities, and associations |
| Unwilling or defrauded donors | Individuals |
| | Businesses |
| | Nonprofit organizations, charities, and associations |
| Sale of goods and services | Legal products and services |
| | Illegal products and services |
| Criminal activity | Crimes committed by terrorists |
| | Crimes committed by others |

Source: Author.

Deeper understanding of fundraising risks will be achieved if the nature of the assets associated with the raised funds and other assets is part of the assessment. Fundraising can involve cash, financial assets, or property of any kind. It is critical to determine whether people in the jurisdiction are donating or obtaining assets, such as gold and precious metals, weapons, IT equipment, cell phones, vehicles, food and other supplies, antiquities, or oil for purposes of terrorism.

Identifying the specific methods used to raise funds and other assets (the types of crimes committed) will also illuminate how funds and other assets are likely raised in the country. Specific examples are best drawn from actual cases.

## Moving Terrorist Financing Funds

Moving funds for terrorist financing includes funds and other assets transferred domestically, transferred into and through the jurisdiction from abroad, and exported to other jurisdictions. When assessing the movement of terrorist financing funds, authorities need to examine all potential methods. Proper assessment will determine the likelihood that each potential method is being used. Authorities may also try to estimate the amount of funds and other assets for financing terrorism that flow through each route.

A first high-level analysis may assess whether terrorist financing funds or other assets are exported from or imported to the jurisdiction. Funds or other assets raised in one jurisdiction may be moved or used there or elsewhere and may or may not return to the origin. Moreover, the import and export of funds or other assets may take place at any step and multiple times. These concepts, illustrated for money laundering by Bartlett (2002), and which are similar in terrorist financing,[26] include three flows that originate with domestic funds or other assets and two that start with foreign funds or other assets (Figure 1.3).

A good starting point for any jurisdiction is to consider its likely exposure to each type of flow. This can be done for the country, for each sector in the

---

[26] For terrorist financing, the main difference is that some of the flows are associated with funds and other assets raised from legitimate sources.

## Figure 1.3. Domestic and International Terrorist Financing Flows[1]

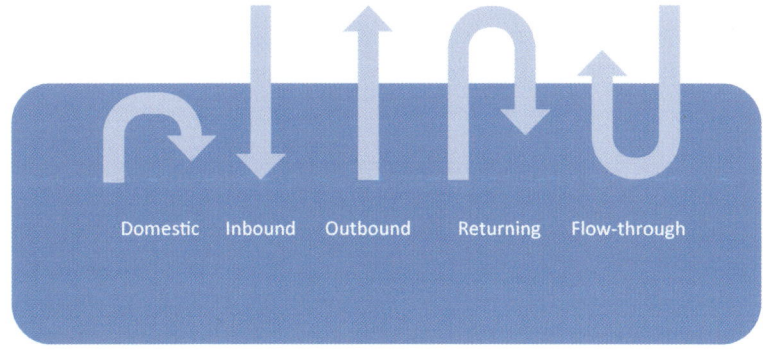

Domestic   Inbound   Outbound   Returning   Flow-through

Source: Adapted from Bartlett (2002).
[1]Domestic terrorist financing flows: Terrorist financing funds and other assets are moved and used for terrorist purposes within the jurisdiction. Inbound terrorist financing flows: Terrorist financing funds from abroad, transferred in formally or smuggled in and used for terrorist purposes in the recipient jurisdiction. Outbound terrorist financing flows: from domestic fundraising, smuggled out or transferred formally and used for terrorist purposes aboard. Returning terrorist financing flows: from domestic fundraising; after being sent out they return to be used in the jurisdiction. Flow-through (or transit) terrorist financing flows: from abroad, enter for processing and depart to be used for terrorism elsewhere.

**TABLE 1.3.**

| Terrorist Financing Flows—Types | |
|---|---|
| **Potential Flows** | **Potential Characteristics** |
| Outflows | Main destination countries |
|  | Main transit countries |
|  | Main terrorist organizations that the funds or other assets are destined for |
|  | Main channels used to transfer the funds or other assets |
| Inflows | Main source countries |
|  | Main transit countries |
|  | Main terrorist organizations or funders that the funds or other assets came from |
|  | Main intended users of the inflows |
|  | Main channels used to transfer the funds or other assets |
| Domestic flows | Main intended users of the funds or other assets |
|  | Main channels used to transfer the funds or other assets |

Source: Author.

financial system, and for designated nonfinancial businesses and professions (DNFBPs).[27] Examples of how to make likelihood estimates are set out later in this chapter (see Table 1.8).

---

[27] Designated nonfinancial businesses and professions include casinos, real estate agents, dealers in precious metals, lawyers, notaries, and other independent legal professionals, accountants, and trust or company service providers.

**TABLE 1.4.**

| Terrorist Financing Transfer Channels | |
|---|---|
| **Domestic Flows** | **International Flows** |
| Formal financial sector | |
| Informal financial sector | |
| Through domestic trade | Through international trade |
| Through movement of cash or physical assets | Through smuggling of cash or physical assets |

Source: Author.

A more granular assessment will determine the main terrorist groups, countries, and channels associated with each type of transfer of terrorist financing funds and other assets. Their potential characteristics are set out in Table 1.3. Authorities could estimate the levels of funds and other assets associated with each type, the proportions that each type represents, or rank them in likely order of occurrence.

Authorities, in determining the countries from where funds or other assets intended to finance terrorism are likely received or exported, could identify factors behind each country's results. These include (1) porous borders that allow transfers of cash and physical assets; (2) financial sector interconnectedness, which facilitates transfers of financial assets; (3) informal financial channels that facilitate informal value transfers; (4) trade links that enable transfers of funds or other assets using trade-based money laundering techniques or smuggling of cash and physical assets; (5) tourism links that pave the way for transfers of cash and physical assets; and (6) community or immigration links that facilitate transfers of financial and physical assets and cash.

Authorities could also try to determine the likely use of the different types of transfer channels, illustrated in Table 1.4.

For transfers involving regulated businesses, ensuring that the analysis is comprehensive and covers domestic and international flows separately is a good practice. For each type of financial institution, DNFBP, or any other type of business that the authorities consider could be exploited for terrorist financing purposes, the most comprehensive analysis covers the items listed in the following points and then combines that analysis to derive a residual or net potential terrorist financing exposure for each business type:[28]

- Inherent likelihood of domestic products and services being exploited
- Inherent likelihood of international products and services being exploited
- Robustness of controls for domestic products and services
- Robustness of controls for international products and services
- Robustness of supervision to ensure that controls are being applied adequately

---

[28] A supervisor for a sector or a firm type will likely also carry out an assessment for each business it supervises, but this may not be necessary for a national NRA on terrorist financing risks. However, if such information already exists, it becomes valuable input to assess country-level exposure. It is also important to stress that if a sector or firm is deemed as low residual risk due to having effective controls, supervisors still need to ensure the controls remain strong.

In one country that followed this approach, the results usefully showed that for one part of the financial sector, the main risk related to a unique international product with low probability but high consequence of being linked to terrorist financing, and for another important part of the financial sector, the risk exposure, while modest, was almost entirely linked to funds transiting the jurisdiction. The analysis also showed that most exposure was likely coming from the international rather than domestic customer base. Without the analysis, it is unlikely these potential exposures would have been identified.

## Terrorist Financing Fund Use

Funds and other assets can be used to carry out attacks (including preparing for them) or to sustain terrorist organizations. A first high-level consideration for any country is to determine how funds and other assets raised in, sent into, or passing through the country are likely to be used. A useful exercise is to estimate the likely share attributable to domestic and foreign use as set out in Table 1.5. This can also be triangulated with other exercises to validate their assumptions. Note that the combination of domestic funds and other assets raised and imported funds and other assets represent a country's total terrorist financing threat.

For domestic funds, authorities need to consider the likely domestic users, the costs of providing support to sustain them, and the likely costs of attacks:

- **Domestic users:** Authorities are advised to use the best available information to list all likely terrorists, terrorist cells, and terrorist organizations that might use terrorist financing funds and other assets inside the jurisdiction. This can include using funds and other assets transferred into the country.[29]
- **Domestic users—intending FTFs:** Separately, they could also estimate how many of the country's nationals might travel to conflict zones each year to become FTFs and the unit cost that each person likely incurs.
- **Costs of terrorist support:** Authorities could consider estimating the annual costs it might take to sustain a terrorist, terrorist cell, or terrorist organization in the country. These include food and shelter, training and infrastructure, communications, propaganda, travel documents (including fake ones), and travel.

**TABLE 1.5.**

| Total Domestic and Foreign Terrorist Financing | | |
|---|---|---|
|  | **Domestic Sources** | **Foreign Sources** |
| For domestic use | a% | b% |
| Sent out or through for foreign use | x% | y% |

Source: Author.

---

[29] A published NRA could summarize such information at a high level, including naming the main organizations known to exist (so long as this information is not too sensitive).

**TABLE 1.6.**

### Costs of Attacks—Types

**Types of Terrorist Acts**

| | |
|---|---|
| Suicide bombing | Vehicle or roadside bomb |
| Assassination of an individual | Assassination of a high-profile individual |
| Damage to infrastructure | Damage to well-protected infrastructure |
| Attacking an individual or a small group | Attacking a large group of people |
| Aircraft hijacking | Shooting down of an aircraft |
| Aircraft explosion | Kidnapping or hostage taking: an individual |
| Kidnapping or hostage taking: a high-profile individual | Kidnapping or hostage taking: a group |
| Rocket or mortar attack | Chemical or biological attack |

Source: Author.

- **Costs of terrorist attacks:** Authorities could estimate the likely annual volume and unit cost of each type of terrorist attack, as set out in Table 1.6, if they were to occur in their country. In doing so, they could describe the volume and nature of any past terrorism incidents in their jurisdiction, including noting whether these were directed toward human targets, property, or infrastructure; the level of fatalities; and whether such incidents are increasing or decreasing in volume, or remaining stable.

More generally, it is good practice for a country to have a very broad approach to defining the potential users of funds or other assets when assessing its terrorist financing risks. Terrorism around the world involves more than Al-Qaida or the ISIL and their affiliates or sympathizers and the high-profile conflict zones. The IMF staff's methodology focuses on a more than 180 possible terrorist organizations. If a country confines its attention too narrowly on certain terrorist groups or doctrines, it runs the risk of ignoring material terrorist financing risks that it might be exposed to.

In at least one country where staff have worked on terrorist financing risk issues, the initial opinion of officials was that their country had no known exposure to Al-Qaida or the ISIL and thus likely had a minimal risk. They altered that view when presented with a list of terrorist organizations recognized by them and other jurisdictions and known to operate in neighboring countries.

## ASSESSING TERRORIST FINANCING RISK ASSOCIATED WITH OTHER ASSETS AND INFORMALITY

### Challenges

Financing terrorism is not just about finance. Many terrorist financing risk assessments have focused predominantly on risks in financial institutions and DNFBPs (mainly related to financial products and assets with value, such as gold), and they overlook the fact that terrorism support and financing can include the supply of other assets, such as weapons, IT equipment, cell phones, vehicles, food and other supplies, antiquities, and natural resources such as oil. Many assessments, by focusing on risks in regulated firms, also overlook that a lot of terrorist financing activity occurs through low-value transfers, often in cash or in the informal sector (see the next section). Some officials also fail to focus on assessing vulnerabilities in the trade sector that can be used to move funds or other assets linked to terrorist activity.

Failing to appreciate these aspects and the subject country's exposure to them could result in a critical risk exposure being ignored and not being subjected to appropriate risk mitigation. The challenges relate to a lack of knowledge, using risk assessment methodologies that do not look at this aspect, and not focusing enough attention on potential exposure through informal money transfers.

## Good Practices

The IMF staff's experience shows that the following good practices will help when assessing terrorist financing risks associated with other assets and informality:

- Officials need to be aware that terrorist financing is broader than financial products and the abuse of financial institutions and DNFBPs.
- Terrorist financing risk assessment methodology needs to address other assets and informality explicitly, including in relation to smuggling risks, and pay particular attention to widely used informal money transfer services in many jurisdictions.

### *Be Aware That Terrorist Financing Involves Other Assets and Informality*

Officials making an assessment need to be aware that terrorist financing often involves low values and transactions outside of firms regulated for AML/CFT. As the FATF 2019 guidance mentions, challenges in assessing terrorist financing risks relate to the low value of funds or other assets, the wide variety of sectors misused for terrorist financing, its cross-border nature, and the fact that the operational needs for attacks can include routine transactional activity (for example, renting a car or purchasing a kitchen knife). Even though the topic is terrorist financing, officials need to think beyond finance. The FATF standard explicitly refers to *"funds and other assets"* (rather than just funds) in recommendations dealing with terrorist financing and proliferation financing. While glossary definitions of these two terms may not suggest much of a difference, the optics are a reminder that terrorists rely on assets beyond those found in financial firms. To proceed without such an awareness could result in a country overinvesting CFT efforts in the formal sector and underinvesting in the informal sector.

### *Include Other Assets and Informality in the Risk Assessment Methodology*

As discussed, a good practice is to ensure that the terrorist financing risk assessment methodology explicitly deals with other assets and informality. Thus, the assessment needs to cover the provision to terrorists of assets such as weapons, IT equipment, cell phones, vehicles, food and other supplies, antiquities, and natural resources such as oil. It needs to cover informality in all three stages of financing: fundraising (such as casual fundraising in the street and online crowdfunding); moving funds (informal money transfers); and fund use (such as the purchase of munitions with cash).

In one country where the IMF staff helped assess terrorist financing risk, officials were convinced it had low exposure because no such financing was happening in their regulated sector (with no cases or foreign requests related to terrorist financing), and they believed that their CFT regime for the regulated sector was robust. They held that view even as their country was situated in a region with many conflict zones. The IMF staff, by applying their methodology, opened the officials' eyes to the possibility that other assets might be transported across the border by relatives of terrorists involved in a conflict with the neighboring government. Up until that point, the officials had not considered that citizens of their country who provided food, vehicles, and other supplies to relatives in the neighboring country might be part of their country's potential terrorist financing risk exposure.

Another good practice is to ensure that the methodology does not inadvertently exclude other assets or informality by relying on inappropriate data sets. Therefore, terrorist financing risk conclusions based solely on STR data cannot be used to assess risk in the informal sector because the sample population for the data is the formal sector. Likewise, drawing conclusions about cross-border risks solely from an analysis of cross-border declarations or disclosures made pursuant to R.32 is also inappropriate because (1) the $/€15,000 threshold for such declarations or disclosures certainly exceeds a lot of terrorist financing activity; and (2) declarations only cover cash and bearer instruments, not other movements of value relevant to terrorist financing. Similar considerations apply to asset or cash transaction reporting based on thresholds.

### Smuggling

Assessing the movement of funds needs to cover smuggling of cash and other assets. For all countries, but especially those near—or with easy transportation links to—conflict zones, assessing the country's exposure to terrorist financing smuggling of cash and other assets is a critical part of a terrorist financing risk assessment.

Countries need to consider the following elements:

- **What is the context?** Does the country border or is it located near countries with terrorism incidents or where terrorist groups are known to or suspected to be based? Is the region known for smuggling networks? How porous are the country's borders?
- **What is likely being smuggled?** Funds (including cash [in which currencies?], bearer instruments, prepaid cards, gold, and precious metals) or other assets (including weapons, IT equipment, cell phones, vehicles, food and other supplies, antiquities, illicit wildlife products such as ivory, counterfeit goods such as luxury goods and medicines, or commodities such as oil)?

- **Where are the assets likely being smuggled?** Into, out of, or through the country? Directly or through transit countries? What mode of transport is likely to be used (air, road, rail, foot, water)?
- **How are the assets being smuggled?** Through the postal system or the trade system, by goods accompanying people, or through sophisticated smuggling networks? Are there any particularly vulnerable time periods?

Data to inform analysis of terrorist financing smuggling risk will likely come from operational agencies. This includes customs or border agency experience and confiscations, intelligence on smuggling networks, and investigations by law enforcement. Other countries' NRAs and FATF typology reports may also be sources.[30] Information about smuggling associated with money laundering could also inform smuggling related to terrorist financing. Details and data on smuggling often cover only what has been found or is known. This makes terrorist financing risk assessment more difficult because border officials will likely be unaware of the intended use in terrorism of assets that can be taken across borders legitimately. Likewise, small amounts of cash are unlikely to draw attention. Thus, the degree of terrorist financing-related smuggling could be understated because it occurs in plain sight. Furthermore, corruption within government agencies cannot be overlooked. Officials should think about whether bribes or added kickbacks for border officials to wave cash or goods through might play a role in successful smuggling operations.

### Informal Money or Value Transfer Services

A good practice for many jurisdictions is to explicitly focus on terrorist financing risks associated with informal money or value transfer services (MVTS). Moving funds using informal remittances is a well-established terrorist financing typology. Assessing terrorist financing risks associated with MVTS could cover issues similar to those for smuggling: which countries, inward or outward, and the like. It could also consider whether such activity is linked to certain immigrant communities with known or suspected links to terrorist activity or terrorist financing, or groups with certain extremist sympathies.[31]

It is good practice to have terrorist financing investigators and MVTS regulators share information about informal MVTS operators. Collectively they have the best available information about the likely use of informal remittances in terrorist financing to inform a risk assessment. They may also hold information on sanctions imposed on informal MVTS—whether for regulatory breaches or criminal activity (for example, aiding and abetting terrorist financing). In ideal conditions, investigators and regulators would work together proactively to bring informal operators into the formal sector or close them down. This

---

[30] FATF typologies report are available at: https://www.fatf-gafi.org/en/publications.html.

[31] Care needs to be taken to ensure that innocent people of the same nationality as a suspect are not subject to discrimination, and to how they as a group are referred to in any public document.

would likely require joint programs targeting informal operators and necessitate investigators to alert regulators if they discover informal MVTS.

Another good input is to assess how effectively the country is mitigating informal MVTS activity. Thus, assessment should include looking at how well it implements FATF R.14. This could involve estimating what percentage of MVTS activity occurs in firms licensed or registered to offer such services and identifying what is being done to detect and act against those operating illegally.

## LACK OF DATA AND INFORMATION TO USE IN TERRORIST FINANCING RISK ASSESSMENT

### Challenges

Officials often complain they have no data to use in terrorist financing risk assessment or that they do not know what type to use. That perceived lack is often associated with not having any known terrorist financing cases.

If officials do not have proper inputs, the assessment results may be too unreliable to provide proper basis for effectively mitigating risks. The potential challenges are numerous: officials are unaware of information to use (including that generated outside of the subject country); agencies do not share relevant information, or they lack the knowledge or willingness to use qualitative data or risk assessment techniques such as scenario analysis; and they are uncertain about how to use classified information.

### Good Practices

The following good practices can overcome an actual or a perceived lack of data related to terrorist financing: (1) using the best information available; (2) sharing information among key stakeholders; (3) relying more on perceptions and other qualitative material; (4) using speculative or "what if" methods; (5) conducting scenario analysis to identify the likelihood that terrorist financing vulnerabilities will be exploited; (6) using open-source information from outside the subject country; (7) combining publicly available data on world terrorism with data on the country's general features to identify potential terrorist financing links; and (8) agreeing in advance on protocols for the use of classified information.

#### Use the Best Information Available

A good practice is to use the best available quantitative and qualitative information as input for an assessment. The types of information that could be relevant are expanded upon in both the FATF's 2013 guidance (Annexes I and II) and 2019 guidance (Parts II and III and Annex B) documents. The IMF staff's approach when assisting countries is to seek information from a wide range of sources to use as input in the NRA. However, the IMF staff also advises countries not to put too much effort into creating new data sets for an NRA and to instead use what they have first.

**TABLE 1.7.**

| NRA Meetings | |
|---|---|
| **Meeting Name** | **Subtopics** |
| Terrorist financing threat | Fundraising |
| | Fund transferring |
| | Fund use |
| Terrorist financing vulnerability | General jurisdiction |
| | Sectors and firms |
| | Financial intelligence unit, law enforcement agencies, criminal justice system |
| Terrorist financing consequence | Short-term |
| | Long-term |

Source: Author.
Note: NRA = National Risk Assessment.

## Share Information

Another good practice is for officials and the private sector to share what they know about vulnerabilities that could be exploited to raise or move funds or other assets for terrorism. By simply sharing information about products and services, past situations where they have been exploited (or even speculating on how they could be exploited), and the ease of smuggling in or out of the country, officials can identify which conditions are more likely to attract terrorist financing activity.[32]

Dialogue between stakeholders is critical during the IMF staff-led NRA process. Open discussions about how to interpret available data and information is the main method used to reach conclusions about threats, vulnerability, and consequences. Such discussion encourages interagency cooperation to forge better CFT working relationships. Table 1.7 illustrates the typical meetings held during an IMF staff-led NRA.

Many countries carrying out a terrorist financing risk assessment find themselves with no known terrorism events or terrorist financing and so regard this as limiting their ability to conduct the assessment. This is not the case. Indeed, a lack of known cases, if verified, can often be used to justify that the country has modest risk exposure.

## Use Perceptions and Qualitative Material

Where quantitative information on terrorism or terrorist financing is scarce, a good practice is to rely more on perceptions and other qualitative material. There is nothing inherently wrong with an assessment that relies on subjective or

---

[32] Many vulnerabilities for terrorist financing are likely to be very similar to those exploited to launder money. Synergies can be created by combining aspects of vulnerability analysis in assessing both sets of risk. It is also important to recognize that a terrorist financier's use of products or services often appears similar to that of most other individuals. That is because financiers derive the funds that they divert into terrorism from legitimately earned income, which can make it more challenging to identify specific products and services.

perceptive input.[33] Qualitative information can include inputs such as brainstorming, perception surveys, structured interviews, focus groups, and scenario building. An IMF staff-led NRA's structured approaches to gathering and interpreting subjective information (as shown in this chapter) can overcome any lack of quantitative material (Galton 1907). This is a conventional approach in risk assessment and is endorsed under international risk standards.

## Use Speculative and "What If" Methods

Another good practice when there is no data available is to use speculative or forward-looking methods to assess terrorist financing risk.[34] In the absence of known cases, officials may find it a challenge to agree that terrorist financing could be happening. It may be easier to focus the assessment more on a "what if?" approach around questions such as the following:

- If fundraising is taking place, how is it likely to manifest? If you were trying to raise funds to finance terrorism, how would you do it?
- If fund transferring is taking place, how is it likely to be occurring? If you were transferring funds or other assets out of or through your country, how would you do it?

Any "what if" scenarios that are not credible can be eliminated. A structured approach is used to score likelihood and consequences for all remaining options. A structured approach can help overcome concerns that speculative exercises are simply guesswork. Tables 1.8 and 1.9 and Box 1.3 contain examples from the IMF staff's methodology of structured approaches.

The IMF staff's experience with applying this approach in one country helped officials to realize their country might be a potential transit point for funds. Up until that point, officials had focused primarily on the lack of any domestic terrorism and the extremely low likelihood of local terrorist sympathizers, largely ruling out any potential terrorist financing exposure.

**TABLE 1.8.**

| Likelihood Scoring Examples | | | |
|---|---|---|---|
| Likelihood Descriptor | Event or Activity Likelihood (%) | Event or Activity Likelihood Frequency | Indicator Score |
| Extremely higher | > 95% | > once a year | 7 |
| Much higher | > 75% | > 3 of every 4 years | 6 |
| Higher | > 50% | > once every 2 years | 5 |
| Medium | > 30% | Around once every 3 years | 4 |
| Lower | < 30% | Once every 5 years or so | 3 |
| Much lower | < 10% | Once every 10 years | 2 |
| Very much lower | < 5% | < once every 20 years | 1 |

Source: Author.

---

[33] The sources and nature of information used in any risk assessment should be fully disclosed.

[34] This can still be done even if information or data are widely available.

**TABLE 1.9.**

**Terrorist Financing Consequences Scoring Examples**

| Score | Descriptor | Social[1] | Incidents[1] | Physical Harm[1] | Funds or Other Assets Involved[2] |
|---|---|---|---|---|---|
| 7 | Huge or severe | Huge, irreversible harm to many members of society | > 50 | > 100 fatalities | Huge value |
| 6 | Very major | Major, irreversible harm to some members of society | > 25 | > 10 fatalities | High value |
| 5 | Major | Major harm to members of society | > 12 | > 1 death or irreversible disability or impairment (OR unknown) | Major value |
| 4 | Moderate | Moderate harm to members of society | > 6 | Injuries—medical treatment in hospital | Moderate value |
| 3 | Minor | Medium harm to members of society | > 3 | Injuries—medical treatment from paramedics or doctors | Medium value |
| 2 | Very minor | Very minor harm to members of society | Up to 3 | Injuries—no medical treatment required | Low value |
| 1 | Negligible | Negligible harm to members of society | 0 | No impact | Negligible value |

Source: Author.

[1] Applied in two contexts: first, in relation to the subject jurisdiction, and second, in relation to the global impact of attacks taking place outside the subject jurisdiction.
[2] A domestic consequence linked to the domestic financial sector and designated nonfinancial businesses and professions and informality.

---

### Box 1.3. Exercise—Marketing Your Country to Terrorist Financiers

Your government has decided that it wants to attract funds or other assets intended to finance terrorism around the world. However, it does not want to draw international attention to this decision by changing the outward appearance of its AML/CFT system. You are tasked with writing and presenting an advertisement that will run on the dark web to attract terrorist financiers to your country. Among other things, the advertisement should explain the following:

- Why your country is an attractive place for them
- How easy it is for them to carry out their activities in your country without being caught or losing their money under the current AML/CFT system

You have 15 minutes in your group to prepare.

Source: Author.
Note: AML/CFT = anti-money laundering/combating the financing of terrorism.

## Carry Out Scenario Analysis

Scenario analysis is another good practice for overcoming data limitations. It can be used to speculate on the likelihood of vulnerabilities being exploited for terrorist financing. Structured scenario building and analysis helps to identify likely and credible typologies and provides qualitative input for risk analysis. This approach is a key part of the IMF staff-led NRA discussions. Two examples are presented in Boxes 1.4 and 1.5.

---

### Box 1.4. Exercise—Terrorist Financing Vulnerability Scenario Exercise

Each table will be given a scenario to fund a terrorist activity. Please describe how you will do the following:

- Prepare to carry out the scheme (for example, create a company)
- Place the funds in the formal sector (if part of the scheme)
- Carry out transactions to make it difficult to trace the funds or other assets back to their origin
- Successfully transfer them to the intended terrorist(s), including through transit countries

Scenarios:

- You are inspired by terrorist propaganda and want to carry out a small-scale, low-tech terrorist attack against people in your country.
- You want to travel to a conflict zone in a neighboring country and fight for the terrorist cause.
- You want to travel to a conflict zone in a faraway country and fight for the terrorist cause.
- Your brother is fighting for a terrorist group in a neighboring country. You want to send him some food and supplies and a small amount of money.
- You are told that your sister and her family who live in a neighboring conflict zone will be killed unless you pay a ransom of $25,000 to the terrorist group controlling that zone.
- You have $1,000 equivalent in local cash to get to a terrorist group in a neighboring country.
- You have $100,000 equivalent in local cash to get to a terrorist group in a neighboring country.
- You have $100,000 equivalent in local cash to get to a terrorist group in a faraway country.
- You have $100,000 in a local bank account to get to a terrorist group in a faraway country.
- You have $100,000 in a local bank account to get to a terrorist group in a neighboring country.
- You work in a large global bank with strong AML/CFT controls. You are told that your sister and her family who live in a conflict zone will be killed unless you facilitate a transfer through your bank of $100,000 for a terrorist organization.
- You are a wealthy industrialist. You want to get a substantial amount of funds (more than $500,000) to the main terrorist organization operating in your region.
- You are the financial controller for a global terrorist organization. You want to invest part of your treasure chest (more than $10 million in cash) in a stable jurisdiction with a standard return on investment.

Source: Author.

Staff experience with using such exercises in workshops with country officials during an NRA showed that they tend to have two useful types of input into the risk assessment:

1. First, they often open officials' eyes to terrorist financing vulnerabilities they had not thought about. For example, in at least two countries, the officials had not thought about valuable jewels being carried on the person to circumvent screening of cash and precious metals in carry-on luggage.

2. Second, they often reinforce or rule out the likelihood of certain vulnerabilities being exploited. For example, in several NRA exercises, officials had ruled out banks being exploited for terrorist financing purposes because AML/CFT controls were stringent. Yet scenario analysis opened their eyes to the potential for trade-based money laundering techniques being used to move value for terrorist financing from their country to others that involve settlement through banks. In other workshop discussions, it became apparent how easy it might be for assets for terrorist financing to be moved across informal border areas without detection.

## *Use Foreign Open-Source Information*

Often public or open-source information, sometimes held outside the country, can be used as input for a terrorist financing risk assessment. Such information includes FATF or FSRB reports into terrorist financing (for example, the regular FATF report on evolving terrorist financing risks associated with the ISIL and its affiliates, which can illustrate generic risk scenarios or may even contain information linked to the country assessing its terrorist financing risks); UN, European Union (EU), or other country lists of designated persons or entities related to terrorism (which can identify whether any of the country's nationals have been listed); the Global Terrorism Database[35] (used to identify national and regional terrorist incidents); Soufan Group[36] reports about FTFs (identifies whether the country has provided FTFs),[37] and *Guidance on AML/CFT Related Data and Statistics* (FATF 2015) can be used as a useful prompt about potential types of data that could inform a risk assessment.

In at least two countries where the IMF staff worked on terrorist financing risk issues, officials were unaware that their nationals were FTFs until staff presented data to them from Soufan Group reports. In another country, the lack of mention in those reports (and other sources) was used along with other factors to conclude that exposure was likely to be very low.

## *Use World Terrorism Data*

A good practice for any country assessing its terrorist financing risk is to combine publicly available data about world terrorism with data about the country's

---

[35] https://www.start.umd.edu/gtd/. Please note that some use is subject to commercial charge.

[36] http://www.soufangroup.com/foreign-fighters/.

[37] INTERPOL Member Countries can consult INTERPOL headquarters on how many of their nationals are reported in INTERPOL databases.

general features. Such data can be used in vulnerability analysis to identify potential linkages between the country and terrorist financing activity around the world. It can help determine what geographic, social, cultural, economic, and other links might be exploited by motivated residents who want to raise and send funds or other assets to a conflict zone.

Authorities can also use indicators based on bilateral relationships between the subject NRA country and terrorist activity. Such indicators help identify some of the potential links that have been mentioned. Box 1.5 has some examples of data relationships that might assist.

---

### Box 1.5. Vulnerability Analysis—Country Relationships with Terrorism

The number of terrorist incidents over recent years in countries that meet any of the following criteria:
- Share borders with your country
- Are the largest sources of migrants
- Share the same official language(s)
- Are the largest destinations for outward remittances
- Are the largest destinations for outward investments
- Are the largest destinations for outward transaction flows (such as through SWIFT)
- Are major import and export partners
- Use the same currencies
- Are the location where the jurisdictions' banks operate or where banks are owned by these entities
- Are the location from which foreign customers of banks originate
- Are involved in inward and outward CFT-related mutual legal assistance and international cooperation requests
- Are assessed by authorities to be main destinations or sources for foreign terrorist financing funds or other assets
- Are the 3–5 largest by value for inward and outward border cash seizures

In relation to the main (for example, 10 most prominent) countries for terrorist incidents in the last five years:
- Number of migrants originating from or destined to a particular country
- Outward remittances to a particular country
- Number of tourist departures to a particular country
- Number of tourist arrivals from a particular country

Source: Author.
Note: CFT = countering the financing of terrorism; SWIFT = Society for Worldwide Interbank Financial Telecommunications.

---

The IMF staff's workshops for sharing this type of analysis find that officials are quite often surprised at the type of links their countries have to conflict zones. In one country, officials had completely overlooked the potential links to another that shared its relatively unique language. In several other countries, officials were unaware of the volume of terrorist incidents in another that was the country of origin for a relatively large source of their expatriate workers.

### Agree on Protocols for Using Classified Information

Finally, it is good practice to agree at the outset on protocols for the use of classified information. These might deal with things such as security clearances needed for assessment participants to access such information, how to sanitize it for discussions when not all participants have appropriate clearances, and how to sanitize the information so that it can be published (if appropriate).

## DISSEMINATING THE RESULTS ABOUT THE TERRORIST FINANCING RISKS

### Challenges

Countries often struggle with communicating the results of their terrorist financing risk assessment, mainly due to concerns about the sensitivity of disclosing some of the information used.

Failure to properly communicate the assessment results may reduce the effectiveness of terrorist financing risk mitigation, especially in the private sector. The main challenges relate to failing to determine in advance a dissemination strategy for the assessment results and not providing the private sector with sufficiently detailed information.

### Good Practices

The IMF staff's experience is that the following good practices will assist with disseminating terrorist financing risk assessment results: (1) agreeing in advance how the results will be shared, (2) creating a public version that includes only terrorist financing risk results and an internal document for recording what underpins the overall conclusions, (3) ensuring that regulated firms are given information on products, services, delivery channels, and transaction corridors assessed as having higher and lower terrorist financing risks, and (4) using briefings and other outreach activities to communicate to key stakeholders and regulated firms.

### Plan for NRA Dissemination

A good plan for assessing terrorist financing risks will cover sharing the risk results. This should be agreed on during the formulative stage of the assessment exercise. Decisions about distributing the results will need to cover the "who," "what," and "how" questions. The "who" should cover the different types of stakeholders (key ministers, senior officials, AML/CFT agencies, foreign counterparts, AML/CFT assessors, and the private sector, among others). The "what" will have to deal with how high-level or detailed the results should be—and this will likely differ across stakeholders. It can also cover issues such as style (narrative, bullets, graphical, and the like). The "how" can detail use of written reports, oral briefings, pamphlets or booklets, and websites, among others. It is also possible that some information can be disseminated through a public–private partnership[38] arrangement with some vetted private sector stakeholders.

### Consider Using Public and Nonpublic Documents

In most cases, publication of terrorist financing risk results requires the release of different versions of the report. It is unlikely that all materials used should be or can be published, and some will likely be classified. It is, therefore, better to create a specific public version of the assessment tailored to the target audience—which in many countries will be firms regulated for AML/CFT. In addition, countries may find it useful to have a private or even a classified version that details the basis for how the risk conclusions were reached. Some countries have at least three versions: a classified version, a version for government agencies that does not contain classified information, and a public version. Countries may also find it useful for any public version to focus more on terrorist financing threats and not dwell too much on weaknesses in the AML/CFT regime that may expose vulnerabilities.

### Disseminate Appropriately for the Private Sector

It is a good practice to ensure that regulated firms are informed about the products, services, delivery channels, and transaction corridors assessed as having both higher and lower terrorist financing risks. This helps private sector actors assess their own terrorist financing risks and plan their mitigation accordingly. The degree of detail communicated may depend on the method adopted and the sensitivity of the information. For example, some countries prefer to communicate publicly about terrorist financing risks associated with regions rather than naming specific countries. However, country names may then be shared in more private briefings.

### Use Briefings and Outreach

In addition to formal sharing of results through written materials, direct communication with key stakeholders and the private sector is good practice. Outreach and briefings allow for more targeted communication of key messages. They also provide an opportunity for sharing more sensitive information. Finally, they give recipients an opportunity to ask for clarification about the findings.

## CONCLUSION

This chapter has discussed challenges associated with conducting terrorist financing risk assessments. It suggests that good practices to deal with these include using a robust methodology that comprehensively defines terrorist financing

---

[38] A public–private partnership is a formal mechanism to facilitate the sharing of financial intelligence among government, industry, and sometimes international partners. An example is the Fintel Alliance set up by the Australian financial intelligence unit, AUSTRAC, in 2017.

activities and a process that assesses such risk separately from money laundering. It is good practice to ensure that security or intelligence agencies, customs or border agencies, and people with expertise on informality are involved. Risks from other assets and informality should be assessed. When it comes to data, agreements should be reached that cover what data to use and how to deal with classified information and that ensure the available data are shared between appropriate agencies. Use of perceptions and other qualitative data should be part of the exercise, as should the use of speculative risk analysis techniques. It is valuable to agree in advance on a strategy for distributing results. And lastly, officials embarking on an assessment are encouraged to read previous reports from other countries and publications from the FATF global network.

## REFERENCES

Bartlett, Brent. May 2002. *The Negative Effects of Money Laundering on Economic Development.* Manila: The Asian Development Bank. http://www.adb.org/Documents/Others/OGC-Toolkits/Anti-Money-Laundering/documents/money_laundering_neg_effects.pdf.

Financial Action Task Force (FATF). 2013. *FATF Guidance: National Money Laundering and Terrorist Financing Risk Assessment.* Paris: FATF. https://www.fatf-gafi.org/content/fatf-gafi/en/publications/Methodsandtrends/Nationalmoneylaunderingandterroristfinancingriskassessment.html.

Financial Action Task Force (FATF). 2019a. *FATF Guidance: Terrorist Financing Risk Assessment Guidance,* Paris: FATF. https://www.fatf-gafi.org/content/fatf-gafi/en/publications/Methodsandtrends/Terrorist-financing-risk-assessment-guidance.html.

Financial Action Task Force (FATF). 2019b. *International Standards on Combating Money Laundering and the Financing of Terrorism & Proliferation: The FATF Recommendations.* Paris: FATF. https://www.fatf-gafi.org/content/fatf-gafi/en/publications/Fatfrecommendations/Fatf-recommendations.html.

Galton, Francis. 1907. "Vox Populi." *Nature* 75 (1949). https://doi.org/10.1038/075450a0.

## RESOURCES

Abuza, Zachary. 2003. "Funding Terrorism in Southeast Asia: The Financial Network of Al Qaeda and Jemaah Islamiya." *Contemporary Southeast Asia: A Journal of International and Strategic Affairs* 25, no. 2 (August): 169–199.

Arbenz, Philipp, Christoph Hummel, and Georg Mainik. 2012. "Copula Based Hierarchical Risk Aggregation through Sample Reordering." *Insurance: Mathematics and Economics* 51, no. 1: 122–133.

Bank for International Settlements. 2010. *Developments in Modelling Risk Aggregation.* Basel: BIS. http://www.bis.org/publ/joint25.pdf.

Bank for International Settlements. 2014. *Sound Management of Risks Related to Money Laundering and Financing of Terrorism.* Basel: BIS. http://www.bis.org/publ/bcbs275.pdf.

Basile, Mark. 2004. "Going to the Source: Why Al Qaeda's Financial Network Is Likely to Withstand the Current War on Terrorist Financing." *Studies in Conflict & Terrorism* 27: 169–185.

Brand, Sam, and Richard Price. 2000. *The Economic and Social Costs of Crime.* London: Home Office.

Center on Global Counterterrorism Cooperation et al. "To Protect and Prevent: Outcomes of a Global Dialogue to Counter Terrorist Abuse of the Non-Profit Sector," June 2013. CGCC_Prevent-Protect-Report_pgs.pdf (globalcenter.org).

Committee of Sponsoring Organizations of the Treadway Commission (COSO). 2004. *Enterprise Risk Management—Integrated Framework.* Durham: COSO.

Committee of Sponsoring Organizations of the Treadway Commission (COSO). 2012. *Risk Assessment in Practice.* Durham: COSO.

Comras, Victor. 2005. "Al Qaeda Finances and Funding to Affiliated Groups." *Strategic Insights* 4, no. 1.

Dawe, Stephen. 2013. "Conducting National Money Laundering or Financing of Terrorism Risk Assessment." In *Research Handbook on Money Laundering*, edited by Brigitte Unger and Daan van der Linde, 110–126. Cheltenham, UK: Edward Elgar Publishing.

European Union Agency for Network and Information Security. 2006. *Risk Management: Implementation Principles and Inventories for Risk Management/Risk Assessment Methods and Tools.* Heraklion: ENISA. http://www.enisa.europa.eu/rmra/files/D1_Inventory_of_Methods_Risk_Management_Final.pdf.

Financial Action Task Force (FATF). 2005. *Money Laundering & Terrorist Financing Typologies 2004–2005.* Paris: FATF. https://www.fatf-gafi.org/content/fatf-gafi/en/publications/Methodsandtrends/Moneylaunderingandterroristfinancingtypologies2004-2005.html.

Financial Action Task Force (FATF). 2008a. *Money Laundering & Terrorist Financing Risk Assessment Strategies.* Paris: FATF. https://www.fatf-gafi.org/content/fatf-gafi/en/publications/Methodsandtrends/Moneylaunderingterroristfinancingriskassessmentstrategies.html.

Financial Action Task Force (FATF). 2008b. *Terrorist Financing Typologies Report.* Paris: FATF.

Financial Action Task Force (FATF). 2010. *"Global Money Laundering and Terrorist Financing Threat Assessment."* Paris: FATF. https://www.fatf-gafi.org/content/fatf-gafi/en/publications/Methodsandtrends/Globalmoneylaunderingterroristfinancingthreatassessment.html.

Financial Action Task Force (FATF). 2013. *Methodology for Assessing Compliance with the FATF Recommendations and the Effectiveness of AML/CFT Systems.* Paris: FATF. Last updated November 2020. https://www.fatf-gafi.org/content/fatf-gafi/en/publications/Mutualevaluations/Fatfissuesnewmechanismtostrengthenmoneylaunderingandterroristfinancingcompliance.html.

Financial Action Task Force (FATF). 2015a. *Emerging Terrorist Financing Risks.* Paris: FATF. https://www.fatf-gafi.org/content/fatf-gafi/en/publications/Methodsandtrends/Emerging-terrorist-financing-risks.html.

Financial Action Task Force (FATF). 2015b. *Financing of the Terrorist Organisation Islamic State in Iraq and the Levant.* Paris: FATF. https://www.fatf-gafi.org/content/fatf-gafi/en/publications/Methodsandtrends/Financing-of-terrorist-organisation-isil.html.

Financial Action Task Force (FATF). 2016a. *Guidance on Criminalising Terrorist Financing.* Paris: FATF. https://www.fatf-gafi.org/content/fatf-gafi/en/publications/Fatfrecommendations/Criminalising-terrorist-financing.html.

Financial Action Task Force (FATF). 2016b. *Terrorist Financing in West and Central Africa.* Paris: FATF. https://www.fatf-gafi.org/content/fatf-gafi/en/publications/Methodsandtrends/Terrorist-financing-west-central-africa.html.

Financial Action Task Force (FATF). 2018a. *Financing of Recruitment for Terrorist Purposes.* Paris: FATF. https://www.fatf-gafi.org/content/fatf-gafi/en/publications/Methodsandtrends/Financing-recruitment-terrorist-purposes.html.

Financial Action Task Force (FATF). 2018b. *Terrorist Financing Disruption Strategies.* Paris: FATF. *Risk Assessment Framework.* London: FSA.

Frey, Bruno S., Simon Luechinger, and Alois Stutzer. 2007. "Calculating Tragedy: Assessing the Costs of Terrorism." *Journal of Economic Surveys* 21, no. 1 (February): 1–23.

Global Terrorism Database. https://www.start.umd.edu/gtd/.

Homeland Security Institute. 2006. *Homeland Security Risk Assessment.* Vols. 1 and 2. Arlington, Virginia: HSI.

Institute of Risk Management, Association of Insurance and Risk Managers, and the Public Risk Management Association. 2002. *A Risk Management Standard*. London.

International Monetary Fund. 2011a. *Anti-Money Laundering/Combating the Financing of Terrorism*. Washington, DC: IMF. http://www.imf.org/external/np/leg/amlcft/eng/.

International Monetary Fund. 2011b. *Anti-Money Laundering and Combating the Financing of Terrorism (AML/CFT)—Review of the Effectiveness of the Program*. Washington, DC: International Monetary Fund (IMF). http://www.imf.org/external/np/pp/eng/2011/051111.pdf.

International Organization for Standardization. 2009a. *Guide 73:2009, Risk Management—Vocabulary*. Geneva: ISO.

International Organization for Standardization. 2009b. *International Standard ISO 31000, Risk Management—Principles and Guidelines*. Geneva: ISO.

International Organization for Standardization. 2009c. *International Standard ISO 31010, Risk Management—Risk Assessment Techniques*. Geneva: ISO.

Kohlmann, Evan F. 2006a. "The Real Online Terrorist Threat," *Foreign Affairs* 85, no. 1: 115. http://heinonline.org/HOL/Page?handle=hein.journals/fora85&div=86&g_sent=1&collection=journals.

Kohlmann, Evan F. 2006b. "The Role of Islamic Charities in International Terrorist Recruitment and Financing. Danish Institute for International Studies." Working Paper No. 2006/7.

Looney, R. 2006. "The Mirage of Terrorist Financing: The Case of Islamic Charities." *Strategic Insights* 5, no. 3: 1-13.

New Zealand Department of Internal Affairs. 2011. *AML/CFT Sector Risk Assessment*. Wellington: DIA.

New Zealand Police Financial Intelligence Unit. 2010. *National Risk Assessment 2010, Anti-Money Laundering/Countering Financing of Terrorism*. Wellington: NZP.

PRS Group. *International Country Risk Guide Methodology*. https://www.prsgroup.com/wp-content/uploads/2022/04/ICRG-Method.pdf.

Quirk, Peter J. 1996. *Macroeconomic Implications of Money Laundering*. Washington, DC: IMF.

Raphaeli, Nimrod. 2003. "Financing of Terrorism: Sources, Methods, and Channels." *Terrorism and Political Violence* 15, no. 4: 59–82.

Reuter, Peter and Edwin M. Truman. 2004. *Chasing Dirty Money: The Fight Against Money Laundering*. Washington, DC: Institute for International Economics.

Roth, John, Douglas Greenburg, and Serena Wille. 2004. *National Commission on Terrorist Attacks Upon the United States: Monograph on Terrorist Financing*. Washington, DC: National Commission on Terrorist Attacks Upon the United States.

Samad-Khan, Ali, Armin Rheinbay, and Stephane Le Blevec. 2006. "Fundamental Issues in OpRisk Management—Misconceptions about Certain Key Concepts Are Causing Confusion throughout the Industry." *OpRisk & Compliance*. Incisive Media. http://www.opriskadvisory.com/docs/Fundamental_Issues_in_OpRisk_Management.pdf.

Schmid, Alex. 2005. "Links between Terrorism and Drug Trafficking: A Case of 'Narco-Terrorism'?" *International Summit on Democracy, Terrorism, and Security*. http://english.safe-democracy.org/causes/links-between-terrorism-and-drug-trafficking-a-case-of-narcoterrorism.html.

Singapore Government (Ministry of Home Affairs, Ministry of Finance, Monetary Authority of Singapore—MAS). 2014. *Singapore National Money Laundering and Terrorist Financing Risk Assessment Report 2013*. Singapore: MAS.

Soufan Group. 2015. *Foreign Fighters: An Updated Assessment of the Flow of Foreign Fighters into Syria and Iraq*. https://www.soufangroup.com/foreign-fighters/.

Standards Australia, Standards New Zealand. 2009. *Australia/New Zealand Standard, AS/NZS ISO 31000:2009—Risk Management—Principles and Guidelines*. Wellington: SNZ.

Standards Australia, Standards New Zealand. 2004a. *Australia/New Zealand Standard, AS/NZS 4360:2004—Risk Management*. Wellington: SNZ.

Standards Australia, Standards New Zealand. 2004b. *HB 436:2004, Handbook: Risk Management Guidelines, Companion to AS/NZS 4360:2004*. Wellington: SNZ.

Treasury Board of Canada. 2001. *Integrated Risk Management Framework.* Ottawa.

Unger, Brigitte, Melissa Siegel, Joras Ferwerda, Wouter de Kruijf, Madalina Busuioic, Kristen Wokke, and Greg Rawlings. 2006. *The Amounts and the Effects of Money Laundering.* Amsterdam: Ministry of Finance.

United Nations. 2009. *CTITF Working Group Report—Tackling the Financing of Terrorism.* New York: UN.

United States Department of Homeland Security. 2010. *Risk Lexicon.* Washington, DC: USDHS. http://www.dhs.gov/xlibrary/assets/dhs-risk-lexicon-2010.pdf.

United States General Accountability Office. 2005. *Strategic Budgeting: Risk Management Principles Can Help DHS Allocate Resources to Highest Priorities.* Washington, DC: USGAO.

United States General Accountability Office. 1998. *Combating Terrorism: Threat and Risk Assessments Can Help Prioritize and Target Program Investments.* Washington, DC: USGAO.

United States General Accountability Office. 2001. *Homeland Security: A Risk Management Approach Can Guide Preparedness Efforts.* Washington, DC: USGAO.

United States Government (various agencies). 2005. *National Money Laundering Threat Assessment.* Washington, DC: USG.

United States Treasury. 2018. *National Terrorist Financing Risk Assessment.* Washington, DC: USG. https://home.treasury.gov/system/files/136/2018ntfra_12182018.pdf.

van der Does de Willebois, Emile. 2010. *Nonprofit Organizations and the Combating of Terrorism Financing: A Proportionate Response.* World Bank Working Paper No. 208. World Bank.

Williams, Phil, 2005. "Warning Indicators, Terrorist Finances, and Terrorist Adaptation." *Strategic Insights* 4, no. 1. https://www.hsdl.org/?view&did=453826.

# CHAPTER 2

# The Role of the Private Sector in Detecting and Disrupting Terrorist Financing Activities

Arz Murr, Terence Donovan, and Yee Man Yu

## CHAPTER IN BRIEF

### The Challenge

According to Europol, less than 1 percent of suspicious transaction reports (STRs) received by European Financial Intelligence Units (FIUs) in 2017 are based on terrorist financing suspicions. Globally, while terrorist financing-related data on STRs is unavailable, they are believed to be low. The low level of reporting suggests that the private sector's role in counter-terrorist financing is significantly underutilized and in urgent need of improvement. However, what steps should be taken to improve the private sector's participation?

### Why It Happens

Counter-terrorist financing measures applied by the private sector are often rules-based and predominantly limited to Targeted Financial Sanctions checks. This poses a fundamental problem as terrorist financing risks remain, therefore, largely unmanaged. The situation is particularly challenging in jurisdictions with less developed financial systems, especially where the large dependence on cash, financial exclusion, the extensive reliance on money remitters, and the prevalence of informal and parallel financial networks makes it difficult to identify and report suspicion of terrorist financing. In addition, private sector participants in most jurisdictions continue to operate with uncertainty regarding information sharing. Legislation and other regulatory-led solutions focused on enabling the sharing of terrorist financing-related information are important to mitigate the risks posed by laws on secrecy and confidentiality of client information.

### The Solution

This chapter provides a diagnosis of the issues and a set of effective best practices that the IMF has observed in certain jurisdictions. The most prominent initiatives include (1) establishing legislated public/private partnerships to combat terrorist financing, (2) pooling private sector data to form shared Electronic Know Your Customer platforms, and (3) adjoining private sector resources/know-how to establish sector-wide training programs. The chapter also offers revolutionary ideas such as establishing a nationwide single platform for all transactions. Such platforms can be adjusted with risk indicators to identify suspicious activity that can potentially reduce the need for STRs.

# ENHANCING THE EFFECTIVENESS OF REPORTING ENTITIES

> *The ongoing risk of terrorist attacks should galvanize countries into resolving weaknesses in efforts to expose terrorist financing networks by deepening cooperation between authorities and the financial industry. The challenge is to nurture a shift in focus for private sector firms from merely meeting legal obligations to becoming active partners in identifying and assessing risks and sharing valuable information with the authorities.*

Private sector financial firms perform an important supporting role in countering the financing of terrorist activity, particularly where effective mechanisms are established that help them do so. Mechanisms need to encompass formal and informal elements if they are to be effective. Examples of formal elements include legislative obligations (for record keeping and reporting of suspicious activity), while informal elements include developing networks for exchanging information and intelligence within countries and across borders. Scope exists to achieve a broader international adoption of formal and informal approaches. A welcome starting point for discussion is how weaknesses in CFT—as identified in past mutual assessments—can be resolved.

Authorities and the private sector must tackle practical challenges in implementing effective CFT measures proportionate to underlying risks. Challenges include lack of awareness of risks and typologies, inadequate training, legislative and operational barriers to information exchange, and the reality that terrorism is often financed through low-value transactions that fall below monitoring thresholds.

Private sector firms have shown a commitment and ability, particularly in the aftermath of terrorist attacks, to cooperate closely with competent authorities in tracing financial activity linked to terrorism. Their support has included taking initiative to provide authorities with targeted information at short notice that helps track transactions and identify the financial activities of suspects and their associates. This cooperation contrasts with results from evaluations of CFT measures that indicate systemic weaknesses and lack of effectiveness in many jurisdictions. With support from authorities, the private sector commitment and determination evident after a terrorist attack could be harnessed to implement day-to-day preventive measures. Initiatives could assist competent authorities in disrupting the activities of terrorist organizations and in preventing attacks.

It is important that the private sector take a risk-prioritized approach to preventive measures. This chapter summarizes recent initiatives that, if implemented more broadly, can significantly improve the effectiveness of the private sector's role and involvement in CFT. These initiatives mainly involve deeper cooperation between the private sector and competent authorities, enhanced channels for exchanging confidential information and intelligence, and risk-focused data harvesting facilitated by investment in more sophisticated IT systems.

While the private sector's contribution to CFT is important, national competent authorities still have the primary role in the detection and disruption of terrorist activity and its financing—as addressed in other chapters of this book. However, the focus here is on the importance of the working relationship between the public and private sectors in enhancing the effectiveness of CFT measures. As competent authorities are best placed to gather information and intelligence about suspected terrorist activity and its financing, it is important they have a means to share information—for example, on typologies and persons of interest—that enables private sector firms to focus their CFT efforts effectively. Financial institutions and other reporting entities, frustrated at the lack of information or guidance from law enforcement regarding the identification of suspicious activity, adopt a defensive approach focused on checking against targeted financial sanctions lists, with the primary aim of avoiding regulatory sanctions for rule breaches, rather than gather information to assess terrorist financing risk.

Meanwhile, from a law enforcement perspective, barriers to timely access to data on the financial activity of persons of interest can delay and undermine investigations. A better approach is needed to bridge the information gap between the public and private sectors and facilitate information access and exchange to strengthen measures that disrupt the financing of terrorism.

## Realistic Expectations for Private Sector Actions

Identifying transactions or other activity that may point to terrorist financing is a challenge. It is important not to create unrealistic expectations about what private sector reporting entities can achieve on their own. The private sector largely depends on the legal environment and on information from competent authorities to inform the preventive measures they put in place. This chapter discusses the resulting limitations and suggests some improvements. That said, the onus is still on the private sector to be more proactive in identifying and reporting suspicions of terrorist financing, given the legal requirements regarding targeted financial sanctions and asset freezing, and to pass on information to competent authorities without delay. Reporting entities must ensure the internal systems and processes needed to complete these tasks are adequately resourced.

The authorities, committees, and structures assigned responsibility for CFT vary by jurisdiction. The approach adopted depends on the legislative and institutional structure in each jurisdiction. While financial intelligence units (FIUs) have a key intermediary role in many countries, this is not always the case. In some jurisdictions, a dedicated authority or an interagency committee deals with CFT reporting and intelligence. In other cases, the intelligence services are assigned that role. In addition, particularly in addressing specific terrorist threats or in response to terrorist activity, informal means can also be used effectively to obtain information needed to deter or investigate terrorist activity or its financing. The term "relevant competent authority" is used in this chapter to cover all such approaches.

In principle, an effective CFT system can use any of the organizational approaches mentioned, provided that the competent authorities can achieve defined objectives. This includes enacting legislation that fully reflects the assessed threats of terrorism and its financing. It also requires effective two-way communication channels and a number of other steps to enhance effectiveness:

- A means to keep reporting entities aware and informed—though without compromising operational intelligence—of typologies, activities of concern, and areas of business on which they should focus due diligence. Raising awareness could also take the form of encouraging more CFT coverage in formal training, including in programs delivered by training academies or private sector providers.

- Adequate steps to ensure that reporting entities have no doubt about their obligation to prioritize and review suspicions of possible terrorist financing activity and to report without delay to the designated authority.

- Clear, unambiguous channels, whether through an FIU or other means, to ensure reports of suspicious activity related to terrorist financing are flagged, prioritized on receipt, and separated for analysis from more routine money laundering or threshold reports. While it might not be feasible for reporting entities to determine in all cases whether a suspicious activity relates to money laundering or terrorist financing, the priority is to file the report of suspicious activity with sufficient supporting analysis and documentation for authorities to determine the most appropriate classification and response.

- Clear lines of communication between all competent authorities to which reports of suspicious activity are required to be filed (where more than one, for example, money laundering reports filed with the FIU and CFT reports with law enforcement). The objective should be to ensure that reports are not misdirected or allowed to fall through interagency gaps.

- Balance CFT reporting obligations against the need to respect human rights and protect privacy. However, some privacy protections (for example, the General Data Protection Regulation obligations in the EU) can create practical barriers to CFT information sharing, particularly on a cross-border basis, that need to be addressed.

- A clear legal basis that supports the cross-border exchange of information and intelligence between the relevant agencies (FIU and/or law enforcement, as appropriate) across relevant jurisdictions. Different approaches and organizational structures currently impede communication and can be an obstacle to international financial service providers having a direct line to authorities in other jurisdictions to discuss a suspicious activity or pattern of transactions. Eliminating communication barriers may require changes to legislation and/or amendments to structural and reporting arrangements so that authorities best placed to act can receive timely information about suspicious activity.

- A meaningful feedback loop to keep reporting entities informed of the usefulness and, where relevant, ultimate outcome of suspicious activity reporting. This needs to be implemented without compromising confidentiality. It can be used to communicate with reporting entities on the negative consequences of delays or gaps in their reporting and to agree on workable remediation measures. It is important that the staffs of reporting entities feel engaged and know what the authorities need and expect.

Steps should be taken to improve CFT supervision, including through additional training on CFT for supervisors. Moreover, the scope of supervision could be defined to include changes to reward structures in reporting entities to place increased stress on effective compliance, including on CFT measures, and reduce emphasis on new business generation or profitability in staff compensation packages and bonuses.[1]

In this chapter, the private sector refers to the full range of categories of reporting entities specified within the recommendations of the Financial Action Task Force (FATF), referred to in this book as the FATF Recommendations (FATF 2012, as amended 2022). Private sector reporting entities comprise banks and other financial institutions and all designated nonfinancial businesses and professions (DNFBPs). This chapter also uses the term "reporting entities" to refer to all private sector firms subject to CFT obligations. It also raises a question regarding the need to widen the scope of coverage of anti-money laundering/combating the financing of terrorism (AML/CFT) requirements to keep pace with recent and emerging developments in financial sector structures, products, and services. The scope could be expanded to include obligations regarding shadow banking, online payment systems, and other cyber-based financial activities, where not already within the scope of AML/CFT obligations.

## Differing Risk Profiles

While the chapter addresses reporting entities, the different categories of financial institutions and DNFBPs may have sharply differing terrorist financing risk profiles. In general, banks and money remitters (money or value transfer services, or MVTS) have the largest risk of being misused. Certain types of authorized electronic money institutions, particularly those issuing prepaid and reloadable cards or facilitating funds transfers and quasi-banking services, also carry higher risk. As low-value transactions are relevant to terrorist financing, transactions conducted by electronic money institutions below thresholds for which due diligence is mandated could present a gap in coverage that is open to exploitation. Similar concerns arise for transactions conducted by virtual asset service providers (VASPs), which should also be considered in assessing terrorist financing risks.

While other categories of financial institutions and DNFBPs should not be discounted, they are in general of less interest to supporters of terrorism. Thus, in applying a risk-based approach to institutions, the expectation is that banks,

---

[1] As with many of the issues discussed in this chapter, the relevance of a well-targeted reward system is much broader than CFT.

money remitters, electronic money institutions, and VASPs should devote particular attention to CFT prevention, as the threat is greater in their case. In assessing terrorist financing vulnerabilities, sharp distinctions may again arise as banks, in general, are likely to be much better placed to conduct customer identification and profiling, as well as record keeping. Given the vulnerabilities of the sector, competent authorities need to pay particular attention to MVTS. While these observations are valid in general, local circumstances must be considered as the significance and profiles of categories of financial institutions vary by jurisdiction. It is beyond this chapter's scope to conduct a more thorough sectoral risk analysis or suggest solutions across different sectors. The analysis, therefore, is rather broad, and its proposals would need to be adapted to the risk profile, size, and complexity of each sector in each country.

### Abuses of Other Nonfinancial Businesses

Taking a broader view of the private sector, some additional nonfinancial businesses can also be abused for terrorist financing. The goods, logistics, or other services they provide can be employed in the organization and execution of terrorist attacks. Therefore, some law enforcement and other competent authorities seek to monitor the activities of, for example, vulnerable travel agents, vehicle-hire businesses, or short-term letting businesses, particularly where services can be arranged online or with a degree of anonymity. In some jurisdictions, categories of business such as travel agents are within the scope of the due diligence and reporting obligations of AML/CFT legislation. In others, FIUs and law enforcement agencies seek to build networks for information exchange and ensure that customer and transaction records can be accessed where needed at short notice. While the focus here is on financial institutions and DNFBPs, countries could usefully consider to what extent their CFT strategy should also encompass non-financial businesses where this is warranted by the perceived risk of terrorist financing.

## IMPEDIMENTS TO UNDERSTANDING TERRORIST FINANCING RISK

Finance for terrorism can take many forms and, where disguised alongside legitimate business activity or exploiting innovative financial products, can be particularly difficult to detect. When considering the challenges undermining the effectiveness of current CFT measures, a number of characteristics specific to analysis of terrorist financing risk can be identified. These include differences between jurisdictions in their understanding and approach as well as the lack of capacity in some to implement effective measures.

The terms terrorism and terrorist financing are not understood consistently across different countries and regions. This reflects local experiences and may create opportunities that could be exploited by terrorists and terrorist organizations. It also results in inconsistencies in the recognition of terrorist financing risk and uneven implementation of preventive measures across the globe. While it is difficult to find published evidence that terrorist financiers have exploited these differences, such potential exists. A further limiting factor is that the capacity to counter terrorist financing varies greatly across jurisdictions, with weaknesses in some jurisdictions undermining global efforts. Less developed jurisdictions lack resources to implement effective CFT measures and require international assistance to make their CFT measures a match for the risks.

## Attempts to Maintain Anonymity

Terrorists and their financiers may use a variety of means to avoid identification and maintain anonymity, ranging in complexity and by size of transactions. In some cases, evidence of the method is clear: frequent small donations in cash and by wire transfer; use of money remitters, both formal and informal; misuse of charities and other nonprofit organizations. Other techniques are more difficult to identify. These may involve the use of fronts, including offshore corporations, false invoicing schemes, value-added tax carousels, and trade financing schemes. In some cases, proceeds of apparently legitimate trade have been diverted to finance terrorism. In other cases, they come from illegal activities, including narcotic production and distribution, kidnapping for ransom, and protection rackets.

When designing risk-based preventive measures, it is best to assume that those seeking to finance terrorism will try to exploit any weaknesses they can identify in the controls of reporting entities. It should also be expected that such financiers can use corporate vehicles and complex structures to achieve their objectives. On the other hand, fundraising for terrorism can involve transfers of legitimately earned income to support terrorist organizations, with no other characteristic to identify them as suspicious. Correspondent banking arrangements can also be manipulated to disguise the movement of funds for terrorist financing purposes.

All of this combines to create a challenging environment for reporting entities in designing effective preventive measures and in ongoing monitoring of activities. The aim should be to effectively implement profiling and exception reporting systems that will highlight transactions, patterns of transactions, and customer behavior that match criteria selected to identify activities from a range of scenarios that could point to terrorist financing. While developing and maintaining such systems is complex and expensive, it should be accepted as a necessary cost of doing business and as a means of protecting the reporting entity from legal and regulatory risk, including regulatory sanctions and potential reputational damage from association with terrorist finance.

Just as financing methods adapt and develop, preventive measures need to be equally agile. The content of current international standards relating to terrorist financing has not changed materially since their introduction post-9/11, although published guidance has sought to keep pace with developments. A valid question is whether reporting entities are also updating their implementation practices to reflect emerging threats. While, as noted in this chapter, constructive initiatives involving the private sector have been introduced in some countries and regions, much work remains to ensure reporting entities are able to respond effectively to the threat of being misused for terrorist financing purposes and are able to support competent authorities with timely and accurate information, including for use in investigations after terrorist attacks.

In response to this difficult landscape, reporting entities are required to implement a range of preventive measures and comply with reporting requirements. CFT requirements comprise rules-based measures, such as targeted financial sanctions and freezing of terrorist assets, and risk-focused due diligence measures. Their aim is to prevent the abuse of reporting entities for the funding of terrorism, to enable the freezing of funds and other assets, and to generate financial intelligence for use in investigations into terrorist financing and terrorism.

Reporting entities adopt measures according to their understanding of the risk to which they are exposed. They are expected to identify and verify information about customers, including their corporate structure and the identity of the beneficial owners. Reporting entities also need to review whether their customers are subject to targeted financial sanctions (see Chapter 4). They are also required to scrutinize their customers' transactions to ensure that they are consistent with their knowledge of the customer, including their business and risk profile. Measures need to be taken, for example, to prevent correspondent banking relationships and MVTS from being abused and to ensure that information on pass-through transactions is available along the entire transaction chain.

> **Link between Beneficial Ownership and Terrorist Financing**
>
> In addition to recorded cases where corporate vehicles and legal arrangements have been misused for terrorist financing, there is anecdotal evidence that financial managers of large terrorist organizations have used front and holding entities to shield their finances (FATF 2015). Limitations in identifying beneficial owners in these cases hindered effective CFT efforts.

Another key obligation is to report any suspicious activities. Reporting entities are also responsible for ensuring that documents, data, and information on these issues are kept up to date, and that account files, business correspondence, and results of any analysis are retained for the period prescribed by law and made available to relevant competent authorities swiftly upon request.

## Anti-Money Laundering Measures Tend to Dominate

AML preventive measures tend to overshadow those of CFT. While evaluations have criticized the effectiveness of CFT measures, it is difficult in practice to separately assess CFT implementation by reporting entities due to the overlap with AML measures. In practice, the overlap can both support and hinder CFT implementation. Although the emphasis should be different, the principal preventive measures are common to AML and CFT, particularly with regard, among other things, to customer identification, risk profiling, identification of ultimate beneficial owners, transaction monitoring, and record keeping. The downside of a common approach is that difficult-to-identify terrorist financing risk can be neglected, as attention diverts toward money laundering risk, which is easier to analyze.

## Separating Money Laundering from Terrorist Financing Risks

Reporting entities need to assess their terrorist financing risk separately from money laundering risk. While terrorist financing risks may be more sporadic and difficult to define than typical money laundering risks, the same broad analytical approach can be usefully followed. Threats can be analyzed by customer, product/service/transaction, geography, and channels of delivery. The reporting entity's terrorist financing vulnerabilities may be generally like those identified in money laundering, but some specific concerns can also be identified. For example, reliable and up-to-date monitoring should be applied to subjects of targeted financial sanctions when analyzing customer categories.

Where indicated by risk, enhanced monitoring may be appropriate for certain charities and other nonprofit organizations linked to persons or regions associated with terrorist activity. Customers who provide money remittance services, certain e-money services, or virtual asset services may also warrant enhanced due diligence, depending on the risk presented by their activities. When assessing geographical factors, customers linked to and transactions to/from war zones and jurisdictions linked to terrorist activity should be considered, as should domestic regions bordering such places. These are some indicative examples of areas that reporting entities should look at when assessing their terrorist financing risk. The FATF's updated guidance for carrying out assessments (FATF 2019) includes useful indicators of potential terrorist financing activities.

## Role of Supervision

Supervision of reporting entities plays an important role in supporting effective CFT measures. Particularly for banks and other financial institutions, supervision should include off-site risk analysis and risk-prioritized on-site inspections. The application of proportionate and dissuasive sanctions to reporting entities with poor CFT implementation can provide incentive to

> **AML/CFT Supervision Needs to Be Risk-Focused**
>
> In line with the Interpretative Note to FATF R.26, the frequency and intensity of on-site and off-site AML/CFT supervision of financial institutions/groups should be based on the money laundering and terrorist financing risks and the policies, internal controls, and procedures associated with the institution/group as identified by the supervisor's assessment of the institution/group's risk profile and on the money laundering and terrorist financing risks in a country.

strengthen preventive measures. Although more detailed analysis of CFT supervision is beyond the scope of this chapter, past evaluations indicate that not all reporting entities are supervised effectively for CFT purposes. A number of countries need to put in place better risk-focused CFT supervision, including for categories of nonfinancial businesses and professions.

Supervisors can influence the behavior of reporting entities and change the focus to identifying and assessing terrorist financing risk. As noted, reporting entities tend to prioritize resources toward managing regulatory compliance risks over financial crime risks (Halliday, Levi, and Reuter 2014).

Supervisors should encourage reporting entities to move beyond a focus on compliance and adopt a risk-focused approach. For this to be effective, supervisors first need to take steps to deepen their own understanding of relevant terrorist financing risks. The outcome of the FATF's fourth round of AML/CFT mutual evaluations shows that supervisory practices need to be risk-based and consider intelligence and law enforcement information and priorities. As far as operational feasibility, although policy coordination with intelligence and law-enforcement agencies should guide the preventive system, this is not yet the case. More cooperation with other supervisors, including foreign supervisors, is also needed. Ideally, this would foster a coordinated approach, which in turn would help reporting entities target their internal monitoring system and controls to areas identified as higher risk and vulnerable (Clearing House 2017).

## LIMITATIONS

Structural and systemic factors constrain the reach and effectiveness of measures to prevent terrorist financing. Some limitations are of particular significance for jurisdictions with less-developed payment and financial systems. Others arise from the sensitive nature of intelligence information.

Use of cash and funds transfers outside the formal financial system can facilitate terrorist financing. Reports show cash prevails in terrorist operations (FATF 2015). Where funds do not pass through reporting entities, preventive measures are not applied. This includes when emerging payment services through social media are used and when virtual assets can be digitally traded, transferred, and used for payment or investment. Informal or underground systems of money transfer (including informal *hawala* arrangements), whether domestic or cross-border, have long been associated with the movement of funds to finance terrorism. This topic was analyzed in detail about two decades ago in a joint IMF/World Bank study (IMF and World Bank 2003). The study's findings are likely still relevant for many jurisdictions as it appears that progress since then to formalize such systems has been limited. As a response to perceived terrorist financing risk, particularly for jurisdictions with large informal or unregulated economies, moves to regulate informal financial services and improve the detection of cash smuggling may have a greater impact on the overall effectiveness of CFT efforts than preventive measures applied by reporting entities (Global Counterterrorism Forum 2018). Therefore, countries should take steps to put in place effective controls to encourage a shift from the use of informal transfer arrangements to the formal sector and to detect cross-border movements of cash.

CFT is undermined by policies or practices that lead to financial exclusion. Efforts to encourage transactions through the formal financial system will not succeed in countries where significant minorities are excluded from access to financial services. Therefore, parallel initiatives are needed to remove significant obstacles to financial inclusion. The barriers may be legislative or related to onerous documentation requirements that some may find difficult to meet. In such cases, pragmatic solutions can be developed without creating undue risks. Barriers may also be cultural or related to known and comfortable patterns of behavior, particularly a preference for using cash, in which case, habits may be more difficult to change. Many international initiatives have been established and best practices published to address this topic, particularly its impact on developing countries.

Structural barriers that may restrict the timely exchange of information need to be removed. Differences in legal systems and structures between jurisdictions can obstruct the timely exchange of information. Moreover, domestic legal or operational constraints on information exchange between relevant competent authorities (for example, intelligence services, FIUs, and supervisors) may undermine CFT measures. These barriers can also impact the reporting of suspicious activity within a time frame that could deter (perhaps imminent) terrorist activity. This constraint is particularly significant for international financial firms holding information of relevance for CFT purposes in multiple jurisdictions. Legislative and structural changes in individual jurisdictions may be needed to lower these barriers, supported by initiatives to expand information-exchange agreements beyond FIUs to also include law enforcement, intelligence, or other agencies with specific CFT responsibilities.

Friction between overlapping public policy objectives can undermine effective CFT measures. For example, steps to improve effectiveness need to be balanced against broader human rights issues and data protection requirements. However, the resulting compromises and technical complexities can have the unintended effect of delaying and undermining the information flows—particularly across borders—needed to deter and detect the financing of terrorism. As terrorists and their financiers may be able to exploit such barriers, authorities should support initiatives that streamline information sharing, subject to appropriate data protection.

Information on terrorism and its financing is sensitive and not made generally available for analysis by reporting entities. Nor do relevant competent authorities share information on the results of disruption and prevention in order to avoid compromising intelligence-gathering and other anti-terrorist measures. Intelligence, data, and information on terrorism and its financing are often treated as classified. Furthermore, there is no international agreement on the interpretation of available data for gauging the effectiveness of CFT measures.

Data in the public domain is incomplete and difficult to counterbalance with anecdotal evidence alone. As a result, assessment of the effectiveness of CFT measures is constrained. Difficulty in establishing the extent to which the measures are effective is compounded by links between terrorism and highly unstable environments that are often linked to armed conflict and political violence by governments. Initiatives to facilitate the release and international collation of sanitized data on disruption of terrorist financing schemes would be helpful. The indications are that international measures such as targeted financial sanctions, countermeasures, and embargoes can be disruptive and may constrain terrorist financing, though it is not possible to quantify the impact.

## CHALLENGES

Even as weaknesses in CFT implementation have been identified, so have many areas for improvement. Solutions to challenges are grouped here to help allocate responsibility, where applicable, to either the public or the private sector, with a view to recommending remedial actions and encouraging positive developments that enhance the effectiveness of CFT measures.

### Sharpen the Focus on Understanding and Assessing Terrorist Financing Risk

Reporting entities need to deepen their understanding of terrorist financing risks relevant to their business. For many, CFT does not go beyond a cursory check against sanctions lists. Overreliance on rules-based compliance is compounded by obliged entities taking insufficient steps to understand how terrorists and their supporters seek to misuse financial services. Terrorist groups have different operational organization models (for example, small cells, command and control terrorist networks, and corporate groups) besides individual terrorists acting alone. Each may use different financing methods (RUSI 2018). Reporting entities, in designing preventive systems, need to understand the distinctions between different types of terrorist groups and individuals and their methods for raising, moving, and using funds. That is essential for implementation of a risk-based approach and effective preventive measures.

It is in authorities' interest to support reporting entities by raising their awareness of terrorist financing and improving their understanding of its threats and typologies. Authorities should consider how best to provide reporting entities with up-to-date risk information and guidance relevant to their operations. They need to maintain a delicate balance between protecting intelligence sources and providing reporting entities with useful information to improve their CFT effectiveness. Intelligence services and law enforcement may be reluctant to share information due to legal, security, and operational concerns. This is reflected globally in national terrorist financing risk assessments, where the participation of reporting entities is often restricted. Moreover, the dissemination of assessment results to reporting entities is often constrained. Recent initiatives in certain countries and regions, as discussed later in this chapter, point to progress in developing controlled ways to share additional information. Reporting entities can also use published guidance (from the FATF, other international organizations, and many national authorities) to develop their own terrorist financing risk assessments and to train staff. Effectiveness can and should be tested as part of CFT supervision, with sanctions applied to reporting entities that cannot demonstrate it.

Terrorist financing risk assessments are not intended to prompt unwarranted de-risking. While compliance with international sanctions is needed, the closing of correspondent banking relationships has extended much more broadly than is warranted. This has had wide-reaching detrimental consequences for jurisdictions and their financial systems. Services to individuals and locations at high risk of exposure to terrorist financing or targeted financial sanctions have been terminated (World Bank 2015; IMF 2016). A range of factors lies behind termination, but featuring among important contributors are compliance costs, fear of withdrawal of a bank's own correspondent banking services, and regulatory pressure. Cutting services is more likely to divert funds to channels less open to detection rather than limit terrorist financing. As such, it is counterproductive to effective CFT. Financial service providers, therefore, should be incentivized to manage risks through improved controls rather than seeking to eliminate all risks by indiscriminate cessation of services.

## Increase Access to Relevant Information

Obstacles in exchanging information have significantly hindered the effectiveness of CFT efforts. Financial institutions report difficulties in implementing measures due to secrecy and privacy laws, including tipping off and similar provisions. These legal restrictions have constrained the exchange of information, including suspicious transaction reports (STRs), and restricted sharing between reporting entities that are not part of the same firm or group.

Legal restrictions can create other barriers to sharing CFT information within the private sector. Although wider sharing between reporting entities of information about suspicious indicators, transaction monitoring, or data on clients could increase detection of suspicious transactions, the FATF Recommendations do not explicitly reference such cooperation. Sharing this type of information is often restricted also within firms that operate internationally. A group-wide view of suspicious activities is impeded by bank secrecy, competition, privacy and confidentiality, and data localization laws (Institute of International Finance 2017). Though national legislation could enable domestic information sharing within the private sector, such provisions are not widely available in most jurisdictions. This topic should be explored with the aim of designing channels for controlled and protected information exchange that lead to a more effective system of preventive measures against terrorist financing.

In some instances, although information sharing and disclosure is allowed, reporting institutions opt not to take the opportunity because they lack clarity about their legal position. In these cases, authorities may need to give clear-cut guidance (FATF 2017). Moreover, competitive concerns may make firms reluctant to share compliance information. Where some reporting entities invest heavily in compliance, this information may be considered a competitive advantage that should be protected. In contrast, some compliance officers have been open to sharing with colleagues from less-resourced firms information on typologies, techniques, and system features. Authorities and industry associations should further encourage the sharing of such expertise.

## Costs of Detection and Reporting of Suspicious Activity

Identification of suspicious activities is resource-intensive, and monitoring may fail to capture a system-wide view. Reporting entities find it challenging and expensive to develop and implement effective monitoring systems that include adequate coverage of targeted financial sanctions and CFT. Their compliance officers typically review transactions against customer profiles and internal rules that prescribe indicators for suspicious activities. In some cases, these processes are conducted manually. In many cases, these processes can be disjointed, with separate focus on customers' profiles and transaction monitoring and no coherent view of overall activity. A piecemeal approach makes it challenging to identify complex patterns or understand transactions on a system-wide basis (Center for Global Development 2018). Partly because of this, even as reporting entities may analyze suspicious activities, they often do not submit reports to the competent authorities. Reporting entities need to reconsider their compliance systems and manual analysis, upgrading where necessary to close current gaps and weaknesses in coverage.

The number of reported transactions relating to suspicions of terrorist financing continues to be low across most jurisdictions. The reporting is intended to prevent and detect abuse of the financial system, to develop intelligence, and to provide leads for investigators to counter terrorist financing and other criminal activities. Global STR data that relates specifically to terrorist financing is not available, but again the numbers are believed to be low. According to Europol, less than 1 percent of STRs that European FIUs receive involve suspicions of terrorist financing (Europol 2017). Although STRs, by their nature, may not lead directly to regular law enforcement investigations, and even though there is no "correct" or ideal level, such reports are considered valuable for investigating terrorist financing and terrorism, particularly when combined with other sources. Their role is considered in detail in Chapter 3.

STRs related to terrorist financing should be encouraged, as they can lead directly to investigations or prosecutions (FATF 2008). Many instances on record show how STRs from reporting entities have led directly to investigations involving the financing of terrorism, the prevention of terrorist attacks, or the detection of terrorist networks (Brzoska 2011; UN Security Council 2011). Nonetheless, most terrorist financing investigations are initiated by traditional law enforcement detection techniques, such as using informants (Waszak 2004).

## GOOD PRACTICES

A number of countries have taken initiatives that seek to respond to the challenges and limitations already discussed. This section explores innovative approaches to improving the efficiency and effectiveness of CFT preventive measures. The innovations are predominantly technology-based and involve methods of accessing, analyzing, and sharing useful indicators of potential terrorist financing activity.

## Reporting Entities Can Find Ways to Strengthen Their Contribution to Effective CFT

Ongoing developments aim to improve the value of STRs for detecting terrorist financing transactions and activities. Reporting entities are working with financial intelligence and investigative authorities to improve risk profiles and develop indicators relating to, for example, the nexus between terrorism and organized crime, the purchase of strategic goods, transactions involving travel, transfers to areas afflicted by terrorist violence, large donations to questionable charities.

Reporting entities are increasingly investing in their ability to counter terrorist financing. Despite, or perhaps due to, challenges in identifying activities and people related to terrorist financing, they are spending more on innovative counterterrorist financing approaches, working on in-house intelligence, and developing collaborations with other entities. A more targeted approach to the disruption of terrorist financing and better allocation and efficacy of compliance spending is the result. This creates a better return on their CFT efforts and improved customer trust and reputation, as well as satisfying ethical responsibilities.

Sharing information with financial intelligence and the law enforcement community is yielding tangible outcomes. Jurisdictions have indicated that targeted ongoing monitoring and record keeping by reporting entities has contributed significantly to investigations into terrorist financing and terrorism, in some cases leading to arrests, prosecutions, and convictions. The information gathered by reporting entities not only serves as intelligence for specific investigations but is also leveraged to analyze financial flows for terrorism and the use of transfer systems and networks between persons and groups (Global Counterterrorism Forum 2018).

> **Examples\* of Public–Private Partnerships (PPPs)**
> 
> - UK Joint Money Laundering Intelligence Taskforce (JMLIT)
> - The Australian Fintel Alliance
> - The Singapore AML/CFT Industry Partnership
> - Hong Kong Fraud and ML Intelligence Taskforce
> - Austrian Public–Private-Partnership (PPP) Initiative
> - The Netherlands Terrorist Financing Taskforce
> - The US FinCEN Exchange
> - Germany Anti-Financial Crime Alliance (AFCA)
> - Ireland Joint Intelligence Group (JIG)
> - Latvia Cooperation Coordination Group
> 
> \*This is not an exhaustive list. Other jurisdictions may have established forms of PPPs more recently.

## Public Sector Can Make a Stronger Contribution to Partnering with Reporting Entities

In a small but increasing number of countries, collaboration through public–private partnership platforms[2] has led to better risk-focused tailoring of preventive measures. This includes work on developing enhanced risk indicators, risk profiling, and jointly developed algorithms that help direct data analysis, including technology-driven analysis.

The creation of joint task forces has enabled ongoing sharing of operational information behind closed doors. For example, the United Kingdom has adopted legislation that enables experimentation with practices to grant formal security clearance to a vetted group of compliance officers from reporting entities and to set up an innovative information-sharing system (Levi 2010; RUSI 2016). Hong Kong SAR and Australia have set up similar public–private information-sharing partnerships (FATF 2017). These platforms convene law enforcement and financial institutions to discuss money laundering and terrorist financing risks. The national authority oversees and facilitates information exchange between government authorities and financial institutions based on law enforcement priorities. Such collaborative innovation can enhance effectiveness significantly. An intelligence-led approach can encourage targeted monitoring and reporting. This would focus efforts on generating information that is of direct benefit to investigations and prosecutions (Clearing House 2017; Europol 2017; RUSI 2017). These types of partnerships to combat financial crimes are becoming more widespread (Levi 2010).

Adequate trust needs to be built when improving information-sharing facilities. Trust can be fostered through better guidance and protective measures (Europol 2017). Risks that the shared information could be leaked or used for other purposes, or that control of the data is lost need to be managed carefully (RUSI 2016).

---

[2] For example, the United Kingdom established JMLIT in 2015 as a partnership between law enforcement and the financial sector to exchange and analyze information relating to money laundering and wider economic threats. Membership includes 40 private sector participants and all relevant public authorities.

In 2017, the AUSTRAC launched Fintel Alliance, a public–private partnership that brings together government, industry, academia, and international partners to harness a new and collaborative approach to combat and disrupt money laundering and terrorist financing. The alliance has since expanded to 25 public and private sector members.

Ireland also established a public–private partnership in 2017 known as the JIG. At present, members are the FIU, the main retail banks, and the largest money remittance firm operating in the jurisdiction.

In Germany, in September 2019, the Federal Financial Supervisory Authority (BaFin) launched the AFCA together with the FIU, the Federal Criminal Police Office (*Bundeskriminalamt*), and 14 banks. As a public–private partnership, these authorities and banks are seeking to strengthen and coordinate the fight against money laundering and terrorist financing under the FIU's leadership.

## Innovations in Technology Can Enhance the Effectiveness of Preventive Measures

Innovations in financial technology can offer solutions to improve the effectiveness and efficiency of efforts to prevent and detect terrorist financing. For example, technology enables efficient record keeping and swift retrieval, and it facilitates communication between different databases that previously operated as separate, unlinked information silos. Data mining can create big data pools, allowing much wider possibilities for analysis. Innovations in artificial intelligence create opportunities for pattern and network recognition, risk profiling, and ongoing monitoring beyond human capabilities.

Some countries are already experimenting with exciting possibilities for the use of innovative technologies. Know Your Customer utilities have been created to reduce the costs and duplication of customer due diligence. Biometrics and Legal Entity Identifiers enable more secure and automated authentication of the identity of customers. Distributed ledger technology presents possibilities to monitor all transactions in the financial system for suspicious activities in real time. This could reduce the need for the current construct for detecting and reporting suspicious activities (Clearing House 2017). Competent authorities could be given access to the network to monitor anonymized transactions flow in real time.

Where investigation would be necessary, a master key could decrypt data, based on a subpoena or other procedural conditions (Center for Global Development 2018; Pisa and Juden 2017). Big data allows for sophisticated and comprehensive analysis, pattern recognition, and improved efficiency of searches using aggregate data. Moreover, financial data could be complemented with machine learning to draw many different factors into the analysis, including customers' social media information and intelligence. That would be a big improvement on current analysis capabilities (Center for Global Development 2018). It should be borne in mind that such tools, though welcome, might be out of reach for smaller financial institutions and DNFBPs due to financial and capacity constraints. Industry associations could help solve these challenges; for example, by pooling resources.

Looking further to the future, improved secure digital communication technology may support direct communication between reporting entities, intelligence agencies, and law enforcement agencies. The need for secure communication channels and working platforms has been identified as a basis to develop financial information sharing partnerships. Rather than improving communication between different technological systems, partners could seek out shared working platforms equipped with advanced cryptography (RUSI 2017). Direct communication would allow reporting entities to increase their intelligence-led monitoring. Through distributed ledger technology, a real time database developed by intelligence services and law enforcement agencies could be accessed by authorized parties and enable cross-matching and searches through their data sources. Response times and the need for intermediation by FIUs would be reduced, freeing up resources for FIUs to concentrate more on other analysis functions. This is an ambitious prospect. Its progress would depend on whether many legal and data protection issues could be resolved.

## Public Sector Support for Reporting Entity Investments in Technological Innovation

The full potential of financial technology can only be realized if policymakers support it. Over time, innovations in financial technology could increase the effectiveness of CFT controls. So far, the adoption of technological innovation has been limited by the current levels of technical expertise. Likewise, reporting entities may be reluctant to invest in technological solutions to improve their compliance on issues that regulators are unable to assess (Center for Global Development 2018).

Policymakers could explore how to best create trust to foster experimentation that increases the effectiveness and efficiency of CFT measures. Regulatory sandboxes are among the chosen approaches. These involve a relaxation of regulatory requirements sufficient to allow innovative technologies to be tested in a live, yet controlled, environment. Supervisors in Malaysia, the Netherlands, Singapore, Thailand, and the United Kingdom, among other jurisdictions, have accommodated innovation through creative use of their laws and interpretation of supervisory rules. This encompasses not only testing of new products and services but also the use of technological solutions for AML/CFT compliance. In due course, such innovative thinking may produce practical solutions for wide application.

Recent international initiatives further encourage and accommodate the use of technology for data analysis and information sharing. Standard setters and other international organizations have been monitoring private sector developments in technology for sharing information—both in the financial sector and in the technology providers—and considering how to facilitate information exchange while respecting privacy rights. Although this work is not focused specifically on terrorist financing, the techniques are relevant since they can be applied to all forms of financial crime. In particular, FATF's July 2021 *Stocktake on Data Pooling, Collaborative Analytics, and Data Protection* includes examples of data pooling and collaborative analytics that can help reporting entities to better understand, assess, and mitigate money laundering and terrorist financing risks. It notes developments in privacy-enhancing technologies that will assist with resolving valid confidentiality and data protection concerns, and it mentions that a technical standard in this area is yet to be developed. The report builds on guidance for information sharing in the private sector (FATF 2017), which deals with issues relating to the exchange of compliance information among financial institutions and across financial groups, including on a cross-border basis. Alongside analysis from the EU and the UN, the ongoing FATF studies signal international support for further development of viable methods of data analysis and information sharing that respects data protection objectives.

## CONCLUSION

Private sector firms have shown on occasion a commitment and ability to cooperate closely with competent authorities in tracing financial activity linked to terrorism. Extending this attitude more generally to ongoing implementation of risk-based preventive measures would assist authorities in disrupting terrorist activity. By contrast, emphasis in the private sector to date has been mainly to meet CFT rules rather than to assess risks. Authorities and reporting entities both point to barriers to information exchange as a key limitation of the effectiveness of CFT preventive measures, and they note that it has generated frustration for both parties. The focus has tended to fall back to implementing the requirements for targeted financial sanctions, with little attention given to CFT risk analysis and effective preventive measures. A better approach is needed to bridge the information gap between the public and private sectors and to pave the way for information access and exchange, subject to appropriate controls, to enhance the effectiveness of risk-based CFT measures.

Action is needed to make CFT preventive measures more effective. Current constraints include (1) a range of inherent limitations that will be difficult to address, and (2) operational challenges for which solutions could be identified and implemented more broadly. As outlined in this chapter, the limitations are most acute in jurisdictions with less-developed financial systems. They include dependence on cash, financial exclusion, the use of money remitters, informal and parallel financial networks, and the small size of many terrorist financing transactions, which makes them difficult to distinguish. Identified constraints create barriers to relevant and timely information flows between reporting entities and relevant competent authorities. The innovative approaches presented in this chapter could enhance these information flows, subject to appropriate confidentiality controls.

Reporting entities need to assess their terrorist financing risk separately from money laundering risk and maintain comprehensive records that can be retrieved promptly. While the threats identified by carrying out a terrorist financing risk assessment may be more sporadic and difficult to define than those associated with money laundering, it is nonetheless useful to follow the same broad analytical approach, with focus on customer profiling and geographical risk. Particularly for terrorist financing cases (including post-terrorist attack), reporting entities can be critical for responding to urgent requests for information on transactions and patterns of transactions. This makes reliable record retrieval systems essential.

Obstacles to exchanging information can significantly hinder the effectiveness of CFT efforts. Innovative mechanisms for exchange of relevant information between the public and private sectors, between reporting entities domestically, between group entities, and, potentially, across borders should be developed. This may require legislative changes to open channels for information exchange, while respecting genuine confidentiality concerns. Innovative reporting entities are investing in technology-based CFT approaches, working on in-house intelligence, and developing collaborations. At the same time, it should be acknowledged that smaller reporting entities and those in less-developed financial systems struggle to invest in such resources.

There is merit in deeper cooperation and information exchange between the public and private sectors. Thanks to developments in communication platforms and technology, law enforcement agencies in some countries can share with selected private sector entities valuable data that improves the effectiveness of risk profiling and data analysis.

The potential of financial technology as an instrument against terrorist financing is being more widely explored. Innovative systems developed by some reporting entities improve risk assessment, ongoing monitoring through pattern recognition, and record keeping. Indeed, technological developments offer the prospect of improving the efficiency and effectiveness of processes to combat terrorist financing, particularly when protocols are developed so the analysis can be accessed by FIUs and used for law enforcement.

These positive initiatives indicate the potential for the private sector to make a greater contribution to CFT. This matters both in the preventive stage and when transaction data and other information is provided to competent authorities following terrorist atrocities. Lastly, technology-based initiatives require private sector investments. From a public sector perspective, there is likely to be a need to amend legislation and the support structures for the exchange of information and intelligence.

## REFERENCES

Brzoska, Michael. 2011a. "Counter-Terrorist Financing—A Good Policy Going Too Far?" *EUSECON Policy Briefing, No. 7*. Accessed September 16, 2021. https://www.diw.de/documents/publikationen/73/diw_01.c.391386.de/diw_eusecon_pb0007.pdf.

Brzoska, Michael. 2011b. "The Role of Effectiveness and Efficiency in the European Union's Counterterrorism Policy: The Case of Terrorist Financing." *Economics of Security Working Paper 51*. Berlin: Economics of Security.

Centre for Global Development. 2018. "Fixing AML: Can New Technology Help Address the De-Risking Dilemma?" Accessed June 2022. https://www.cgdev.org/sites/default/files/fixing-aml-can-new-technology-help-address-de-risking-dilemma.pdf.

Clearing House. 2017. *A New Paradigm: Redesigning the U.S. AML/CFT Framework to Protect National Security and Aid Law Enforcement*. Accessed September 16, 2021. https://bpi.com/wp-content/uploads/2018/07/20170216_tch_report_aml_cft_framework_redesign.pdf.

Europol. 2017. *From Suspicion to Action: Converting Financial Intelligence into Greater Operational Impact*. The Hague, Netherlands ql-01-17-932-en-c_pf_final.pdf.

Financial Action Task Force (FATF). 2008. *Terrorist Financing*. Paris. https://www.fatf-gafi.org/content/fatf-gafi/en/publications/Methodsandtrends/Fatfterroristfinancingtypologiesreport.html.

Financial Action Task Force (FATF). 2012–2022. *International Standards on Combating Money Laundering and the Financing of Terrorism & Proliferation*. https://www.fatf-gafi.org/content/fatf-gafi/en/publications/Fatfrecommendations/Fatf-recommendations.html.

Financial Action Task Force (FATF). 2015a. *FATF Report: Emerging Terrorist Financing Risks*. Paris. https://www.fatf-gafi.org/content/fatf-gafi/en/publications/Methodsandtrends/Emerging-terrorist-financing-risks.html.

Financial Action Task Force (FATF). 2015b. *Terrorist Financing: FATF Report to G20 Leaders—Actions being taken by the FATF*. Paris. https://www.fatf-gafi.org/content/fatf-gafi/en/publications/Fatfrecommendations/Terrorist-financing-fatf-report-to-g20.html.

Financial Action Task Force (FATF). 2017. *FATF Guidance: Private Sector Information Sharing*. Paris. https://www.fatf-gafi.org/content/fatf-gafi/en/publications/Fatfgeneral/Guidance-information-sharing.html.

Financial Action Task Force (FATF). 2019. *FATF Report: Terrorist Financing Risk Assessment Guidance*. Accessed September 16, 2021. https://www.fatf-gafi.org/content/fatf-gafi/en/publications/Methodsandtrends/Terrorist-financing-risk-assessment-guidance.html.

Financial Action Task Force (FATF). 2021. *Stocktake on Data Pooling, Collaborative Analytics and Data Protection*. Paris. https://www.fatf-gafi.org/content/fatf-gafi/en/publications/Digitaltransformation/Data-pooling-collaborative-analytics-data-protection.html.

Global Counterterrorism Forum. 2018. "The Hague Good Practices on the Nexus between Transnational Organized Crime and Terrorism." Accessed September 16, 2021. https://www.thegctf.org/Portals/1/Documents/Framework%20Documents/2018/GCTF-Good-Practices-on-the-Nexus_ENG.pdf?ver=2018-09-21-122246-363.

Halliday, Terence C., Michael Levi, and Peter Reuter. 2014. "Global Surveillance of Dirty Money: Assessing Assessments of Regimes to Control Money-Laundering and Combat the Financing of Terrorism." Center on Law & Globalization.

Institute of International Finance. 2017. *Financial Crime Information Sharing Survey Report*.

International Monetary Fund (IMF) and World Bank. 2003. *Informal Funds Transfer Systems: An Analysis of the Informal Hawala System*. Washington, DC. https://www.imf.org/external/pubs/nft/op/222/index.htm.

Levi, Michael. 2010. "Public and Private Policing of Financial Crimes: The Struggle for Co-Ordination." *Journal of Criminal Justice and Security* 12, no. 4: 343–354.

Maxwell, Nick J., and David Artingstall. 2017. "The Role of Financial Information-Sharing Partnerships in the Disruption of Crime." *RUSI Occasional Paper*. Accessed September 16, 2021. https://static.rusi.org/201710_rusi_the_role_of_fisps_in_the_disruption_of_crime_maxwwell_artingstall_web_4.2.pdf.

Pisa, Michael, and Matt Juden. 2017. "Blockchain and Economic Development: Hype vs. Reality." Centre for Global Development. https://www.cgdev.org/sites/default/files/blockchain-and-economic-development-hype-vs-reality_0.pdf.

UN Security Council. 2011. *Eleventh Report by the Analytical Support and Sanctions Monitoring Team*, S/2011/245. New York.

Waszak, J. D. G. 2004. "The Obstacles to Suppressing Radical Islamic Terrorist Financing." *Case Western Reserve Journal of International Law* 36: 673–710.

World Bank. 2015. *Withdrawal from Correspondent Banking: Where, Why, and What to Do about It*. Washington, DC. https://documents1.worldbank.org/curated/en/113021467990964789/pdf/101098-revised-PUBLIC-CBR-Report-November-2015.pdf.

# RESOURCES

Biersteker, T. J., S. E. Eckert, and M. Tourinho. 2016. "Targeted Sanctions: The Impacts and Effectiveness of United Nations Action." Accessed September 16, 2021. https://scholar.google.com/scholar?q=related:GEuRli3r0vUJ:scholar.google.com/&scioq=&hl=en&as_sdt=0,5.

Counter-Terrorism Implementation Task Force (CTITF). *Working Group Report—Tackling the Financing of Terrorism*. Accessed September 16, 2021. https://www.un.org/counterterrorism/ctitf/sites/www.un.org.counterterrorism.ctitf/files/ctitf_financing_eng_final.pdf.

De Goede, Marieke, and Mara Wesseling. 2017. "Secrecy and Security in Transatlantic Terrorist Financing Tracking." *Journal of European Integration* 39, no. 3: 253–269.

Deloitte. 2009. *Facing the Sanctions Challenge in Financial Services: A Global Sanctions Compliance Study*. Accessed September 16, 2021. Facing the sanctions challenge in financial services.pdf (deloitte.com).

De Oliveira, Inês Sofia. 2016. "Challenges to Information Sharing. Perceptions and Realities." *RUSI Occasional Paper*. Accessed September 16, 2021. https://static.rusi.org/20160708_ines_challenges_to_info_sharing_final1.pdf.

Erbenová, Michaela, Yan Liu, Nadim Kyriakos-Saad, Alejandro López-Mejía, Giancarlo Gasha, Emmanuel Mathias, Mohamed Norat, Francisca Fernando, and Yasmin Almeida. 2016. "The Withdrawal of Correspondent Banking Relationships: A Case for Policy Action." Fund Staff Discussion Note SDN/16/06. Accessed September 16, 2021. https://www.imf.org/external/pubs/ft/sdn/2016/sdn1606.pdf.

Financial Action Task Force (FATF). 2007. *Guidance on the Risk-Based Approach to Combating Money-Laundering and Terrorist Financing, High-Level Principles and Procedures*. Accessed September 16, 2021. https://www.fatf-gafi.org/content/fatf-gafi/en/publications/Fatfrecommendations/Fatfguidanceontherisk-basedapproachtocombatingmoneylaunderingandterroristfinancing-highlevelprinciplesandprocedures.html.

Financial Action Task Force (FATF). 2015. *Terrorist Financing: FATF Report to G20 Leaders—Actions Being Taken by the FATF*. Paris. https://www.fatf-gafi.org/content/fatf-gafi/en/publications/Fatfrecommendations/Terrorist-financing-fatf-report-to-g20.html.

Graduate Institute of International and Development Studies. 2014. "UN Targeted Sanctions." Qualitative Database. Accessed September 16, 2021. https://www.graduateinstitute.ch/research-centres/global-governance-centre/targeted-sanctions-initiative.

Heißner, Stefan, Peter R. Neumann, and John Holland-McCowan. 2015. "Caliphate in Decline: An Estimate of Islamic State's Financial Fortunes." The International Centre for the Study of Radicalisation and Political Violence and Ernst and Young. Accessed September 16, 2021. https://icsr.info/wp-content/uploads/2017/02/ICSR-Report-Caliphate-in-Decline-An-Estimate-of-Islamic-States-Financial-Fortunes.pdf.

Keatinge, Tom, Florence Keen, and Anton Moiseienko. 2018. "From Lone Actors to Daesh: Rethinking the Response to the Diverse Threats of Terrorist Financing." *RUSI Newsbrief* 38, no. 1 (January). Accessed September 16, 2021. https://rusieurope.eu/sites/default/files/20180123_terrorist_financing_proof1.pdf.

Levi, Michael. 2010. "Combating the Financing of Terrorism: A History and Assessment of the Control of 'Threat Finance,'" *British Journal of Criminology* 50, no. 4: 650–669.

Neumann, Peter R. 2017. "Don't Follow the Money: The Problem with the War on Terrorist Financing." *Foreign Affairs* (July/August). Accessed September 16, 2021. https://www.foreignaffairs.com/articles/2017-06-13/dont-follow-money.

O'Donoghue, Cynthia. 2013. "Data Protection vs. Anti-Money Laundering, Counter Terrorism and Traceable Money Transfers." *Technology Law Dispatch* (August 21). Accessed September 16, 2021. https://www.technologylawdispatch.com/2013/08/global-data-transfers/data-protection-vs-antimoney-laundering-counter-terrorism-and-traceable-money-transfers/.

Oftedal, Emilie. 2014. "The Financing of Jihadi Terrorist Cells in Europe." *Forsvarets forskningsinstitutt, FFI-rapport 2014/02234*. Accessed September 16, 2021. https://publications.ffi.no/nb/item/asset/dspace:2469/14-02234.pdf.

Passas, N. 2012. "Terrorist Finance, Informal Markets, Trade and Regulation: Challenges of Evidence Regarding International Efforts." *Evidence-Based Counterterrorism Policy*, vol. 3.

UN Office on Drugs and Crime. 2007. *Study on Fraud and the Criminal Use and Falsification of Identity*.

UN Security Council. 2012. *Thirteenth Report by the Analytical Support and Sanctions Monitoring Team*, S/2012/968.

UN Security Council. 2013. *Fourteenth Report by the Analytical Support and Sanctions Monitoring Team*, S/2013/467.

Vlcek, William. 2007. "Hitting the Right Target: EU and Security Council Pursuit of Terrorist Financing." London School of Economics.

# CHAPTER 3

# The Production and Use of Financial Intelligence to Counter Terrorism and Terrorist Financing

Sabrina Lando and Marilyne Landry

## CHAPTER IN BRIEF

### The Challenge

In most jurisdictions, financial investigations are often perceived as too complex or time consuming in time-sensitive cases or as requiring extensive financial and technical skills. Consequently, some investigators might disregard looking into the financial aspect of their cases, and some agencies may fail to appreciate the strategic value of financial intelligence to better orient their operations. Current perceptions prevent concerned authorities from achieving outcomes possible from the adequate production/use of financial intelligence.

### Why It Happens

The sources of financial intelligence to counter terrorism and terrorist financing are beyond reporting entities and include a web of data sources from both the public and private sectors. The IMF's experience suggests that most jurisdictions find it difficult to design a jurisdiction-specific web of public and private data sources. Useful data sources to counter terrorism and terrorist financing include stakeholders that may not be immediately identified by investigators, such as travel agents and social media platforms. As for traditional sectors that are expected to produce financial intelligence—such as financial institutions (FIs), designated non-financial businesses and professions (DNFBPs), and virtual asset service providers (VASPs)—concerned authorities must ensure that appropriate preventative measures are maintained to produce useful financial intelligence. Adequate risk understanding, due diligence, suspicious reporting, and record-keeping procedures are essential to producing financial intelligence. For DNFBPs and VASPs (primarily due to its emerging nature), this is especially challenging for concerned authorities to maintain due to (1) lack of scoping for terrorism and terrorist financing issues, (2) the size of the sectors, and (3) the evolving level of financial crime sophistication seen within those sectors. Even within FIs, terrorism- and terrorist financing-related indicators are often overwhelmed by money laundering indicators—which may result in a lower degree of focus on terrorism and terrorist financing. Furthermore, two-way communication mechanisms between concerned authorities and the private sector are not always in place, which results in outdated information maintained by the private sector and lower quality reports.

> **The Solution**
>
> This chapter explains how to facilitate access to information among public entities themselves—as well as the private sector—by way of public/private partnerships. Examples of stakeholders and the types of mechanisms to use are explained in detail to facilitate the design of a jurisdiction's financial intelligence infrastructure. Oversight on the informal remittance sector is essential to obtaining terrorism- and terrorist financing-related financial intelligence. Countries should establish the required procedures with consideration to human rights and economic implications. Financial Intelligence Units (FIUs) are at the helm of financial intelligence, and this chapter explains how they should be legally set up, empowered, trained in terrorism and terrorist financing, appropriately resourced, as well as achieve international interconnectedness.

## AN ADDED-VALUE CONTRIBUTION TO INVESTIGATIONS

> *The gathering and dissemination of intelligence should be at the center of all work to combat terrorist financing. Yet its strategic value in orienting counterterrorism operations is too often overlooked in favor of other leads. All evidence, however, points to the increasing value of financial investigations—if practitioners can get comfortable with their complex challenges.*

Financial investigation[1] is becoming integral to effective counterterrorism efforts in many jurisdictions. Financial intelligence has gathered valuable information in efforts to disrupt the financing of terrorist organizations, identify terrorist networks, and reconstruct events by providing the law enforcement and intelligence community with information they would not otherwise have. While some questions surround the actual contribution of financial intelligence to the prevention of terrorist attacks, recent efforts and potential to maximize the work of intelligence agencies and the effectiveness of financial investigations increasingly emphasize that such intelligence provides added value (Levitt and Bauer 2017, Neumann 2017).

Financial investigations have helped not only unveil the complex financial structure of terrorist organizations, but also retrace the activities and networks of small cells and lone actors. Disrupting complex terrorist organizations that have become state actors requires a comprehensive and multiagency approach in which

---

[1] The Financial Action Task Force (FATF) defines financial investigations as "an enquiry into the financial affairs related to criminal conduct. The major goal of a financial investigation is to identify and document the movement of money during the course of criminal activity." — FATF, *Operational Issues Financial Investigation Guidance*, 2012. https://www.fatf-gafi.org/content/fatf-gafi/en/publications/Methodsandtrends/Operationalissues-financialinvestigationsguidance.html

extensive financial investigation is among the imperatives. As some terrorist organizations rely on trade of goods or commodities generated within the territory they control, the upstream and downstream domestic and cross-border funding ramifications of such operations must be disrupted while letting legitimate transactions continue. On the other end of the spectrum, terrorist attacks by small cells and lone actors are difficult to prevent. Their financing is problematic to detect because of the small amounts involved and the multiplicity of ways that terrorism can be perpetrated. However, through financial intelligence gathering and financial investigations, FIUs and law enforcement have identified associates and financiers and, in all likelihood, have been able to prevent additional attacks.

Financial intelligence is most likely to be used as a means to uncover new intelligence and evidence. Financial intelligence can contribute to the initiation and development of investigations by identifying and detecting networks and associates before and after attacks. For example, finding portions of a credit card number at the scene of an attack or tracking down the number of an account used to purchase chemicals in a bomb can help law enforcement and intelligence agencies to identify facilitators of terrorism. Financial intelligence can also add value by linking individuals under surveillance to a known terrorist organization and acquiring imagery from retailers or ATMs to identify terrorists. This intelligence can often be the missing link in a counterterrorism investigation and can uncover information and evidence not otherwise available.

Strategic analysis of terrorist financing cases has been useful in post-attack investigations. The identification of recurring financial trends has helped detect affiliates and supporters. It has also been instrumental in the disruption of financial networks developed to support terrorists or terrorist organizations, most notably with respect to the Islamic State of Iraq and the Levant (ISIL), where complex and expansive financial networks allowed the organization to spread its governance over large territories.

Financial intelligence could add value to or help better focus the efforts of agencies with a counterterrorism mandate. Financial investigations are often regarded as too complex or time-consuming, or are thought to require extensive financial and technical skills. Consequently, some investigators might disregard the financial aspect of their case, and some agencies may not appreciate the strategic value of financial intelligence to better orient their operations. However, law enforcement agencies, the military, intelligence services, and customs agencies have debunked this perception and made financial intelligence and exchange of information with the national FIU integral to their activities. In doing so, they have developed more informed strategies and actions.

## EVOLUTION OF INTERNATIONAL NORMS AND PRACTICES

The evolution of international standards on CFT recognizes that harnessing the full potential of financial intelligence should be part of any CFT strategy. The first requirements regarding reporting suspicious transactions related to terrorism and physical cross-border transportation of currencies were introduced by the 1999 International Convention for the Suppression of the Financing of Terrorism (United Nations 1999) and the 2001 Special Recommendations of the Financial Action Task Force (FATF). Since then, detection and reporting of suspicions have evolved, and the growing volume of filed reports has generated important metadata. In July 2017, G20 leaders called for further steps to refine this practice, notably developing new financial intelligence tools to better track terrorist finance transactions. They also encouraged law enforcement to bridge the intelligence gap and improve the use of financial information in counterterrorism investigations (G20 Leader's Declaration 2017).

The 1990 FATF Recommendations and 1999 International Convention for the Suppression of the Financing of Terrorism called for the adoption of requirements for financial institutions to report suspicious transactions to competent authorities but without indicating who this authority should be. It was only with the issuance of the 2003 Recommendations that the FATF recognized the need for an FIU as part of the AML/CFT national framework. The first FIUs were established in the early 1990s in response to the need for a central agency to receive, analyze, and disseminate financial information to combat money laundering. The Egmont Group of FIUs is an international network of FIUs created in 1995 and designed to improve communication, information sharing, and training coordination among its membership, which now numbers 166.

FATF and the Egmont Group have worked hard to improve financial intelligence practices and better define the role of FIUs. The 2013 FATF Methodology requires that financial intelligence and all other relevant information be used for terrorist financing investigations, including by mobilizing resources and skills to use this information to conduct analysis and financial investigations, to identify and trace the assets, and to develop operational analysis. It also expects that national coordination and cooperation between law enforcement agencies, customs agencies, and national and international FIUs will be effective. FATF and the Egmont Group have provided guidance on best practices in this respect and have reinforced this priority, notably with the FATF strategy on CFT first issued in 2015 and the Egmont Group 2016 Communiqué on CFT.

The effectiveness of the CFT regimes with respect to financial intelligence is difficult to evaluate. FIU capabilities and mandates are evolving at different speeds and developments in the financial intelligence field have been uneven. While similarities exist in the overarching mandates of FIUs, their structures and powers can be widely different. It is, therefore, difficult to compare their effectiveness, particularly as their place in the national intelligence community is not formally established in many countries. A number of mutual evaluation reports against the 2013 FATF Methodology on IO.6 provide little insight into the use of intelligence for counterterrorism/CFT purposes, with the focus mostly on money laundering and FIU effectiveness. As discussed in the upcoming section about the challenges regarding the analysis of information, these are not always at the center of the financial intelligence cycle for counterterrorism/CFT. Nonetheless, the contribution of FIUs and their intelligence products to counterterrorism efforts has been improving (see Figure 3.1).

### Figure 3.1. Ratings of Countries Against the FATF Standards on the Effective Use of Financial Intelligence for Money Laundering/Terrorist Financing Investigations (IO.6)[1]

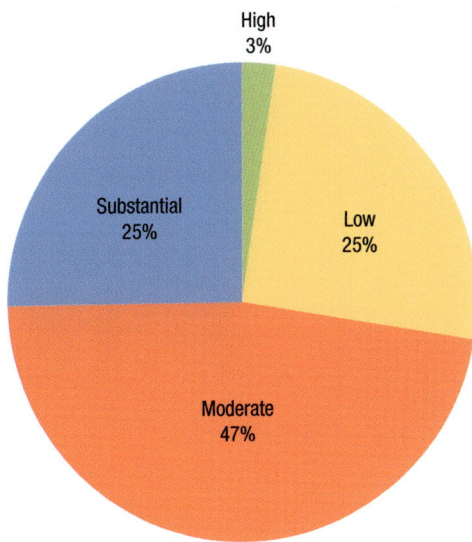

Source: Financial Action Task Force (FATF).
[1] Based on 127 mutual evaluation reports published by June 2022.

# THE FINANCIAL INTELLIGENCE CYCLE

Analysis in this chapter is organized along the main points of the financial intelligence cycle, as depicted in Figure 3.2. The cycle consists of three phases: receipt and collection, analysis, and dissemination. These three key FIU functions are in line with the FATF standard and provide a condensed version of the intelligence cycle outlined in the Egmont Tactical and Strategic Analysis Courses. Although initially referenced in the context of FIU operations, this financial intelligence cycle is also relevant for law enforcement and intelligence agencies undertaking their own financial intelligence activities.

The receipt and collection phase is the gathering of the raw information needed to produce finished intelligence. In the collection phase, financial analysts are called to plan their data collection activity, evaluate information they have gathered, and collate it. Information is provided by the private sector (including through transaction monitoring and suspicious transaction reports [STRs]), government agencies (for example, law enforcement, intelligence, and revenue agencies), and publicly available information (such as the internet, commercial databases, and the like).

At the analysis phase, the analysts from FIUs, intelligence agencies, and law enforcement agencies convert the information into intelligence through the integration, evaluation, and interpretation of all source data. To identify and bring together disparate pieces of information, the analyst must have in-depth

### Figure 3.2. Financial Intelligence Cycle

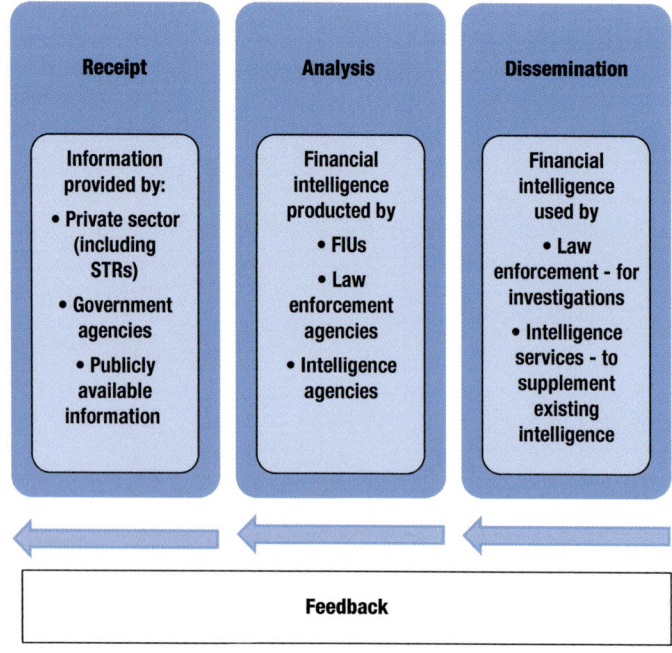

Source: IMF staff.
Note: FIU = Financial Intelligence Unit; STR = suspicious transaction reports.

understanding of the subject and the strength/reliability of sources, the operating environment, and end user's requirements. It is at the analysis stage that the financial intelligence product is prepared.

Finally, the dissemination phase is where analyzed intelligence information is distributed in the most appropriate format to the recipient competent authority and ultimately used by law enforcement in financial and other investigations, and by intelligence agencies and defense agencies for intelligence purposes.

Feedback is essential to every phase of the intelligence cycle. Analyzed information can provide feedback to the intelligence and law enforcement agencies that produced the intelligence and to private sector sources that gathered information for the intelligence. This feedback loop can help private and public sector actors to better understand indicators of suspicious behaviors and so provide more pertinent and targeted information.

The effectiveness of this cycle is influenced by many other parts of the CFT regime. For example, the quality of information collected will depend on the sophistication and efficiency of reporting systems, including the scope of the obligations imposed on the private sector in relation to identification of customers and filing of STRs. The cycle functions properly when reporting entities' understanding of risks is based on their own knowledge of a client risk profile as well as efforts and proper communication by national authorities on risk assessment results. These challenges were discussed in greater detail in Chapters 1 and 2. Similarly, the effectiveness of dissemination and use of financial intelligence is a function of the effectiveness of national coordination mechanisms and international cooperation, which are discussed in Chapter 6.

The financial intelligence community of FIUs, law enforcement, customs, and intelligence agencies must face challenges related to the production and use of financial intelligence in their efforts to combat terrorism and terrorist financing. These can occur at different stages of the cycle and relate to cumbersome processes of accessing information and intelligence as well as impediments to sharing and using financial intelligence. They are discussed in the following sections of this chapter.

A number of good practices to facilitate and enhance the use of financial intelligence to counter terrorism and terrorist financing have been identified to deal with these issues. Good practices stem both from domestic innovations and efforts by international organizations such as the IMF, the Egmont Group, FATF, INTERPOL, Europol, and the UN to identify and promote best practices for financial intelligence analysis and investigations. Some of these are discussed in the next section.

The critical issues and good practices were partially identified through an expert meeting on the use of financial intelligence to support CFT efforts.[2] The meeting included participants from international organizations and representatives from a cross-section of national law enforcement and intelligence agencies, including FIUs, police, and specialized teams focused on terrorism investigations. Although some tactical good practices were identified, discussions centered around institutional measures that hinder the production and use of financial intelligence.

## CHALLENGES IN ACCESSING AND COLLECTING INFORMATION AND INTELLIGENCE

### Diversity and Accessibility of Information Sources

The wide diversity of information sources and access mechanisms poses important challenges in the collection of useful information. The nature of intelligence on terrorist financing requires access to a wide range of information held across public authorities and private organizations with differing infrastructure, record-keeping standards, and levels of responsiveness. Besides information from financial institutions and designated nonfinancial businesses and professions (DNFBPs), the production of financial intelligence also benefits from connecting the dots with information from other competent authorities, such as customs and tax authorities, social services, birth and death registries, and company registries.

---

[2] The Experts Meeting was co-organized by the the UN Counter-Terrorism Centre of the UNOCT and the IMF's Legal Department from February 28 to March 1, 2019. It took place in Vienna, Austria.

Maintaining access and querying several external databases in a single case can be time consuming and involve significant bureaucracy.

In addition to requirements to report to FIUs, intelligence and investigative authorities should have access to information from open or public sources, to information collected and/or maintained by, or on behalf of, other authorities and, where appropriate, to data held by commercial entities. Commercial data could include information from credit card and credit reporting companies, cell phone companies, travel agencies, airlines, and social media platforms. This information can provide vital information for preventing or identifying the perpetrator of a terrorist act. Complications in accessing this information may arise because of data privacy issues and limitations on a country conducting surveillance on its own citizens.

Lack of interoperability among IT systems, including governmental databases, greatly limits the timely collection and exploitation of the wide range of information needed to identify terrorist financing. Production of financial intelligence is predicated on the ability to receive and analyze a significant amount of data and, when dealing with time-sensitive cases, the ability to quickly access the information. Lack of interoperability between the FIU, law enforcement, and intelligence agencies often makes it challenging to fully leverage the data available for the production of terrorist financing–related financial intelligence. In other cases, the lack of IT systems and reliance on physical databases can make the timely production of terrorist financing cases impossible.

Important information sources often are held within unregulated or underregulated sectors, with diverse terrorist financing channels constantly shifting to take advantage of this and emerging payment methods. The use of cash and money or value transfer services (MVTS) presents an important challenge in following the terrorist financing money trail. Many regions affected by terrorism use MVTS and cash, as opposed to bank accounts, for financial transactions. The often informal operation of MVTS makes it difficult, if not impossible, to obtain information that can contribute to financial intelligence. Furthermore, banks with MVTS service agreements do not always receive the customer due diligence information from the MVTS needed to file a comprehensive STR with FIUs. Regulated financial institutions can also become complicit in terrorist financing activities stemming from a shared ideology with the terrorists, pressure from the state (in instances of state-sponsored terrorism), infiltration by criminals, or profit motivations. In addition, the emergence of new payment systems, such as virtual asset services and crowdfunding platforms, is raising technological and legal barriers to accessing information. Finally, when private sector firms have information that could contribute to cross-border investigations, national legislation often prevents them from sharing this information with FIU, law enforcement, and intelligence agencies from other jurisdictions.

## Limits to Private Sector Contributions to Identifying Terrorist Financing

The regulated financial and nonfinancial sectors continue to face challenges in identifying terrorist financing and feeding the financial intelligence cycle. In their efforts to identify suspicious transactions, regulated entities continue to have difficulty specifically identifying suspicions. Factors contributing to this include a lack of understanding of the risks related to terrorist financing; difficulty cross-referencing terrorism-related lists of designated individuals or entities; weak monitoring systems; lack of specialized software for identification of suspicious transactions or clients, especially in nonbanking financial institutions and the DNFBP sector; lack of sufficient guidance, red flags, and risk indicators; the continuously evolving nature of terrorist financing threats; and difficulty establishing indicators for lone actors. To illustrate this point, a study conducted by Europol determined that terrorist financing reports accounted for less than 1 percent of all reporting received by FIUs across Europe in 2013–14.

Lack of understanding among some regulated entities about terrorist financing often results in poor quality STRs. Despite concrete efforts by reporting entities, STRs can at times be the result of religious or other profiling that may not have any intelligence value. Reporting entities, rather than making independent assessments of MVTS activities, can engage in automatic reporting where supervisory authorities identify a provider of MVTS as high risk. Automatic reporting can divert important FIU resources from higher risk and more relevant cases. In many instances, there is defensive reporting applied toward vulnerable groups of the society, which may also lead to low quality and limited added value. In more extreme circumstances, where a financial institution decides to limit or cease its services to certain geographies or types of customers altogether, important intelligence can be lost as customers turn to less-regulated or unregulated providers.

Use of cryptocurrencies in terrorist financing also poses new challenges for competent authorities who are expected to keep up with these issues and to offer solutions for tracking transactions that may relate to terrorism. Obtaining information on financial transactions conducted through virtual channels can present a challenge as most countries have yet to extend obligations to virtual assets, and customer due diligence in this emerging area outside of traditional finance is often seen as weak.

Terrorist financing lists derived from domestic regional and international data are often a primary indicator of intelligence on terrorist financing. These lists provide important information for reporting entities to consult when determining whether a transaction or activity is suspicious. Yet sharing and using them can be a struggle for reporting entities and competent authorities alike. Reporting entities with limited resources do not systematically check relevant terrorist financing lists. When they do, false positives can create challenges when confirming whether the person identified is the same individual as in the listing. Finally, supervisory authorities and FIUs do not always have mechanisms to communicate changes in lists to financial institutions and DNFBPs, and reporting entities do not always update their automated systems to reflect such changes.

Difficulties in identifying suspicions can also be more systemic. Reporting entities may have weak transaction monitoring systems and procedures that hamper their ability to identify suspicious transactions of any type. Furthermore, the quality of the information submitted to competent authorities, including suspicious and threshold reporting to FIUs, may be poor if reporting entities do not comply with customer due diligence requirements, including proper identification of clients and beneficial owners.

Supervisory authorities cannot always identify compliance failures because they do not have the ability to scope terrorist financing issues generally nor specifically for transaction monitoring needed for anti-money laundering/combating the financing of terrorism (AML/CFT) inspections. An absence of risk-based supervision can result in a rules-based compliance approach that fails to focus on terrorist financing risk. The sampling of transactions during inspections may not always be sufficiently comprehensive, particularly on the identification of beneficial owners. Also, FIUs may not advise supervisors about data quality issues related to suspicious transaction and threshold reporting, which makes it difficult for the supervisory authority to determine the underlying cause of poor reporting. (Chapter 2 included a broad discussion of issues related to the implementation of preventive measures and the effectiveness of CFT supervision.)

Competent authorities developing terrorist financing intelligence can often be reluctant to share information with reporting entities because of its classified or sensitive nature, and so deprive reporting entities of useful risk indicators. Even when CFT authorities can request information from reporting entities, the nature of information related to terrorist financing often prevents them from even sharing elements of it with reporting entities. Furthermore, lack of trust that reporting entities will keep information confidential can contribute to that reluctance.

## Shortcomings in the Mandate of Financial Intelligence Units

Despite their CFT mandate, some FIUs lack the requisite authority to carry out their mandate effectively. While FIUs receive, analyze, and disseminate financial information on CFT, some still do not have authority to collect the information needed in a timely manner. In particular, some FIUs lack powers to request additional information from reporting entities. This limits their ability to develop a comprehensive financial profile of the persons of interest and can ostensibly handicap their financial analysis if data holdings are limited to STRs as it severely limits the financial information that can be analyzed. It also hinders their ability to respond to foreign counterparts' request for complete banking information. Restrictions on FIUs' ability to share information can impede the flow of intelligence to competent authorities.

# GOOD PRACTICES FOR ACCESSING AND COLLECTING INFORMATION AND INTELLIGENCE

## Facilitating Access to Information

Timely sharing of information between different competent authorities can play an important role in gathering details that paint a more comprehensive picture of terrorist financing activities. This can be facilitated through direct access to pertinent databases as well as by outlining information exchange procedures that reduce bureaucracy and increase timeliness and efficiency while respecting confidentiality and privacy rights.

FIU powers to request and exchange information should be strengthened to ensure effective and timely conduct of their missions. As required by criteria 29.3 of the FATF Methodology, FIUs should have the ability to request information from reporting entities, competent authorities, and commercially held data regardless whether the request stems from an analysis of a suspicious transaction report or a request from a foreign counterpart. As required by criteria 40.11 (a) and (b), and subject to the principle of reciprocity, the FIU should have the power to exchange all domestically sourced information it can access or—directly or indirectly—obtain, along with any other information that its powers permit it to obtain or access.

Reporting entities should be able to share all relevant information with competent authorities and should report suspicious transactions to FIUs, as per FATF R.29. Specifically, reporting entities should be able to provide information about transactions that have been made outside the FIU's jurisdiction and information obtained from affiliates and subsidiaries without being impeded by domestic data privacy and protection rules. The prerequisite to sharing this information with authorities is collection in the context of customer due diligence and record keeping of such information as well as an effective supervisory and sanctioning regime to enforce these obligations.

The receipt of low-threshold cross-border wire transfer information can substantially enhance an FIU's capacity to produce financial intelligence, since terrorism and terrorist financing is often international. In receiving cross-border wire transfers, FIUs can establish links between the domestic financial activities of terrorists and determine whether other jurisdictions are involved. This can be crucial for developing the profile of both the person of interest and that of the terrorist network. As amounts involved in terrorist financing are often low, higher thresholds for these transactions may exclude some activity of interest.

Another important and easily accessible source of information is regional and international information exchange platforms or databases. For example, INTERPOL's National Central Bureau databases include information related to criminal records, lost passports, and other details that can provide leads and insights into persons of interest to FIUs, law enforcement agencies, and intelligence agencies.

Human rights and data protection questions should be considered as these good practices are implemented. As authorities strive to expand the effectiveness of their CFT activities by obtaining the necessary powers, resources, and access to information, they need to ensure that legislation and mechanisms put in place continue to meet the best standards of human rights and privacy protection.

## Sensibly Addressing the Information Gap from Unregulated and Informal Sectors

Countries should establish strategies to formalize the MVTS sector. MVTS provide a critical role in the provision of financial services in many jurisdictions affected by terrorism and therefore can be misused. Countries should establish a licensing or registration regime for MVTS to integrate them into the formal economy as required by FATF R.14. These efforts should be accompanied by AML/CFT monitoring of licensed/registered entities and a strategy to identify natural and legal persons that carry out transfers without a license or registration. Amid efforts to formalize the sector, consideration should be given to the human rights and economic implications of arbitrarily closing remittance operations and the alienating economic and social effects this may have on affected communities.

## Sharing Targeted Risk Indicators and Leads Through Trusted Channels

FIUs and law enforcement agencies provide the private sector with indicators, trends, and typologies, particularly when a new sector is being brought under the terrorist financing reporting regime. To reinforce the private sector's capacity to correctly identify terrorist financing, FIUs and law enforcement agencies should publish specific indicators through the assistance of supervisors, which should be updated regularly. Updating the indicators becomes important in fast-changing environments, such as the rise and fall of the Islamic State of Iraq and the Levant in recent years. Terrorist financing trends and typologies can also help private entities understand how they can be abused by terrorists. These measures have contributed to better-quality transactions and intelligence reports to FIUs and intelligence and law enforcement agencies (Box 3.1).

---

### Box 3.1. Strategic Intelligence on Lone Actors and Small Cells

Development of strategic intelligence through international partnerships can give reporting entities information about important trends and assist competent authorities in disrupting terrorist financial networks. Such an example is the strategic analysis undertaken by the Egmont Information Exchange Working Group on lone actors and small cells.[1]

The report was produced following the analysis of 122 incidents (100 lone actor and 22 small cell incidents) that took place between 2004 and 2018. The Egmont Group published eight key findings deemed appropriate for public release and derived from a more comprehensive report.

1. Lone actors are often influenced by the ideologies of terrorist organizations.
2. Traditional indicators of terrorist financing alone are unlikely to expose the financing activity of lone actors, although they remain relevant.

[1] https://egmontgroup.org/wp-content/uploads/2021/09/20190712-IEWG-Lone-Actors-and-Small-Cells-Public-Sumary.pdf

> 3. New lone actor and small cell indicators are related to the procurement of means, like firearms, other weapons, and chemicals used as precursors for building improvised explosive devices or homemade explosives.
> 4. Some financial institutions, such as payment processors for online retailers or large FIs, are able to employ threshold monitoring and may be better positioned than others to observe more granular transactional data. In nearly 40 percent of cases examined, lone actors and small cells conducted cash transactions.
> 5. FIs may be more likely to file suspicious transaction reports on premeditated lone actor terrorist attacks versus spontaneous lone actor terrorist attacks.
> 6. Most of the pre-attack reporting reviewed was based on other anti-money laundering indicators, which may indicate a close nexus between terrorism and other crimes, such as possible fraud or structured transactions.
> 7. Firearms were the weapon most frequently used in attacks. Special attention from reporting entities could identify when individuals suddenly purchase large amounts of firearms and the presence of other suspicious activity indicators.
> 8. Explosives were the second most common means of attack used by lone actors. Educating reporting institutions on suspicious chemical purchases may not always help identify attackers, unless the institutions have access to granular transaction data and can observe precisely which chemicals are being purchased.
>
> Source: Authors, based on The Egmont Group of Financial Intelligence Units.

Public–private partnerships (PPPs) give FIUs and select reporting entities the opportunity to share more sensitive information to improve the quality of the information provided by the private sector. Countries have increasingly established PPPs between FIUs, law enforcement, and major reporting entities to share sensitive tactical and strategic information that can inform reporting entities' identification of suspicious transactions in domestic and international terrorism. In certain circumstances, private sector entities can share information between each other, helping make links between transactions and activities that would not otherwise be identified.

PPPs can encourage the joint development of targeting indicators for the banking and financial services industries, delivering greater understanding for law enforcement, government agencies, and FIs. Sharing knowledge allows for greater insight into how terrorist financing could exploit financial systems and services, and into actions that can mitigate risks and disrupt illicit activity.

By establishing trust and relationships, PPPs also allow for the identification of joint training or learning development opportunities for law enforcement, government agencies, and FIs. Closer collaboration through shared learning and partnerships presents opportunities for the development of relationships, streamlining of information sharing, and increased capability to identify terrorist financing (Box 3.2).

> **Box 3.2. Financial Information-Sharing Partnerships**
>
> Financial information-sharing partnerships are increasingly being established to deepen collaboration between the private sector, FIUs, and law enforcement agencies. Australia, Canada, Hong Kong SAR, Singapore, the United Kingdom, and the United States have all established different models of financial information-sharing partnerships. These engage the public sector and private sector firms to support case investigations through activities such as the development of public–private typologies, the sharing of details about specific entities of concern by law enforcement agencies, and the colocation of law enforcement and private sector analysts to allow for real-time exchange.
>
> The Royal United Service Institute for Defense and Security Studies (RUSI) published a 2017 paper, *The Role of Financial Information-Sharing Partnerships in the Disruption of Crime*. It listed five principles to guide countries in the establishment of financial information-sharing partnerships: leadership and trust; legislative clarity; governance; technology and analytical capability; and adaptability and evolution. It formulated 26 recommendations for supporting implementation of the five principles. The publication can be found at https://rusi.org/publication/occasional-papers/role-financial-information-sharing-partnerships-disruption-crime.
>
> Source: RUSI.

Through PPPs, FIUs and law enforcement agencies share targeted information with sectors that do not have reporting obligations under the CFT legislative framework. Sharing of reclassified identification information, such as names, physical addresses, emails, and phone numbers, can result in the private sector sharing information with significant intelligence value. The information can be shared with trusted entities in sectors that terrorists can abuse by supplying goods related to a terrorism act, such as online retailers, car rentals, airlines, hardware stores, beauty parlors, and the like. In establishing these relationships, it is important for law enforcement agencies not only to foster local contacts but also to include senior executives of large entities in information exchange initiatives (Box 3.3).

Some FIUs and other law enforcement and intelligence agencies have developed the capacity to monitor social and other forms of media to supplement information received through other sources. Terrorists often use mass media, social media, and crowdfunding platforms to publicize and finance their activities as well as to recruit members. By running this information against databases and other information sources, FIUs, law enforcement, and intelligence agencies can identify additional leads for inclusion in their intelligence products and exchanges with the private sector. As competent authorities undertake this type of monitoring, it is important that domestic activities are coordinated to avoid duplication of effort and Potentially tipping off targets.

> **Box 3.3. Information Sharing by Law Enforcement Leads to STR**
>
> FINTRAC (FIU Canada) has seen instances where individuals under investigation for terrorism-related offenses, including attempts to leave the country to carry out acts of terror, have used crowdfunding websites prior to leaving or attempting to leave Canada. In one example, a reporting entity received information from law enforcement that an individual had left Canada. This prompted an account review and a suspicious transaction report sent to FINTRAC. It contained details about a crowdfunding website. Specifically, the reporting entity stated, "This account was used for four transactions, totaling Can$61.56 (approx. $47) with a known crowdfunding website [web address provided]. This merchant is categorized by its merchant bank as "Professional Services." The company's website describes itself as an International Crowdfunding site, allowing people to easily set up a fundraising webpage and collect donations. Most of the donation options are related to conflict relief in Country A, Country B, and Country C."
>
> Source: 2016 APG Yearly Typologies Report.

## Targeted Supervision of Terrorist Financing Suspicious Transaction Monitoring and Reporting

AML/CFT supervisory authorities should in their inspections include the review of reporting entities' transaction monitoring system to specifically detect suspicions of terrorism. They should examine whether monitoring systems adequately integrate terrorist financing indicators and whether reporting entities have put in place the systems and procedures needed to identify suspicions of terrorism. Furthermore, supervisory authorities should work with FIUs to resolve data quality issues regarding the reporting of terrorist financing suspicions. This could include the FIU pointing out recurring data quality issues to the supervisory authority before inspections are conducted. Communication of these issues should be undertaken without sharing specific information contained in the STR with the supervisory authority.

# KEY CHALLENGES IN ANALYZING FINANCIAL INFORMATION

## Exploiting Large Amounts of Information

Counterterrorism, in particular efforts to prevent attacks, is often like trying to find a needle in a haystack.[3] As was discussed in the previous section, efforts require gathering a large amount of data from diverse sources. This is a particular

---

[3] The use and sharing of large amounts of information and metadata raises important security, legal, and ethical concerns which are not discussed in this book. The authors are not weighting in or against the use of metadata but are highlighting the particular challenges of exploiting the information CFT authorities already hold and that might amount to metadata.

challenge, as the pool of information to process reaches metadata levels and access to and interoperability between different databases are needed. In that context, technology plays a crucial part in linking information to identify intelligence and investigative leads as well as trends and typologies in terrorist financing. The absence of robust IT systems limits the ability of FIUs, law enforcement, and security agencies to produce comprehensive financial intelligence, and it means that smaller jurisdictions may rely on larger, allied countries' intelligence communities. The availability of technological tools is now a basic requirement for processing information and reaching acceptable effectiveness in the production of financial intelligence. This challenges not only smaller FIUs but also smaller reporting entities that lack technological tools to establish links electronically.

## Limitation of Financial Intelligence Unit Mandates and Authority

While most FIUs are in charge of analyzing STRs received, including against other information sources, limited powers can hinder their ability to produce actionable intelligence. For example, some FIUs cannot initiate analysis outside of the STRs received. This hamstrings the FIU's ability to initiate analysis based on intelligence it receives or the information it can access. This can present a significant challenge when wanting to respond to requests from domestic and international counterparts.

Limited information can make it difficult for the FIU to analyze an STR and reach the necessary threshold required to disseminate information to relevant competent authorities. FIUs may find it difficult to establish a direct link between the suspicion outlined in the STR and terrorism or terrorist financing activities. If an FIU only has limited access to additional information, this can make it difficult to reach the threshold required to share information with law enforcement or intelligence agencies.

Furthermore, the exclusion of FIUs in some jurisdictions from the terrorism intelligence community deprives the community of targeted financial expertise and valuable financial information, and it prevents FIU products from meeting the needs of investigation agencies. In many countries, FIUs are not involved in terrorism cases and the terrorist financing value chain, which means law enforcement, security, and military agencies are not always aware of their role and the information they can access. The absence of FIU involvement in terrorism cases and intelligence gathering also makes failure to explore the financial aspects of a terrorism case more likely. Underutilization of an FIU's expertise can deprive intelligence and law enforcement agencies of potentially valuable intelligence and actionable leads.

Composition of the counterterrorism value chain will vary in each domestic context and can result in certain relevant law enforcement agencies being excluded from the intelligence gathering phase. This further limits the effectiveness of counterterrorism and CFT activities.

## Allocation of Resources to CFT

A focus on imminent or immediate threats to public safety can compete with terrorist financing investigations as a priority. Understandably, priority has been placed on ensuring the safety of the public when dealing with terrorism cases. Resource allocation to leverage the financial intelligence aspect of counterterrorism is often not a priority despite the potential of producing timely intelligence from financial investigations. This lack of prioritization and resources may also lead law enforcement to neglect looking into the financial aspects of terrorism investigations and miss potentially vital intelligence.

Lack of dedicated resources in FIU, law enforcement agencies, and intelligence agencies is undermining the effectiveness of terrorism and terrorist financing intelligence gathering and investigations. Even as many national governments identify terrorism as a priority issue, resource constraints remain a challenge, particularly regarding their allocation. Although most FIUs will prioritize terrorist financing cases and information requests, many lack resources to focus a specialized team on terrorist financing analysis or to analyze information in a timely or comprehensive manner. Similarly, lack of law enforcement resources for financial investigations impacts the ability to respond to financial intelligence related to terrorism and terrorist financing. Many countries have a dearth of capacity regarding financial investigations, compounded by inexperience in utilizing legislative tools designed to assist financing investigations. This shortage of resources and experience makes it difficult for law enforcement agencies to investigate financial intelligence and conduct investigations.

## Building Financial Investigation Expertise in CFT

The lack of specialized terrorist financing expertise and financial investigations presents a challenge for FIUs, law enforcement, and intelligence agencies. Many FIUs have limited expertise to analyze cases and, as has been shown, are not always included in the terrorism value chain because they are not considered intelligence agencies. A similar lack of capacity in law enforcement results in failures to conduct financial investigations. Investigators do not necessarily understand that financial intelligence can provide information not only on the financial profile of a suspect but also on the financial footprint that will help identify a suspect's location, associates, meeting places, and so on.

## Misconception about the Value of Financial Intelligence

Financial intelligence and analysis is a bit of a novelty in the traditionally hands-on field of investigative work. Some law enforcement and intelligence services are put off by its perceived complexity. It is also seen as requiring a different skill set than field agents might possess. As law enforcement and intelligence services in many countries have limited training in financial intelligence or are not aware of ways by which they can tap into such expertise, they can be reluctant to include financial analysis in counterterrorism investigations.

Similarly, the value of financial intelligence is not always understood by senior management of law enforcement agencies, and they might decide to allocate resources elsewhere. These decision makers do not always appreciate that a financial investigation team can provide a large amount of reliable, cheap, and fast operational intelligence that supports other counterterrorism operations. This can result in limited to no investment in financial intelligence gathering.

## GOOD PRACTICES FOR ANALYZING FINANCIAL INFORMATION

### Acquiring the Right Analytical Tools

Implementation of robust IT solutions, mindful of ethical and legal privacy concerns, can facilitate the linking of transactions and identification of trends. As the amount of information keeps increasing, the need for IT solutions that allow large data sets to be analyzed becomes essential. Through IT solutions, it becomes possible to link disparate sets of data and identify patterns that can initiate tactical cases and strategic analysis. It is important to highlight that the cost of such IT tools may be prohibitive for some FIUs and law enforcement and intelligence agencies.

### Giving Financial Intelligence Units the Requisite Authority

FIUs that are able to initiate an analysis from any information source can considerably enhance the value of their intelligence products. Many FIUs do not have authority to initiate a financial intelligence case in the absence of an STR. Criteria 29.4 of the 2013 FATF Methodology requires an FIU to conduct operational and strategic analysis using available and obtainable information to identify specific targets (operational analysis) and trends and patterns in money laundering and terrorist financing (strategic analysis).

### Investing Resources in Building Financial Investigation Practice

Effective internal procedures for terrorist financing analysis should be established. Clearly outlined operational procedures provide analysts and investigators with a road map to conduct their work and ensure a consistency of approach within the FIU, law enforcement, and security agencies. For example, the Egmont Group has developed an Emergency Terrorist Financing Response Checklist to help FIUs make the same high-quality response.

Specialized FIU teams can help build terrorism-specific expertise and contribute to timely dissemination. Many FIUs have analytical teams that focus exclusively on terrorist financing cases. This can help deal with the lack of expertise as specialists can train other analysts and liaise with intelligence agency and law enforcement teams working on terrorism cases. Some countries have also assigned specific analysts to financial intelligence and investigations on specific terrorist organizations, creating centers of expertise within specific organizations.

## Coordination and Collaboration between Competent Authorities

Many jurisdictions have set up national coordination bodies to discuss operational issues and analytical priorities for investigating terrorist financing. These bodies provide an opportunity for domestic competent authorities to tackle operational and bureaucratic impediments directly and reduce the chance that information and investigative silos are created. Some jurisdictions have even allowed vetted AML/CFT experts in financial institutions to participate.

Trusted relationships between FIUs and other CFT agencies allow for a better understanding of operational needs and more targeted information collection, while acknowledging the central role that intelligence agencies play in the fight against terrorism and terrorist financing. When bilateral relationships between FIUs, law enforcement, and security services are strengthened, the result can be improved collaboration and information exchange. Bilateral collaborations can also be expanded to financial institutions that are able to share the results of their own intelligence capacity. Maximizing the use of financial intelligence in terrorism and related financing cases requires strong trust between the FIU, intelligence, and law enforcement agencies. FIUs should understand the needs of recipients, establishing bilateral mechanisms for sharing information between competent authorities and providing training on financial intelligence and how it can improve investigations. It is here where memoranda of understanding, secondments, liaison officers, or joint training opportunities are also important in fostering trust and establishing mechanisms that can respond to the urgent nature of terrorism and terrorist financing.

Furthermore, joint task force investigations which include the FIU, law enforcement, and intelligence agencies can help expedite both the development of intelligence and the resolution of investigations by having all relevant competent authorities share their expertise.

It is also important for FIUs to schedule reviews of the quality of their analysis to ensure that financial intelligence products meet the need of recipients. Feedback from the recipient agency is critical in helping FIUs ensure that the intelligence being shared has value.

## KEY CHALLENGES IN DISSEMINATION AND USE OF FINANCIAL INTELLIGENCE

### Limitation of Powers

Some FIUs do not have the authority to share their intelligence with all counter-terrorism or CFT agencies. Certain domestic legislation can limit their authority to pass on case files, and the one designated recipient might not be the agency able to make best use of CFT information. Where dissemination to intelligence agencies in particular is essential for a timely response to a terrorist threat, this limitation can be a significant obstacle to the initiation of investigations or the use of financial intelligence.

## Distrust and Institutional Barriers Creating Silos

Counterterrorism or CFT agencies often face institutional challenges in exchanging terrorism information. Given the sensitive nature of terrorist financing, law enforcement and security agencies involved in intelligence gathering and investigations are at times reluctant to share information with other government agencies. Concerns about corruption in government agencies or lack of trust that the receiving agency will be able to protect the information exacerbate this trait.

Reluctance to share can create information silos where different law enforcement and intelligence agencies, FIUs, and the military hold information about a terrorism threat or case but are unable to link it with information held by partner agencies. Although many countries have established terrorism coordination committees and integrated teams, silos between national agencies continue to undermine effectiveness.

The sensitivity of terrorism and terrorist financing cases can engender the creation of specialized bureaucratic processes that impact efficiency and hinder the exchange of information. With the increasing focus on terrorism and terrorist financing, specific procedures have been established to deal with terrorism-related cases within agencies and counter the risk of information leakage due to corruption. In some instances, these have streamlined standard operating procedures. In others, they require higher levels of the organizational hierarchy to be involved, which can slow the dissemination of important information to other competent authorities.

## Navigating Information (Over)classification and Protection

Barriers to exchanges also include information classification and confidentiality rules. Intelligence and information related to terrorism and terrorist financing cases is often given the highest classification. This can make exchange between agencies difficult, particularly if certain government agencies lack the highest security designation. Rules regarding the confidentiality of information received from a counterpart can also be challenging when wanting to exchange information. As law enforcement, intelligence, and military agencies receive information from their domestic and international counterparts, data protection legislation often prevents them from distributing it, even if they believe the information would help another national authority.

Lack of experience in working with data privacy legislation can limit the accessibility of intelligence and information related to terrorism and its financing. The presence of data privacy legislation, although necessary to protect important fundamental and civil rights, can hinder the exchange of intelligence and information if officers perceive it as an obstacle or do not have experience with related operational procedures. The impact of such legislation, especially absent mechanisms to allow access to information for national security matters, will vary from country to country, and at times it might impose restrictions on the type and extent of information that can be shared. Law enforcement and intelligence agencies should be involved in policy discussions to ensure a good understanding of the practical implications of policy and legislative initiatives. Inability to share specific information with the private sector can hinder efforts to identify a suspicion or threat and can undermine the quality and speed of the information cycle.

## Turning Financial Intelligence into Evidence

Lack of experience among investigative bodies in using financial intelligence can present challenges in turning financial intelligence into evidence. Authorities are often unaware of how to use financial intelligence—including the different ways to "parallel reconstruct" a case by collecting closed-circuit television, witness statements, DNA/fingerprints from a crime scene, interviews, and covert recordings or by using undercover officers or subpoenaing/getting a warrant to require a bank to produce bank statements in court as evidence and other specialized investigative tools. In some jurisdictions, investigative agencies have had to restart data collection because some intelligence information (including information provided by the FIU) cannot be used in court. Furthermore, the conversion of intelligence into evidence can tip off key players in the terrorist organizations that investigative agencies have suspicions—a risk particularly difficult to negotiate when trying to prevent a specific terrorist attack.

The absence of effective internal terrorist financing procedures can also hinder effective use of financial intelligence. Competent authorities do not always have adequate internal procedures in place to investigate terrorist financing. This can affect the timeliness, comprehensiveness, and overall effectiveness of terrorist financing investigations.

## Exchanging Information with International Counterparts

Given that terrorism is often transnational in nature, the barriers to information exchange between international counterparts can be a significant challenge in advancing intelligence gathering and investigations. They mirror many of the same challenges that plague the domestic exchange of information. Trust between international counterparts is not always easy to establish, particularly when sensitive information is at stake and tipping off bad actors can have disastrous consequences. While some international partners have established solid communication channels, less trusted channels prevent the gathering of information or intelligence. In addition, while information exchanges between similar agencies (for example, law enforcement to law enforcement) can be well established, exchanges between agencies of different nature are often problematic and require the involvement of an intermediary agency.

A few FIUs have had difficulty obtaining financial intelligence internationally, particularly when requesting information from an FIU that lacks authority to request information from reporting entities. Not all FIUs can request additional information from reporting entities, despite this being a requirement in criteria 29.3 of the FATF Methodology and a requirement of the Egmont Group Principles for Information Exchange. For some that can, at times they are only allowed to request information linked to an STR already filed. Both FATF, through mutual evaluations, and the Egmont Group, through its support and compliance working group, are working with FIUs to resolve these deficiencies. Inability to request additional information from reporting entities can be extremely limiting for an FIU where information on account opening and activities is crucial to a financial investigation.

Important delays in receiving responses from foreign partners can be a deterrent to seeking international exchange of information and ensuring the effectiveness of the intelligence cycle. Domestic priorities often take precedence over international requests. With limited resources, FIUs, law enforcement, and security agencies tend to prioritize domestic cases before responding to international requests. In addition, delays can happen when the requested FIU has no prior consent to forward information to competent authorities. This can result in the requesting agency having to wait months and sometimes longer to receive a response, if indeed a response is given. Chapter 6 features a more comprehensive discussion of international cooperation issues.

## GOOD PRACTICES FOR THE DISSEMINATION AND USE OF FINANCIAL INTELLIGENCE

### Putting a Premium on Parallel Financial Investigation

Parallel financial investigations are initiated for terrorism investigations in anticipation of an attack, following an attack, or when terrorists are publicly identified. The parallel financial investigation has the dual purpose of disclosing terrorist financing offenses and supporting the investigation with operational leads for financial intelligence sources. Besides providing a financial profile on persons of interest, parallel financial investigations have the potential to deliver vital information on location and links between individuals and provide insights about the activities of persons of interest, which can generate additional intelligence and investigative leads. Achieving this will entail a significant increase in trained financial investigators and analysts within law enforcement, FIUs, and the intelligence services. As terrorist financing investigations are initiated, coordination with intelligence agencies will be essential to avoid tipping off bad actors and hampering the work of intelligence agencies.

### Breaking Silos by Establishing Integrated Investigative Teams

The creation of integrated terrorism investigative teams can help ensure that financial intelligence is reviewed and used in a timely manner. Integrated teams provide a center of expertise for officers from intelligence, law enforcement, and sometimes FIUs to work cooperatively, with the easy exchange of both information and expertise having a positive impact at both the information collection and analytical phases. Specialized teams increase the likelihood that financial intelligence will be shared, understood, and used to investigate terrorism. They also create CFT career streams that consolidate terrorist financing expertise, and—depending on their mandate and resources allocated—can contribute to investigating a greater number of cases.

## Use of Financial Intelligence by Customs Agencies

FIUs, intelligence agencies, and law enforcement should proactively exchange financial intelligence with their national customs counterparts. Also, their activities should be coordinated with intelligence agencies to avoid tipping off bad actors. Customs agencies use financial intelligence to better target suspicious border activity related to terrorism. Operational and strategic financial intelligence can provide customs agencies with information on persons of interest as well as on trends and typologies of terrorism-related behaviors.

## Providing the Financial Intelligence Unit with the Requisite Authority

FIUs have the authority to share financial intelligence with all competent authorities. The FATF Recommendations requires that they can disseminate—spontaneously and upon request—information and the results of analysis to other competent authorities, and that they should use dedicated, secure, and protected channels. This will allow FIUs to direct the financial intelligence they produce to government agencies, particularly to the intelligence services leading the fight against terrorist financing.

## The Exchange of Bilateral Operational Information with Trusted Foreign Counterparts

The international community has established a number of best practices related to the exchange of financial intelligence between foreign counterparts. These include fostering bilateral relationships that outline information-sharing procedures and foster a climate of trust. In addition, practitioners have identified informal channels of communication as offering efficient and rapid means of sharing information that should not be neglected. These relationships are often built between individuals and may also include the sharing of expertise and other professional activities. FIUs can also use established domestic channels to intelligence services for international cooperation on matters unrelated to ongoing criminal terrorist financing or terrorism investigations. This would facilitate control of the information, vetting of the value added from the international exchange, and prevent tipping off.

## Using Multilateral Information-Sharing Platforms and Task Forces

Multilateral and regional operational working groups have recently been established to collaborate on terrorist financing cases. These include, among others, work undertaken on ISIL by FATF and the Egmont Group as well as the latter's work on lone actors and small cells (see Box 3.1 for more details). Working groups can help identify trends and patterns to help competent authorities and the private sector identify terrorist financing activity. Working groups can also collaborate on operational cases where each participant coordinates their activities related to a specific case. When establishing these working groups, the objective should be clearly stated, whether it is to provide financial intelligence to support ongoing criminal investigations or to identify new targets. That clarity will help determine who should lead and participate in the information-sharing platform.

The use of information-sharing platforms provided by the Egmont Group, INTERPOL, and Europol as well as other multilateral task forces, such as Five Eyes and G-5 Sahel Joint Forces, can facilitate international information exchange and cooperation between FIUs, law enforcement, and intelligence services. FIUs can use the Egmont Secure Web (ESW) and FIUNET (for FIUs in the EU) to share information between FIUs. FIUNET can also help identify which EU jurisdiction may possess information that could be related to the person on which information is being requested. These encrypted mechanisms address the challenge of exchanging information securely. INTERPOL has established an information-sharing platforms that law enforcement and, to a certain extent, FIUs can leverage. Also, the Financial Intelligence Consultative Group[4] is developing an Information Sharing Platform (ISP) pilot to strengthen information sharing between regional FIUs in Southeast Asia.

International events, such as meetings of the FATF-Style Regional Body (FSRB) network, can be leveraged for building capacity and overcoming lack of trust between international counterparts. For example, GAFILAT (the FSRB for South America) has a terrorist financing working group to discuss best practices for the analysis, production, and dissemination of financial intelligence, including sharing examples of successful investigations.

## CONCLUSION

The nexus for producing financial intelligence related to terrorism and terrorist financing has gone beyond FIUs to include law enforcement, intelligence, and customs agencies as well as the military. Financial intelligence gathering efforts now look beyond suspicious transactions and financial information from traditional reporting entities to also focus on information gathered at the site of terrorist acts and collaboration with retailers whose goods (such as component materials of bombs) and services are used to carry out a terrorist act. Continued monitoring of how financial intelligence is developed by different competent authorities can lead to an exchange of expertise—and beyond that, potentially to

---

[4] This is the operational arm of the CFT Summit, consisting of the heads of intelligence from the Association of Southeast Asian Nations, Australia, and New Zealand.

expanding the scope of financial intelligence activities as currently set up by the FATF to include more sharing of financial intelligence with intelligence services in a speedy and timely manner.

Deeper exploration of specific tactics for gathering and analyzing financial intelligence used by intelligence and law enforcement agencies can complement the institutional measures proposed in this chapter. Experts consulted for this chapter of the book focused overwhelmingly on institutional challenges that hinder the production and use of financial intelligence in terrorism and terrorist financing cases and their corresponding good practices. Future studies could specifically examine innovative operational practices used in the production and use of financial intelligence that supports the fight against terrorism and its financing—and how to implement the good practices highlighted in this chapter.

Furthermore, increasing use of the internet for remittance of funds and organizing activities presents a series of emerging challenges that are ripe for detailed exploration, particularly relating to cryptocurrencies, cyberterrorism, and the monitoring of social media platforms.

## REFERENCES

Egmont Group. 2016. *Communiqué: The Egmont Group of Financial Intelligence Units Reinforces Its Efforts in Combating Terrorist Financing.* Monaco. https://egmontgroup.org/wp-content/uploads/2021/09/2016_Monte_Carlo_Monaco_-_Working_Group_Meetings_Communique.pdf.

Europol. 2017. *From Suspicion to Action: Converting Financial Intelligence into Greater Operational Impact.* Luxembourg. https://www.europol.europa.eu/sites/default/files/documents/ql-01-17-932-en-c_pf_final.pdf.

Financial Action Task Force (FATF). 2013a. *FATF Guidance: National Money Laundering and Terrorist Financing Risk Assessment.* Paris. https://www.fatf-gafi.org/content/fatf-gafi/en/publications/Methodsandtrends/Nationalmoneylaunderingandterroristfinancingriskassessment.html.

Financial Action Task Force (FATF). 2013b. *Methodology for Assessing Compliance with the FATF Recommendations and the Effectiveness of AML/CFT Systems.* Paris. Last updated October 2021. https://www.fatf-gafi.org/publications/mutualevaluations/documents/fatf-methodology.html.

Financial Action Task Force (FATF). 2015. *Emerging Terrorist Financing Risks.* Paris. http://www.FATF-gafi.org/media/FATF/documents/reports/Emerging-Terrorist-Financing-Risks.pdf.

Financial Action Task Force (FATF). 2016. *Consolidated FATF Strategy on Combatting Terrorist Financing.*

Financial Action Task Force (FATF). 2018. *Terrorist Financing Disruption Strategies.* Paris.

Group of 20. 2017. *G20 Leader's Declaration: Shaping an Interconnected World*, July 8, 2017, Hamburg. http://www.g20.utoronto.ca/2017/2017-G20-leaders-declaration.html.

Levitt, Matthew, and Katherine Bauer. 2017. *Can Bankers Fight Terrorism?* Foreign Affairs. https://www.foreignaffairs.com/articles/2017-10-16/can-bankers-fight-terrorism.

Neumann, Peter R. 2017. *Countering Violent Extremism and Radicalisation That Lead to Terrorism: Ideas, Recommendations, and Good Practices from the OSCE Region.* International Centre for the Study of Radicalisation. https://www.osce.org/files/f/documents/1/2/346841.pdf.

United Nations 1999. The International Convention for the Suppression of the Financing of Terrorism (UN CFT Convention 1999).

## RESOURCES

Financial Action Task Force (FATF). 2008a. *Money Laundering & Terrorist Financing Risk Assessment Strategies*. Paris. https://www.fatf-gafi.org/content/fatf-gafi/en/publications/Methodsandtrends/Moneylaunderingterroristfinancingriskassessmentstrategies.html.

Financial Action Task Force (FATF). 2008b. *Terrorist Financing Typologies Report*. Paris.

Financial Action Task Force (FATF). 2010. *Global Money Laundering and Terrorist Financing Threat Assessment*. Paris. https://www.fatf-gafi.org/content/fatf-gafi/en/publications/Methodsandtrends/Moneylaunderingterroristfinancingriskassessmentstrategies.html.

Financial Action Task Force (FATF). 2013. "International Best Practices: Targeted Financial Sanctions Related to Terrorism and Terrorist Financing (R.6)." Paris.: Documents - Financial Action Task Force (FATF) (fatf-gafi.org)

Financial Action Task Force (FATF). 2019a. *International Standards on Combating Money Laundering and the Financing of Terrorism & Proliferation: The FATF Recommendations*. Paris. https://www.fatf-gafi.org/content/fatf-gafi/en/publications/Fatfrecommendations/Fatf-recommendations.html.

Financial Action Task Force (FATF). 2019b. *FATF Guidance: Terrorist Financing Risk Assessment Guidance*. Paris. https://www.fatf-gafi.org/content/fatf-gafi/en/publications/Methodsandtrends/Terrorist-financing-risk-assessment-guidance.html.

# CHAPTER 4

# Investigating, Prosecuting, and Sanctioning Terrorist Financiers

## Giuseppe Lombardo and Chady El Khoury

### CHAPTER IN BRIEF

*The Challenge*

A comparative analysis of mutual evaluation reports (MERs) by IMF staff reveals that a limited number of countries have achieved a high level of effectiveness on Immediate Outcome (IO) 9. Interestingly, several countries with relatively high technical compliance ratings for R.5 have been rated Moderate on IO.9. This trend could support the conclusion that capacity issues, combined with a poor understanding of the terrorist financing risk, are a major factor that impacts the effectiveness of terrorist financing-related investigations and prosecutions.

*Why It Happens*

Countries often lack a strategy for combating terrorist financing. However, the IMF staff identified countries with successful outcomes following the implementation of an appropriate strategy based on the results of the National Risk Assessment. Strategies focus on, for example, (1) large terrorist organizations such as Da'esh or (2) lone-wolf attackers. As a result, investigators need to understand the various types of terrorism to adequately examine them. The financial needs of a complex and structured terrorist organizations differ greatly between those of a small group or a lone wolf and those of a person who wishes to travel to join a terrorist organization (Foreign Terrorist Fighters, FTFs). Often, the amounts used to fund FTFs are very small compared with those that finance large terrorist organizations. Moreover, countries may find it difficult to prosecute terrorist financing cases and secure a conviction if the relevant legislation is not drafted properly. Prosecutors sometimes opt to charge other criminal offenses, which may result in less severe sanctions than those brought on by terrorist financing. This chapter includes case studies of acquittals by courts in various jurisdictions resulting from the prosecution's inability to prove intent (knowledge that the funds will be used for terrorism). Thus, legislation must be wide enough to capture all possible terrorist financing scenarios, including funding peaceful activities by a terrorist organization. Judges who specialize in terrorist financing are often lacking, a factor which may also lead to unintended consequences.

> **The Solution**
>
> This chapter begins with an overview of the evolution of legislation since the Financial Action Task Force (FATF) adopted terrorist financing in its recommendations. Understanding these developments paves the way for governments to adequately tailor their legislative frameworks to address terrorist financing including its nuanced and related activities. In addition, the chapter includes terrorist financing investigative and prosecutorial techniques for achieving convictions. As a result, offenders will receive terrorist financing sanctions, which are harsher than other criminal offenses. In this chapter the reader will learn more about other terrorist financing disruptive measures that a country can adopt when a conviction cannot be achieved.

# THE EVOLUTION OF EFFECTIVE INTERNATIONAL REGULATION

> *Terrorist financing convictions are more likely achieved when well-equipped investigators are backed by strong financial intelligence and prosecutors have intimate knowledge of legal precedents for bringing perpetrators to justice. The objective of every stage of due process is to subject financiers of terrorism to effective, proportionate, and dissuasive actions.*

Investigations and prosecutions aim to identify and disrupt terrorist financiers and bring them to justice. They complement the goals of targeted financial sanctions, which are to prevent terrorism and to deprive terrorist organizations and terrorists of assets and financial means that can be used to support their activities.

This chapter describes the key issues in disrupting and sanctioning terrorist financing offenses, as identified by the analysis of criminal judicial cases related to terrorism and terrorist financing and the findings of selected evaluations. After discussing the evolution of international regulations and the definition of the terrorist financing offense, it highlights challenges and good practices related to the key issues. Some apply to all judicial phases (investigations, prosecutions, convictions), while others are more specific.

## Defining the Terrorist Financing Offense

The introduction of terrorist financing in the 2001 revision of the Financial Action Task Force (FATF) Recommendations mandated all countries to criminalize it. FATF R.5 requires that offenses apply to those who meet the following criteria:

> [. . .] any person who willfully provides or collects funds or other assets by any means, directly or indirectly, with the unlawful intention that they should be used, or in the knowledge that they are to be used, in full or in part (i) to carry out a terrorist act; or (ii) by a terrorist organization; or (iii) by an individual terrorist. (FATF 2012–2020)

Therefore, the terrorist financing offense covers two distinct types of activity: *providing funds or other assets* and *collecting funds or other assets*. Countries are also required to criminalize the following ancillary offenses: (1) attempting to finance terrorism, (2) participating as an accomplice, (3) organizing or directing others to finance terrorism, and (4) contributing to the commission of terrorist financing by a group of persons acting with common purpose.[1]

The definition of "funds or other assets" encompasses not only financial assets but also every possible kind of property regardless of its corporeality, tangibility, or movability.[2] The terrorist financing offense should cover such funds or other assets and—unlike for money laundering, where funds are raised from criminal acts—the offense should apply regardless of whether the funds or other assets originate from legitimate or illegitimate sources. Typology studies have shown that legitimate sources of funds or other assets, such as income from employment, social assistance, family support, and loans are a primary source of funding for foreign terrorist fighters and small terrorist cells.[3]

The 2012 revision of the FATF standard did not significantly alter the scope of criminalization. The FATF clarified that criminalization is based on the 1999 UN Convention on the Suppression of Terrorist Financing (the UN Convention), and applies even when no link has been established to a specific terrorist act or acts. Recently, UN Security Council Resolution (UNSCR) 2462/2019 strongly urged all states to implement the comprehensive international standards embodied in the revision to the FATF's *Recommendations on Combating Money Laundering and the Financing of Terrorism and Proliferation* and its interpretive notes (FATF 2012. Last update in March 2022).

These are very important clarifications, as the FATF standard goes further than the UN Convention. Both the FATF and the UN Convention[4] require

---

[1] Such contribution shall be intentional and shall either (1) be made with the aim of furthering the criminal activity or criminal purpose of the group, where such activity or purpose involves the commission of a terrorist financing offense; or (2) be made in the knowledge of the intention of the group to commit such an offense (Financial Action Task Force [FATF], *International Standards on Combating Money Laundering and the Financing of Terrorism & Proliferation* [Paris: FATF, 2012–2020], https://www.fatf-gafi.org/en/publications/Fatfrecommendations/Fatf-recommendations.html. Updated in March 2022.).

[2] "The term "funds or other assets" means any assets, including, but not limited to, financial assets, economic resources (including oil and other natural resources), property of every kind, whether tangible or intangible, movable or immovable, however acquired, and legal documents or instruments in any form, including electronic or digital, evidencing title to, or interest in, such funds or other assets, including, but not limited to, bank credits, traveler's checks, bank checks, money orders, shares, securities, bonds, drafts, or letters of credit, and any interest, dividends or other income on or value accruing from or generated by such funds or other assets, and any other assets which potentially may be used to obtain funds, goods or services." (Financial Action Task Force [FATF], *International Standards on Combating Money Laundering and the Financing of Terrorism & Proliferation* [Paris: FATF, 2012–2020], https://www.fatf-gafi.org/en/publications/Fatfrecommendations/Fatf-recommendations.html. Updated in February 2023.)

[3] See, for example, the FATF Report on Financing of the Terrorist Organization ISIL (February 2015), p. 22, or the FATF Report on Emerging Terrorist Financing Risks (October 2015), p. 26.

[4] Article 1(3) of the UN Convention: "For an act to constitute an offence set forth in paragraph 1, it shall not be necessary that the funds were actually used to carry out an offence referred to in paragraph 1, subparagraphs (a) or (b)."

criminalization regardless of whether terrorist acts are committed (or even attempted), but the FATF clarifies that the provision or collection does not need to be linked to a specific terrorist act. The FATF requires criminalization of terrorist financing for all the "treaty offenses" referenced by the UN Convention, whereby the convention contains an exception.[5]

Most important, the FATF requires the criminalization of providing to and collecting for a terrorist organization or an individual terrorist for any purpose. The funds collected or provided do not need to be specifically for the commission of terrorist acts by a terrorist organization or an individual, but could be for recruitment, training, travel, and even for legitimate activities, such as social services provided to a community.

If the funds are willfully collected for or provided to a terrorist organization or an individual terrorist, this should suffice to criminalize terrorist financing. There is no need to prove, for example, specific intent to further the aim of the organization, or awareness that the funds will be used to commit terrorist acts, or the intention to provide the funds for legitimate activities of an organization.

The offense should also extend to the funding of travel for foreign terrorist fighters. To apply the requirement of UNSCR 2178/2014 to foreign fighters, in October 2015, the Interpretative Note to FATF R.5 clarified that terrorist financing should also include "financing the travel of individuals who travel to a State other than their States of residence or nationality for the purpose of the perpetration, planning, or preparation of, or participation in, terrorist acts or the providing or receiving of terrorist training."

As regards the elements of the offense, the meanings of the terms "terrorist act," "terrorist organization," and "individual terrorist" are important to understand. The FATF defines "terrorist act" (in the Glossary) in line with Article 2 of the UN Convention as follows:

> (a) An act which constitutes an offence within the scope of, and as defined in one of the following treaties: (1) Convention for the Suppression of Unlawful Seizure of Aircraft (1970); (2) Convention for the Suppression of Unlawful Acts against the Safety of Civil Aviation (1971); (3) Convention on the Prevention and Punishment of Crimes against Internationally Protected Persons, including Diplomatic Agents (1973); (4) International Convention against the Taking of Hostages (1979); (5) Convention on the Physical Protection of Nuclear Material (1980); (6) Protocol for the Suppression of Unlawful Acts of Violence at Airports Serving International Civil Aviation, supplementary to the Convention for the Suppression of Unlawful Acts against the Safety of Civil Aviation (1988); (7) Convention for the Suppression of Unlawful Acts against the Safety of Maritime Navigation (2005); (8) Protocol for

---

[5] Article 2, paragraph 2 (a): "On depositing its instrument of ratification, acceptance, approval or accession, a State Party which is not a party to a treaty listed in the annex may declare that, in the application of this Convention to the State Party, the treaty shall be deemed not to be included in the annex referred to in paragraph 1, subparagraph (a). The declaration shall cease to have effect as soon as the treaty enters into force for the State Party, which shall notify the depositary of this fact."

the Suppression of Unlawful Acts against the Safety of Fixed Platforms located on the Continental Shelf (2005); (9) International Convention for the Suppression of Terrorist Bombings (1997); and (10) International Convention for the Suppression of the Financing of Terrorism (1999).

(b) Any other act intended to cause death or serious bodily injury to a civilian, or to any other person not taking an active part in the hostilities in a situation of armed conflict, when the purpose of such act, by its nature or context, is to intimidate a population, or to compel a government or an international organization to do or to abstain from doing any act. (FATF 2012)

The FATF also defines the terms "terrorist organization" and "terrorist." A terrorist organization is defined as follows:

[. . .] any group of terrorists that: (1) commits, or attempts to commit, terrorist acts by any means, directly or indirectly, unlawfully and willfully; (2) participates as an accomplice in terrorist acts; (3) organizes or directs others to commit terrorist acts; or (4) contributes to the commission of terrorist acts by a group of persons acting with a common purpose where the contribution is made intentionally and with the aim of furthering the terrorist act or with the knowledge of the intention of the group to commit a terrorist act. (FATF 2012)

The term "terrorist" refers to individuals who can be described as follows:

[. . .] any natural person who: (1) commits, or attempts to commit, terrorist acts by any means, directly or indirectly, unlawfully and willfully; (2) participates as an accomplice in terrorist acts; (3) organizes or directs others to commit terrorist acts; or (4) contributes to the commission of terrorist acts by a group of persons acting with a common purpose where the contribution is made intentionally and with the aim of furthering the terrorist act or with the knowledge of the intention of the group to commit a terrorist act. (FATF 2012)

Absent internationally agreed on definitions of "terrorist organization" and "terrorist," countries are left with flexibility to choose how they define "terrorist organization" and "terrorist." Therefore, these definitions need to provide specific content in the criminal law of a given country. As case studies show, it is relevant to prove that the funds were collected for or provided to a terrorist organization or to a terrorist. In the context of a criminal trial, it is usually for courts to determine whether an organization or individual should be considered a terrorist organization or terrorist, based on the criminal law of the country.

## STATUS OF IMPLEMENTATION

According to the FATF, the aim of IO.9, which deals with terrorist financing, is not only to *punish and deter crime* (unlike IO.7 for money laundering), but also to *detect and disrupt terrorist activities*, and so prevent the occurrence of planned or potential terrorist acts. The need to prevent such acts means that law enforcement or security services may be required to intervene to prevent an attack—by arresting suspects and seizing goods and funds—before they have gathered enough evidence to make a terrorist financing prosecution. Therefore, the core issues focus also on achieving the IO by employing other criminal justice, regulatory, or other measures to disrupt terrorist financing activities where it is not practical to secure a conviction. This includes prosecution for a different terrorist or other criminal offense, prosecution for a lesser offense, or the use of administrative powers, which are frequently used to disrupt terrorist activity and may make a terrorist financing prosecution impossible, while bearing in mind the fundamental principles of human rights. It is important to understand that recourse to these alternate measures should not itself be considered a priority response, and that, according to FATF, a country must assess the practicability of securing terrorist financing convictions before administrative measures can be applied (FATF and APG 2016).

Comparative analysis of selected mutual evaluation reports (MERs) adopted by the FATF and its related national bodies shows that only four countries[6] have achieved a High rating for effectiveness on IO.9. However, in countries that have received a Substantial rating, the low number of investigations and prosecutions seems at odds with the terrorist financing risk that these countries may be facing. These ratings may have been justified by the country's combating the financing of terrorism (CFT) efforts or framework, or by the country's capacity to disrupt terrorist activities.

That said, it is difficult to conclude whether the relative dearth of terrorist financing investigations and prosecutions results from having disrupted activities or can be attributed to other issues, such as the capacity of investigators and prosecutors to handle terrorist financing investigations, difficulties finding evidence to support prosecution, or broader concerns such as a poor understanding of the terrorist financing risk. The fact that several countries with high technical compliance ratings for R.5 have been rated Moderate on IO.9 could support the conclusion that capacity issues—combined with poor understanding of risk—may significantly undermine the effectiveness of terrorist financing investigations and prosecutions.

## CRITICAL ISSUES FOR EFFECTIVE PROSECUTION

### Definition of Terrorist Financing and Terrorism, and Countries' Efforts to Disrupt Certain Terrorist Groups

The first critical issue to ensuring effective enforcement is related to the definition of a terrorist financing offense in a jurisdiction's criminal law. In the FATF Recommendations, the offense should not require that the funds or other assets be linked to a specific terrorist act. Rather, it occurs if one willfully collects or provides funds with the intention or knowledge that they are to be used by a terrorist organization or an individual terrorist. Therefore, the acts are considered

---

[6] These countries are Israel, the Russian Federation, the United Kingdom, and the United States.

terrorist financing if one provides funds to an organization, knowing that it is a terrorist organization. This criterion applies even if the funds are provided under the assumption that they will be used for lawful activities or services (for example, if the organization provides assistance to the poor).

However, there are instances when prosecuting a particular conduct could be more challenging. An example is when funds are provided to the family of a suicide bomber after the terrorist act has been committed. As analysis of judicial cases will show, if the prosecution is not carefully crafted, it may be a challenge to establish the *mens rea* (intent) or to prove a terrorist financing offense has occurred.

One of the most challenging issues, given its political dimensions, is the definition of "terrorist organization." As analysis of the cases will make clear, the question of whether the organization for which funds are collected or to which they are provided is, in fact, a terrorist organization is central to proving a terrorist financing offense has been committed. Absent an internationally agreed on definition of "terrorist organization" or "terrorist," countries choose how they define these terms, provided that their definitions cover persons or entities who commit or attempt to commit terrorist acts as defined by the FATF and the UN Convention, or who otherwise participate in, organize, direct, or contribute to the commission of such acts.

International debate continues on the difference between terrorism and legitimate resistance or liberation movements. Since the UN considers Al-Qaida, Taliban, and ISIL (Da'esh) as terrorist groups under a system of sanctions established in UNSCR 1267, all countries are expected to consider these to be terrorist groups. For other groups, some countries consider them terrorist organizations while others do not. For example, whereas the United States and other countries consider Hizballah to be a terrorist organization, Iran regards it as a resistance movement. Opinions may also shift. For example, the EU did not initially consider Hamas to be a terrorist organization.

Furthermore, the Council of Arab Ministers of the Interior and the Council of Arab Ministers of Justice adopted a Convention for the Suppression of Terrorism in Cairo in April 1998[7] that provides a broad definition of "terrorism." The struggle, including armed struggle, against foreign occupation and aggression for liberation and self-determination is specifically excluded.[8] Article 2, paragraph 1 of the Convention notes the following:

> [. . .] all cases of struggle by whatever means, including armed struggle, against foreign occupation and aggression for liberation and self-determination, in accordance with the principles of international law, shall not be regarded as an offence. This provision shall not apply to any act prejudicing the territorial integrity of any Arab State.

---

[7] Refer to Annex IV for the full text of the Convention.
[8] Paragraph 4 of the Preamble affirms as follows: "the right of peoples to combat foreign occupation and aggression by whatever means, including armed struggle, in order to liberate their territories and secure their right to self-determination, and independence and to do so in such a manner as to preserve the territorial integrity of each Arab country, of the foregoing being in accordance with the purposes and principles of the Charter of the United Nations and with the Organization's resolutions."

Article 41 of the Convention prohibits the contracting state from making reservations that explicitly or implicitly violate its provisions or are incompatible with its objectives.

Influenced by the 1998 Convention, several countries party to the UN Convention[9] made declarations and reservations on some provisions. Three countries (Egypt, Jordan, Syria) made reservations on Article 2 of the UN Convention and considered acts of resistance to foreign occupation to not be acts of terrorism.[10]

Many countries objected to these reservations by stating that they unilaterally limit the scope of the UN Convention and contradict its object and purpose, in particular to suppress the financing of terrorist acts wherever and by whomever they may be committed. They also stressed the following:

> [. . .] the reservation is further contrary to the terms of Article 6[11] of the UN terrorist financing Convention, according to which States Parties commit themselves to adopt such measures as may be necessary, including, where appropriate, domestic legislation, to ensure that criminal acts within the scope of this Convention are under no circumstances justifiable by considerations of a political, philosophical, ideological, racial, ethnic, religious, or other similar nature. (United Nations 1999)

Therefore, most objections noted that, according to customary international law, as codified in the Vienna Convention on the Law of Treaties, reservations that are incompatible with the object and purpose of a convention are not permissible.

## Investigative Techniques Considering Varied Nature of Financing and Funding Needs

The financial needs of a complex and structured terrorist organization are very different from those of a small group, a lone wolf, or a person who wishes to travel in order to join a terrorist organization (that is, a foreign terrorist fighter) (FATF 2015). Often, the amounts used are much smaller than those used to finance large terrorist organizations. A study by the *Forskningsinstitutt* (FFI)[12] on the financing of 40 jihadi terrorist cells that plotted attacks in Europe shows that jihadi terrorist attacks in western Europe have generally been cheap, with three-quarters

---

[9] Thirteen out of 18 countries (72 percent) in the region joined the Convention.

[10] For more details, please refer to Annex III.

[11] Article 6 of the ICSFT has attempted to address some of the problems, attendant upon the lack of a terrorism definition by refusing to allow political exceptions to the offense.

[12] The Norwegian Defence Research Establishment works on behalf of the Norwegian Armed Forces and provides expert advice to political and military defense leaders. See https://publications.ffi.no/nb /item/asset/dspace:2469/14-02234.pdf.

estimated to cost less than $10,000. In contrast, the financial needs of a terrorist organization like ISIL are much higher.[13]

Funding can come from illegal or legal sources. Criminal activities that may generate the required proceeds include, for example, looting of natural resources, extortion or kidnapping for ransom, or drug trafficking, while examples of legitimate origins include salaries or social benefits, particularly for small groups and foreign terrorist fighters (FATF 2015). Funds may be collected through illicit means (for example, unlicensed remittance systems) or from licit sources (such as loans or crowdfunding). The FFI study shows, for example, that the jihadi cells operating in Europe have primarily relied on funding from the cell members' own salaries and savings, that 90 percent of the cells studied were involved in income-generating activities, and that half were entirely self-financed. In contrast, larger terrorist organizations appear to rely more on funds generated from illicit activities. The *World Atlas of Illicit Flows*, compiled by INTERPOL, RHIPTO (a Norwegian UN-collaborating center), and the Global Initiative Against Transnational Organized Crime, says the following:

> Collectively, for the seven main extremist groups of insurgents and terrorists (referred to above)—al-Shabaab, Boko Haram, [Revolutionary Armed Forces of Colombia] (FARC), [Hay'at Tahrir al-Sham] (HTS), [Jama'at Nusrat Al-Islam Wal-Muslimin] (JNIM), Islamic State and the Taliban, plus the [Democratic Republic of Congo] (DRC) fighters, the combined funding totals about US$1–1.39 billion a year. Taxation of natural resources and drugs is the most significant, readily available and accessible source of income, ranging from taxation of vehicles at checkpoints, agricultural produce, protection money targeting commercial activity to religious taxes.

Although the financing operations could go through the formal sector (for example, banks and licenses remitters), evidence suggests that they often occur in complete informality, with cash and unlicensed money value transfer services (MVTS) as examples. These differences in techniques can have an impact on the ability of financial institutions and designated nonfinancial businesses and professions (DNFBPs) to identify and detect suspicious transactions, which, in the conceptual approach underlying the FATF Recommendations, is among the triggers for criminal investigations into activities related to terrorist financing, such as money laundering.

These different financial needs and modalities for obtaining funds may affect the effectiveness of investigations and prosecutions. For instance, even when the amounts are small, a parallel financial investigation could help yield new information to support a terrorism investigation. However, in some cases where the amounts are small, pursuing specific terrorist financing charges may add only to the burden of prosecutors without adding much value to the prosecution or sentencing, since charging for recruitment or for membership in a terrorist organization may

---

[13] See https://www.fatf-gafi.org/content/fatf-gafi/en/publications/Methodsandtrends/Fatf-action-against-terrorist-financing-june-2019.html.

carry a similar or harsher punishment than terrorist financing and may be easier to prove.

In general, the number of terrorist financing investigations (and prosecutions and convictions) across the world appear to be relatively small, particularly when set against the risk profile of the country or compared to the number of terrorist financing–related suspicious transaction reports (STRs), of which there are often very few. The reasons for this may not necessarily indicate a lack of or poor investigations.

Comparing the number of STRs to investigations and prosecutions (or assessing whether STRs related to terrorist financing are in numbers commensurate to the risk in a jurisdiction) may not be a good indicator. In some countries where the number of STRs related to terrorist financing is high, this could be the result of reporting false positives. In countries where the main risk of terrorist financing is related to foreign terrorist fighters or small groups, the lack of STRs may be because funding comes from legitimately derived sources (salaries, social benefits, family contributions), or from petty crime (theft), small loans, or because the operations take place in the informal sector (using cash). In these cases, the funding does not involve financial institutions or DNFBPs subject to STR requirements. When it does (as with loans, for example), the amounts are small and lacking suspicious elements that would typically trigger an STR.

In some offshore financial centers—although the risk of terrorism could be low—the terrorist financing risk may be elevated and relate to the jurisdiction's ability to channel funds to terrorist organizations operating within or nearby conflict zones (for example, the United Arab Emirates in relation to conflicts in Iraq and Syria or Malta in relation to risks of terrorism in sub-Saharan Africa). Whether this type of jurisdiction can be exposed to terrorist financing risk could be established by, for example, analysis of the outflows to conflict areas or to regions close to them.

One of the main challenges for suppressing terrorist financing is related to the difficulty of pursuing investigations and charges that relate to money supporting terrorists in other countries (further details are included in the section on international cooperation in Chapter 6). An example of this difficulty is the Paris attacks of November 2015. Investigations required following the terrorist financing trail across several jurisdictions, including analysis of attempted transactions the attackers conducted while traveling from Syria to France through Turkey and Italy. Also, as noted in the MER of Australia, "the money trail becomes difficult to follow as funds are first transferred to conduit countries—generally countries neighboring conflict zones making it difficult to prove the final destination of the funds."

Reviews of case studies underline the need for careful consideration when filing charges for terrorist financing offenses. In some cases, it is easier to subsume terrorist financing elements under other charges that often carry similar or harsher penalties, such as membership or participation in a terrorist organization, recruiting, aiding, and abetting terrorism or a terrorist organization, for which it is easier to establish guilt. The MER of Austria notes the following:

[. . .] most of the investigations do not result in criminal prosecutions due to the lack of sufficient evidence for the Public Prosecutor's Office to formally initiate criminal charges on terrorist financing crimes but may result in prosecutions on terrorist association crimes. The large number of terrorist financing investigations compared to prosecutions is largely due to the fact that terrorist financing-related STRs almost automatically trigger an investigation, although STRs are not the only basis for terrorist financing investigations[14]

While gathering evidence for terrorist financing can prove more challenging than for other terrorism-related or ancillary offenses, a preference in prosecutorial practice for not bringing separate charges for terrorist financing (where conducts may be reclassified as different, easier-to-prove criminal offenses) can reduce the dissuasiveness of the criminal sanctions, and, ultimately, undermine the effective pursuit of terrorist financing criminal offenses.

Specific terrorist financing activity is not always evident during an investigation. Sometimes elements of it appear at a later stage of investigation into a terrorism-related offense when the case is ready for trial. Including the terrorist financing component may delay the trial while not adding much to the potential sentencing of the perpetrators, especially for multiple offenses where the punishment for a "lesser" offense (terrorist financing) may be absorbed by a "higher" offense (for example, terrorism). The case in Box 4.1 is extracted from the MER of Albania.

---

**Box 4.1. Financing Travel to a Conflict Zone**

In a case reported in the mutual evaluation report of Albania,[1] nine people were convicted for various terrorism-related offenses. An examination of terrorist financing aspects was conducted in relation to the recruitment of some 70 individuals in Albania and the funding of their travel to Syria as foreign terrorist fighters (where it could be proven that some were directly involved in atrocities requiring explosives). The nine perpetrators were indicted and then convicted of recruitment of persons for the commission of terrorist offenses (Art. 231 of Criminal Code), encouraging public invocation and propaganda for the execution of terrorist offenses (Art. 232/a of Criminal Code), and inciting hatred or quarrel (Art. 265 of Criminal Code). It was proven during the trial that the defendants had purchased tickets for some of the recruits to fly to Syria and so had covered their travel expenses, and at least in one case, they gave financial compensation, in the form of cash, to the family of a militant who was killed in Syria. However, there was no indictment for terrorist financing, as further investigation would have been needed to secure a conviction.

Source: Albania Fifth Round Mutual Evaluation Report, July 2018.
[1] http://www.FATF-gafi.org/publications/mutualevaluations/documents/fur1-albania-2019.html.

---

[14] https://www.fatf-gafi.org/en/publications/Mutualevaluations/Mer-australia-2015.html.

Investigators often lack financial skills or human resources, which affect their capacity to effectively investigate offenses. Investigations can require financial skills to examine complex, large-scale transactions often involving many people across different countries.

## Good Practices

The analysis of MERs shows more effective results when terrorist financing investigations are part of a broader strategy to counterterrorism, with a strong policy and operational framework that ensure systematic investigations (and adoption of countermeasures). The FATF acknowledges that both policy and operational coordination is the most common failure in this IO—given the range of different agencies involved, and that they may not have long records of working together in other contexts. Countries that have achieved important results include the United Kingdom, where the strategy to convict foreign terrorist fighters involves interactions among all relevant authorities. The MER of the United Kingdom notes as follows:

> [The country] actively pursues two terrorist financing aspects with respect to these individuals: the funding of travel to the conflict zone; and subsistence in-country potentially through the support of relatives or contacts in the United Kingdom or the abuse of legitimate benefits. Law enforcement agencies work with [Her Majesty's Revenue and Customs] HMRC and the Department of Work and Pensions to suspend benefits wherever intelligence indicates a claimant has left the United Kingdom for extremist purposes. These terrorist financing aspects integrate with a broader counter-[foreign terrorist fighter] FTF policy. This includes utilizing available powers to remove passport facilities, imposing travel restrictions, and depriving individuals of British citizenship. (FATF 2018)

Spain has a strategy of dismantling the organizational and support network of Euskadi Ta Askatasuna, which has a highly sophisticated economic arm to finance operations. This has resulted in a few successful cases targeting the organization's different funding modalities (FATF 2014). Another good practice is to conduct parallel financial investigations into the funds and roles of terrorist financing financiers when investigating terrorism-related crimes, also because financial information could identify contacts with known subjects or identify previously unknown subjects in a terrorist network. Specialized officers or units best conduct these investigations.

Financial investigations should look at the funding element related to terrorist organizations and individuals, not only in the actual provision of funds or other assets but also at the collection stage, in line with the country's terrorist financing risk profile. For example, the MER of Denmark notes that every counterterrorism investigation assesses potential terrorist financing, and all financial elements of foreign terrorist fighters are analyzed. The Danish Security and Intelligence Service (PET) has a dedicated financial intelligence team responsible for collecting, analyzing, and documenting financial intelligence. In Sweden, terrorist financing cases are investigated by a specialized unit of terrorist financing investigators at Säpo, and by other units trained in financial investigation and terrorist financing. All counterterrorism investigations include a financial dimension, and financial intelligence is used routinely as a source of intelligence in all counterterrorism investigations. In Spain, once terrorist financing activity is identified, the authorities bring to investigations their full range of investigative tools and available sources of information, including the full range of financial intelligence, in cooperation with other countries. Every terrorism investigation involves a parallel investigation of terrorist financing.

## Difficulty of Prosecuting and Securing a Conviction

Several MERs note that most investigations do not result in criminal prosecutions due to a lack of sufficient evidence to formally initiate criminal charges for terrorist financing offenses. In some cases, prosecutors have identified potential difficulties in demonstrating a connection with a terrorist act when pursuing an individual, as well as difficulties in proving an organization is terrorist when not formally designated as such. This section takes a deep dive into some key challenges related to the prosecution of terrorist financing offenses, particularly how to establish *mens rea*, on the characteristics of terrorist organizations and groups and on circumstantial evidence that may be sufficient to prove them, from an analysis of several court rulings.

### *Proving Intent*

One of the most significant challenges concerns the specific level of knowledge a defendant is required to have had in order to prove intent. The terrorist financier must be acting with knowledge that the funds or other assets are intended for the commission of a terrorist act or for a terrorist organization or an individual terrorist. Therefore, it is only the terrorist financier's unlawful intention/purpose that is relevant (and should be proven) for a terrorist financing prosecution to go to trial. The FATF, in its *Guidance on Criminalising Terrorist Financing* (FATF 2016), made the following remarks:

[T]he following aspects are not relevant to the scope of the terrorist financing offense (and to prove the mental element):

i. The purpose for which the terrorist financier intended those funds or other assets to be used by the terrorist organization/individual terrorist;
ii. Any knowledge that the terrorist financier may have had about how the terrorist organization/individual terrorist was using or intending to use the funds or other assets;
iii. The use to which the terrorist organization/individual terrorist actually put (or intended to put, or tried to put) the funds or other assets; and
iv. Whether or not the funds or other assets were used to plan, prepare for or carry out a specific terrorist act.

The way the criminal statutes are written is fundamental to avoid challenges, particularly in the interpretation of courts. For example, in the United States, it is explicit that it shall not be necessary that the funds collected were actually used to carry out a predicate act in order to violate the statute.[15] Therefore, US courts have stated that statutory law does not require a showing of specific intent that the defendant acted to further the organization's terrorist activities or that the defendant intended to aid or encourage the particular attack.

> The government needs to prove two intent requirements: (1) that the aid was intentional and (2) that the defendant knew the organization he is aiding is a terrorist organization or engages in acts of terrorism. The prosecution is not required to show a specific intention that the defendant intended his aid to support the terrorist activity of a terrorist group.[16]

The courts also stated that it is irrelevant whether the defendant donated the funds to support "peaceful activities of a designated terrorist organization."

In Indonesia, a cleric, suspected of being a key member of the jihadist Jemaah Islamiah network—the Indonesian cell of Al-Qaida—was convicted for having funded a paramilitary group of the network, with funds then diverted to the network itself. Although the defendant claimed he did not know the funds were diverted to the terrorist group, the Supreme Court upheld the conviction.[17]

In Denmark, some individuals were charged with terrorist financing because they sold T-shirts to help fund FARC and the Popular Front for the Liberation of Palestine (PFLP)—both designated by the EU as terrorist organizations. The Supreme Court of Denmark upheld the conviction, even though the defendants argued, among other claims, that the proceeds of the sale were aimed at supporting the "humanitarian projects" of FARC and the PFLP.[18]

However, in Finland, before the law was amended to criminalize terrorist financing for the provision of funds or assets to a terrorist group regardless of the

---

[15] Although the specific intent is not necessary, at least mere knowledge that the funds provided and collected would be used to carry out the predicate act is essential to proving the violation of § 2339C. This is because § 2339C punishes the financing of terrorist acts. In contrast, § 2339B does not require even mere knowledge that the funds provided and collected would be used to carry out the predicate act. It is enough to prove the aid was intentional and that the defendant knew the organization he is aiding is a terrorist organization or engages in acts of terrorism because § 2339B prohibits the financing of terrorists or terrorist organizations, not terrorist acts.

[16] The United States Court of Appeals, Second Circuit, *United States v. Monzer al-Kassar* (Decided September 21, 2011).

[17] AsiaNews.it: http://www.asianews.it/news-en/Jakarta-confirms-sentence-for-Abu-Bakar-Bashir:-He-was-financing-the-jihadists-38231.html; *South China Morning Post*: http://www.scmp.com/news/asia/southeast-asia/article/1999167/abu-bakar-bashir-loses-appeal-against-15-year-sentence.

[18] Danish Supreme Court, *Katrine Willumsen v. Prosecutor* (March 25, 2009). Reference to this case can be found in the Library of Congress: http://www.loc.gov/law/foreign-news/article/denmark-convictions-for-terrorism-t-shirts/; and Sam Jones and Helen Pidd, "Danish T-shirt Sellers Convicted of Financing Terrorism," *The Guardian*, March 25, 2009, https://www.theguardian.com/world/2009/mar/25/danish-t-shirt-sellers-financing-terrorism.

purpose, it used to be that a conviction for providing financial support to a terrorist group required the defendant to have known that the money would be used for terrorism.

The cases described in Box 4.2 show differences in case law stemming from different legal drafting of the relevant criminal provisions. What is interesting is that, in both cases, prosecutors were able to prove that the defendants knew they were providing funds to a terrorist organization.

---

### Box 4.2. Proving Knowledge and Intent

United States Court of Appeals, Fourth Circuit, *United States v. Mohamad Youssef Hammoud* (Decided on September 8, 2004)[1]

**Legal principle:** 18 USC § 2339B, which lacks a specific intent requirement for furthering a Foreign Terrorist Organization (FTO)'s illegal aim and therefore punishes the conduct of providing material support to a designated FTO, including a case where the defendant had intended to give aid only for peaceful activities of the FTO, does not violate the First Amendment right of association.

**Category:** Protected right (right of association); knowledge/intent

**Type:** Preventing financial support to terrorists and terrorist organizations (§ 2339B)

**Background:** Mohamad Hammoud donated $3,500 of his own money to Hizballah, a designated FTO. The US district court convicted him of providing material support through currency to the designated FTO under 18 USC 2339B. Hammoud appealed to the US federal appellate court. He argued that Hizballah engages in both legal and illegal activities, and he provided the support for peaceful activities of Hizballah and claimed that 18 USC. § 2339B violates the First Amendment right of association.

**Excerpts:** "More fundamentally, money is fungible; giving support intended to aid an organization's peaceful activities frees up resources that can be used for terrorist acts [. . .] [T]he prohibition on material support is adequately tailored to the interest served and does not suppress more speech than is necessary to further the Government's legitimate goal. We therefore conclude that § 2339B does not infringe on the constitutionally protected right of free association."

Helsinki Appeals Court (April 2016)[2]

**Legal principle:** The court found that a defendant did not know that the money would be used for a terrorist attack, although the defendant knew that the money was going to a terrorist organization. It acquitted the defendant of financing terrorist acts.

**Category:** Knowledge/intent

**Type:** Criminalizing the financing of terrorist acts (Finnish law)

**Background:** The defendant was accused of sending money to the terrorist group al-Shabaab in Somalia and Kenya. A district court sentenced the defendant to a suspended prison term.

**Description of legal principle:** The Appeals Court overturned the conviction. The court found that at the time of their actions, providing financial support to a terrorist group had not yet been criminalized under Finnish law except in cases where it was clear that the money would be used for terrorism. Therefore, the court was not able to apply law for preventing financial support to terrorists and terrorist organizations to this case.[3] Thus, it examined only application of law for criminalizing the financing of terrorist acts. The court found that the defendant did not know the money would be

### Box 4.2. *(continued)*

> used for a terrorist attack, although the defendant knew it was going to the terrorist organization al-Shabaab. The court acquitted the defendant of financing terrorist acts.
>
> Source: United States v. Hammoud, US Court of Appeals, Fourth Circuit (2004). https://www.ca4.uscourts.gov/opinions/034253.P.pdf.
>
> [1] 381 F.3d 316.
>
> [2] See https://yle.fi/uutiset/osasto/news/court_acquits_four_in_finlands_first_terror_case/8762843.
>
> [3] If the court had been able to apply law for preventing financial support to terrorists and terrorist organizations to this case, the court would have found the defendant guilty because the knowledge that the money was going to a terrorist organization is enough to satisfy the subjective element of the crime, and it does not require that the defendant knew that the money would be used for the terrorist attack (see the case # 1.1).

The cases presented in Box 4.3 concern indirect collection/provision. Providing proof for these cases was more challenging because the courts were not satisfied that the persons to which the funds were provided would be acting with or at the direction of a designated terrorist organization, or because the prosecution could not prove that the funds provided indirectly had in fact reached the designated terrorist organization.

### Box 4.3. Objective Elements of the Terrorist Financing Offense

Denmark—Rachid Mohamad Issa and Ahmad Mohamad Suleiman (February 2008)[1]

**Legal principle:** Judges found the evidence presented in court to be insufficient for proving that defendants transferred money to a terrorist organization. The evidence failed to prove that the recipient organizations were part of the terrorist organization.

**Category:** Objective elements of the crime; evidence; burden of proof/standard of proof

**Type:** Preventing financial support to terrorists and terrorist organizations (EU sanctions prohibiting support to Hamas)

**Background:** Defendants were charged with breaking EU sanctions prohibiting support to Hamas. Although the defendants agreed that they had collected money and transferred it to charities, they denied being aware that the recipient organizations were part of Hamas or that the purpose was to finance terrorism.

**Description of legal principle:** Judges found no decisive evidence that leaders of the recipient organizations were working in conjunction with or at the direction of Hamas, regardless of whether some leaders were also members of Hamas. The court acquitted the defendants.

Denmark, Lower Court (October 22, 2014)[2]

**Legal principle:** The court found the defendants not guilty on the grounds that they did not know that the money went to a terrorist organization.

**Category:** Knowledge/intent; evidence; burden of proof

**Type:** Preventing financial support to terrorists and terrorist organizations

**Box 4.3. (continued)**

> **Background:** Defendants were accused of collecting approximately $23 million for the Kurdistan Workers' Party (PKK), which is designated as a terrorist organization in Denmark. The prosecution argued that the defendants channeled money to the PKK through the Kurdish-language broadcast station Roj TV. The prosecution submitted evidence gathered over several years, including extensive material from wiretapping and bugging, detailed bank statements, and company accounts.
>
> **Description of legal principle:** The lower court found the defendants not guilty on the grounds that prosecutors could not prove they knew that the money raised for the TV station went to the PKK. The prosecution appealed, and the Eastern High Court of Appeals upheld the acquittal of eight defendants but overturned the acquittal of two defendants in June 2016.
>
> Source: Flashback. https://www.flashback.org/p29131034
>
> [1] https://jamestown.org/program/scandinavian-trials-demonstrate-difficulty-of-obtaining-terrorist-financing-convictions/
>
> [2] The FATF's mutual evaluation report for Denmark, p. 69. https://www.fatf-gafi.org/en/publications/Mutualevaluations/Mer-denmark-2017.html.

## *Proving the Existence of a Terrorist Organization or Group*

Another significant challenge is to prove that the organization or group to which funds are destined is a terrorist organization. A prosecutor of a civil law country would not typically need to prove that an entity such as Al-Qaida or ISIL is a terrorist organization, since this would be considered a known fact that does not need to be proven.[19] If an organization was designated as terrorist through a UN Security Council Resolution, this could serve, for example, as a *prima facie* indication of the terrorist nature of the organization.

However, what if the organization is not a designated entity pursuant to the UN or other domestic mechanisms? The prosecution would have to establish two things: (1) that it is an organization, and (2) that its aim is to commit terrorism. This entails proving a structured organization exists (in civil law countries, this would typically require a minimum of three people) that is capable of executing the common purpose/criminal goal of the organization (for example, committing terrorist attacks, even if abroad) with the members acting in concert to execute a "criminal plan" ("acting with a common purpose," in this case the execution of terrorist acts [Tribunal de Première Instance Francophone de Bruxelles 2015[20]]), with a duration exceeding the amount of time needed to carry out the criminal acts. The criminal plan should entail the execution of multiple, unspecified acts, not just one single, specific act, and it is irrelevant whether the acts are committed or not.

---

[19] This refers to a fact with such a level of certainty that it is undisputed (for example, in the public domain).

[20] https://www.stradalex.com/fr/sl_src_publ_jur_be/document/tprem_F-20151106-5.

What about the case of small terrorist cells, groups, or networks? Typologies have shown that they can operate with an extremely flexible structure, in more countries and at different times, with sporadic and discontinuous contacts among them (including by phone, email, or other electronic means), and that the members/cells contribute in different ways to the goal of the organization. Could these smaller cells, groups, or networks be considered an "organization" for the purpose of applying the terrorist financing provision? Looking at the elements required by the jurisprudence of some countries to prove criminal organizations or associations established to pursue terrorist ends or to support terrorist organizations (therefore not strictly speaking the jurisprudence concerning terrorist financing), it can be seen that the approach is quite flexible. The following needs to be established:

- Prove *mens rea*. They are aware of contributing to the criminal goal of the organization or to the commission of the offense, however modest the assistance or however far removed the actual crimes may be.
- Prove at least one support activity (such as proselytism, propaganda, assistance, and assistance, including funding members of the organization, provision of false documents, weapons, and so on).
- It does not matter if the cell does not have violent purposes. If it provides support to a parent organization, no matter in which country, that has violent or terroristic purposes, then it has committed a terrorist financing offense.[21]

Also of interest are the types of circumstantial evidence that, considered as a whole, could be deemed sufficient to demonstrate the "terrorist" character of the group. This class of evidence would include actions such as visiting websites of extremist organizations (for example, with almost daily access); accessing restricted websites of terrorist organizations (which require passwords shared only among trusted members); downloading and duplicating extremisms/terrorism-related materials; and possessing materials that incite terrorism or violence. It also includes particular conduct by members that is aimed at keeping activities confidential (such as using cryptic language to avoid detection or "splitting" information among the members of the organization so that most members are party only to some information and lack the whole picture).

Circumstantial evidence, as shown in the case in Box 4.4, has also been deemed sufficient to prove that the funds collected were intended for a terrorist organization.

---

[21] See Italian Court of Cassation ruling n. 46308, July 12, 2012.

> ### Box 4.4. Solicitation to Fund Terrorist Organizations
>
> **Legal principle:** The crime of soliciting funding for terrorist organizations can be proven by the cumulation of circumstantial evidence (first conviction of solicitation to funding of terrorist organizations)
>
> **Relevant provision:** Criminalizing solicitation to funding of terrorist organizations under Section 3 of the Act on Punishment for Public Enticement and Education Regarding Terrorist Crimes and Other Extraordinarily Serious Crimes (the Act)
>
> **Background:** A person was charged with the crime of soliciting funding for terrorist organizations, including ISIL, under Section 3 of the Act. Swedish law distinguishes Section 3 of the Act for criminalizing the solicitation from the Swedish Act on Funding of Serious Crimes, where it punishes the direct collecting of funds for terrorist organizations. The defendant denied the solicitation. Therefore, the prosecution tried to prove his guilt by cumulating circumstantial evidence.
>
> **Description of legal principle:** The district court found the defendant guilty of soliciting funding for terrorist organizations through the cumulation of circumstantial evidence. The court found that he had made the following message available on his Facebook page: "[h]elp us supply our brothers at the front with weapons to avenge our siblings." The court also found that he had provided two known funders of terrorism with contact information. The court further found that the defendant was the owner of the account, despite the alias used; that the defendant's objection that he had been given the Facebook account to access other accounts was improbable; and that considering full circumstances, including updates being made on his employer's network, he had indeed exercised control over the account and intentionally provided information on the account to solicit funding for terrorist organizations. The defendant was sentenced to six months in prison.
>
> Source: "Sweden/Syria, Can Armed Groups Issue Judgments?" International Committee of the Red Cross. https://casebook.icrc.org/case-study/swedensyria-can-armed-groups-issue-judgments

## Disruption Measures When Conviction Cannot Be Secured

In certain cases, where it is not possible to secure a final terrorist financing conviction, authorities use alternative criminal justice, regulatory, or other measures to disrupt terrorist financing. Mutual evaluation results show that many countries disrupt terrorist financing activities early instead of pursuing a terrorist financing prosecution. This is often done in the interest of public safety in time-sensitive cases, or where available evidence is not admissible or sufficient to support a terrorist financing prosecution. Alternative measures include pursuing other criminal charges (such as association with a terrorist organization, immigration violations, fraud, and tax crimes) or using broader counterterrorism powers, financial disruptions, and civil penalties.

While the following examples may demonstrate varying efficacy, alternative measures should not replace investigations and prosecutions dedicated to disrupting terrorism and its financing. Alternative measures should be viewed in the context of broader counterterrorism strategies and terrorist financing risk profiling. These strategies should rely on investigations and prosecutions and on the criminal process in general to disrupt and repress terrorism.

Box 4.5 highlights examples of alternative measures used by countries, derived from MERs. On the one hand, alternative measures can be preventive because they are applied in advance, before the commission of an act, to reduce the threat within a country (for example, "soft" approaches such as deradicalization, harmonization, and poverty alleviation). On the other hand, they can be punitive and even repressive (for example, revocation of social benefits or citizenship, deportation, and confiscation of funds) to the extent that they impose restrictions and, in some cases, are used as sanctions. While the "soft" approaches can be good as long-term strategies to reduce the risk of terrorism and terrorist financing, they do not impose disrupting effects on immediate threats. Especially in the deportation of potential terrorists, the approach might only mean that risks are transferred to other jurisdictions.

---

### Box 4.5. Alternative Measures Used to Disrupt Terrorist Financing Activity

#### *Deportation*

**Italy** has used deportation of foreign residents widely as a means to disrupt potential terrorist activities. In 2015, the Italian government adopted a new regulation with measures against terrorist activities, such as strengthening deportation powers and the adoption by the National Anti-Mafia Prosecutor (currently, the National Anti-Mafia and Counterterrorism Prosecutor) of new counterterrorism measures. Italian law provides that, for purposes of public order or state security, the Ministry of the Interior can order the deportation of a foreign citizen.

#### *Disruption through investigation and arrests, freezing/ confiscation of funds, and other criminal charges and measures*

In **the United Kingdom,** when criminal prosecution is not possible, authorities seek to disrupt terrorist financing through freezing, seizing, or forfeiting terrorist funds or assets. The Home Secretary also has powers to restrict the activities of suspected terrorists where necessary for public protection by issuing a notice under the Terrorism Prevention and Investigation Measures (TPIM) Act of 2011. TPIM notices can restrict the amount of cash individuals can hold, their access to electronic communication devices, residency requirements, travel, and association with certain individuals. They can require the individual to report regularly to authorities.

When unable to use the Terrorism Law of 2014, **the United Arab Emirates** has utilized others, including a law on charities (Federal Law No. 2 of 2008) to prosecute, convict, and confiscate funds of terrorist financiers.

In cases with insufficient evidence and where the suspect is a foreigner, the United Arab Emirates will often deport the suspect back to their home country. This happened to several couriers carrying large amounts of cash, who were deported with the funds. The emirate notifies the receiving country of the deportation and provides the suspect's identifying information and other background details, making it likely that these individuals will be detained when they return home.

**Box 4.5.** *(continued)*

> In **Greece,** authorities consider the most effective measures to be the designation of a suspect as a "person related to terrorism" by the anti-money laundering and combating the financing of terrorism (AML/CFT) authority. In accordance with the AML/CFT law, this designation results in immediate freezing of assets and a ban on making any transaction with an obliged entity. Greece has successfully used this measure since the creation of the counterterrorism unit to disrupt financial flows and reduce the assets available for terrorist activities or to support individual terrorists or terrorist groups.
>
> In **Denmark**, where a terrorist financing conviction is not possible and the individual is committing a tax violation, the PET may refer the case to the tax authority for administrative action. This may alert the target of the investigation with the intention of a further disruption of terrorist financing activities. Denmark may seize or deny passports of those suspected of traveling abroad to engage in activities that may pose a threat to its national security or that of other states.
>
> In **Sweden**, when authorities do not identify an alternative terrorist financing activity, they can use preventive measures, including Prohibitions on Disposal of Property, which target funds directly, giving the ability to "freeze" any funds and prevent travel during the duration of an investigation. This expands the range of disruption tools available.
>
> *Prevention: Deradicalization, Harmonization, and Poverty Alleviation*
>
> **Malaysia** has placed an emphasis on "soft" approaches to combating terrorism and terrorist financing. The initiatives center on rehabilitation and disengagement programs for detainees and close family members, and countering radicalization through the internet.
>
> **Bangladesh** has pursued a number of approaches, including educational reforms in religious and educational institutions and preventive measures to address root causes of radicalization.
>
> Source: Authors.

## CONCLUSION

Deterring terrorist financing requires imposing dissuasive sanctions against its perpetrators. Cases should be (1) investigated by highly trained and well-equipped law enforcement agencies building on strong financial intelligence, (2) presented to courts by qualified prosecutors who are well aware of the evolution of precedents in terrorist financing offenses worldwide, and (3) adjudicated by professional and specialized judges who can inflict appropriate sanctions to deter future perpetrators from committing those crimes and potentially preventing future terrorist attacks.

Absent convictions on terrorist financing offenses, alternative techniques (such as deportation, undercover operations, and adjudicating for different crimes) can function as deterrents. Although most countries face significant challenges to achieving effective enforcement against terrorist financiers, some have achieved good outcomes that could be built on for further success.

## REFERENCES

Financial Action Task Force (FATF). 2012–2020. *International Standards on Combating Money Laundering and the Financing of Terrorism & Proliferation*. Paris. Updated in March 2022. https://www.fatf-gafi.org/en/publications/Fatfrecommendations/Fatf-recommendations.html.

Financial Action Task Force (FATF). 2014. *Spain's Measures to Combat Money Laundering and Terrorist Financing*. Mutual Evaluation Report. Paris. https://www.fatf-gafi.org/en/publications/Mutualevaluations/Fur-spain-2018.html.

Financial Action Task Force (FATF). 2015a. *Report on Emerging Terrorism Financing Risks*. Paris.

Financial Action Task Force (FATF). 2015b. *Report on Financing of the Terrorist Organization ISIL*. Paris. https://www.fatf-gafi.org/en/publications/Methodsandtrends/Terrorist-financing-risk-assessment-guidance.html.

Financial Action Task Force (FATF). 2016. *Guidance on the Criminalisation of Terrorist Financing (Recommendation 5)*. Paris. https://www.fatf-gafi.org/content/fatf-gafi/en/publications/Fatfrecommendations/Criminalising-terrorist-financing.html.

Financial Action Task Force (FATF). 2018a. *FATF President's Paper: Anti-money Laundering and Counter-Terrorist Financing for Judges and Prosecutors*. Paris. https://www.fatf-gafi.org/content/fatf-gafi/en/publications/Fatfgeneral/Aml-cft-judges-prosecutors.html.

Financial Action Task Force (FATF). 2018b. *The United Kingdom's Measures to Combat Money Laundering and Terrorist Financing*. Mutual Evaluation Report. Paris. https://www.fatf-gafi.org/en/publications/Mutualevaluations/Mer-united-kingdom-2018.html.

Financial Action Task Force (FATF), and APG. 2016. *Anti-money Laundering and Counter-Terrorist Financing Measures—Singapore*. Fourth Round Mutual Evaluation Report. Paris and Sydney. https://www.fatf-gafi.org/en/publications/Mutualevaluations/Mer-singapore-2016.html.

INTERPOL, RHIPTO, and the Global Initiative Against Transnational Organized Crime. 2018. *World Atlas of Illicit Flows*. London.

Tribunal de Première Instance Francophone de Bruxelles. 2015. *Federal Prosecutor v Hamza B, Harris C-K, Abdelfattah A, Younnes HA, Kamal A and Sami L*. Brussels. https://www.internationalcrimesdatabase.org/Case/3288.

United Nations (UN). 1999. *International Convention for the Suppression of the Financing of Terrorism*. New York: UN. https://treaties.un.org/doc/Publication/CN/2020/CN.368.2020-Eng.pdf.

## RESOURCES

Financial Action Task Force (FATF). 2018. *Australia's Measures to Combat Money Laundering and Terrorist Financing*. Mutual Evaluation Report. Paris. https://www.fatf-gafi.org/publications/mutualevaluations/documents/fur-australia-2018.html.

Financial Action Task Force (FATF). 2016a. *Austria's Measures to Combat Money Laundering and Terrorist Financing*. Mutual Evaluation Report. Paris. http://www.fatf-gafi.org/publications/mutualevaluations/documents/mer-austria-2016.html.

Financial Action Task Force (FATF). 2016b. *Italy's Measures to Combat Money Laundering and Terrorist Financing*. Mutual Evaluation Report. Paris. http://www.fatf-gafi.org/publications/mutualevaluations/documents/mer-italy-2016.html.

Financial Action Task Force (FATF). 2016c. *Switzerland's Measures to Combat Money Laundering and Terrorist Financing*. Mutual Evaluation Report. Paris. https://www.fatf-gafi.org/publications/mutualevaluations/documents/mer-switzerland-2016.html.

Financial Action Task Force (FATF). 2017a. *Denmark's Measures to Combat Money Laundering and Terrorist Financing*. Mutual Evaluation Report. Paris. http://www.fatf-gafi.org/publications/mutualevaluations/documents/mer-denmark-2017.html.

Financial Action Task Force (FATF). 2017b. *Sweden's Measures to Combat Money Laundering and Terrorist Financing*. Mutual Evaluation Report. Paris. https://www.fatf-gafi.org/publications/mutualevaluations/documents/mer-sweden-2017.html.

Financial Action Task Force (FATF). 2019a. *Finland's Measures to Combat Money Laundering and Terrorist Financing*. Mutual Evaluation Report. Paris. http://www.fatf-gafi.org/publications/mutualevaluations/documents/mer-finland-2019.html.

Financial Action Task Force (FATF). 2019b. *Greece's Measures to Combat Money Laundering and Terrorist Financing*. Mutual Evaluation Report. Paris. http://www.fatf-gafi.org/publications/mutualevaluations/documents/mer-greece-2019.html.

Financial Action Task Force (FATF), and APG. 2015. *Malaysia's Measures to Combat Money Laundering and Terrorist Financing*. Mutual Evaluation Report. Paris. https://www.fatf-gafi.org/publications/mutualevaluations/documents/mer-malaysia-2015.html.

Financial Action Task Force (FATF), and APG. 2016. *Bangladesh's Measures to Combat Money Laundering and Terrorist Financing*. Mutual Evaluation Report. Paris. http://www.fatf-gafi.org/publications/mutualevaluations/documents/mer-bangladesh-2016.html.

Financial Action Task Force (FATF), and APG. 2017. *Cambodia's Measures to Combat Money Laundering and Terrorist Financing*. Mutual Evaluation Report. Paris. http://www.fatf-gafi.org/publications/mutualevaluations/documents/mer-cambodia-2017.html.

Financial Action Task Force (FATF), and MENAFATF. 2020. *United Arab Emirates' Measures to Combat Money Laundering and Terrorist Financing*. Mutual Evaluation Report. Paris. https://www.fatf-gafi.org/publications/mutualevaluations/documents/mer-uae-2020.html.

Financial Action Task Force (FATF), and Moneyval. 2018. *Czech Republic's Measures to Combat Money Laundering and Terrorist Financing*. Mutual Evaluation Report. Paris. http://www.fatf-gafi.org/publications/mutualevaluations/documents/mer-czech-republic-2018.html.

Financial Action Task Force (FATF), and Moneyval. 2019. *Moldova's Measures to Combat Money Laundering and Terrorist Financing*. Mutual Evaluation Report. Paris. http://www.fatf-gafi.org/publications/mutualevaluations/documents/mer-moldova-2019.html.

Financial Action Task Force (FATF), and Moneyval. 2021. *Albania's Measures to Combat Money Laundering and Terrorist Financing*. Mutual Evaluation Report. Paris. http://www.fatf-gafi.org/publications/mutualevaluations/documents/mer-albania-2018.html.

# CHAPTER 5

# Terrorism-Related Targeted Financial Sanctions

## Jay Purcell, Delphine Schantz, and Jacqueline Shire

### CHAPTER IN BRIEF

*The Challenge*

Targeted Financial Sanctions (TFS) are a powerful tool for combating terrorism and its financing, but their effectiveness is too often constrained by (1) limited awareness, understanding, and/or use of the designation tool at the UN and national levels in compliance with UN Security Council Resolutions (UNSCRs) 1267 (1999) and 1373 (2001); (2) a lack of implementation without delay; (3) inconsistent implementation by the private sector and; (4) the need for greater clarity and accessibility in delisting. Of the 127 jurisdictions that had completed the fourth round of anti-money laundering and combating the financing of terrorism (AML/CFT) mutual evaluations as of May 2022, only 19 were assessed to be sufficiently effective in their implementation of terrorism-related TFS.

*Why It Happens*

The constraints described above can often be explained by inadequate sensitization, guidance, or supervision on the part of relevant authorities; cumbersome or poorly adapted procedures for the implementation of new UN listings and the handling of delisting requests at the national level; and wide disparities in the resources and motivation of private sector actors. As such, bolstering the effective implementation of terrorism-related TFS will require tailored and efficient national processes that are designed and executed in coordination with the financial institutions (FIs), designated non-financial businesses and professions (DNFBPs), and virtual asset service providers (VASPs) on the front lines.

*The Solution*

The international good practices presented in this chapter were generated from (1) the insights and recommendations found in the References and Resources; (2) the wide range of approaches currently applied by IMF members; and (3) the authors' professional experiences. Sensitization of the relevant public sector actors, speed in implementing new UN listings, and support of the private sector—including via the provision of useful tools and timely guidance—are key.

## UNDERSTANDING A FLEXIBLE TOOL FOR COMBATING TERRORIST FINANCING

> *Targeted financial sanctions are a key preventive measure as well as a potent alternative to prosecution when the available evidence is insufficient to meet the applicable criminal threshold. Moreover, the possibility of their removal can function as a strong incentive for a designated person or entity to change their behavior. Sanctions are most effective when implemented globally and without delay.*

Targeted financial sanctions are a key tool for CFT and for countering terrorism more broadly.[1] The concept is likely familiar even if the term is not. In short, sanctions may be broadly or narrowly applied (such as to entire states or sectors or to specific individuals or firms) and may take a variety of forms (arms embargoes, travel bans, and financial restrictions are examples). The term "targeted financial sanctions" refers to an obligation to freeze the funds or other assets[2] of specified or "designated" persons or entities, combined with a prohibition on providing funds or other assets, economic resources, and financial or other related services to those persons or entities, whether directly or indirectly.[3]

Terrorism-related targeted financial sanctions may be levied at the international or regional levels (by the UN or regional organizations) and then implemented by individual states on a mandatory basis. States may also levy and implement sanctions of their own accord. Regardless, targeted financial sanctions are ultimately imposed and implemented under national laws that should reflect the obligations detailed in relevant UN Security Council Resolutions (UNSCRs)[4] and applicable

---

[1] As in the other chapters of this book, the names of specific states or groups of states have been largely omitted, both to avoid compromising the confidentiality of the meetings and documents from which many of the insights were derived and to emphasize the broad applicability of those insights.

[2] In this context, the term "funds or other assets" refers to everything of value owned or controlled by a person or entity. Indeed, the Financial Action Task Force (FATF), as the global standard setter for anti-money laundering and combating the financing of terrorism (AML/CFT), defines "funds or other assets" as follows: "any assets, including, but not limited to, financial assets, economic resources (including oil and other natural resources), property of every kind, whether tangible or intangible, movable or immovable, however acquired, and legal documents or instruments in any form, including electronic or digital, evidencing title to, or interest in, such funds or other assets, including, but not limited to, bank credits, travellers cheques, bank cheques, money orders, shares, securities, bonds, drafts, or letters of credit, and any interest, dividends or other income on or value accruing from or generated by such funds or other assets, and any other assets which potentially may be used to obtain funds, goods or services." Moreover, the Interpretive Note to FATF R.15 clarifies that virtual assets shall also be considered funds or other assets (FATF 2022).

[3] Depending on the design of a given sanctions regime, designated persons or entities may be subject to an arms embargo or a travel ban *in addition to* the financial measures described here.

[4] Including UNSCRs 1267 (1999), 1373 (2001), 1452 (2002), 1989 (2011), 2253 (2015), and 2462 (2019).

FATF standards.⁵ Once a national legal requirement to implement targeted financial sanctions is triggered, it applies to all persons and entities under the given state's jurisdiction, including ordinary individuals; formal or informal groups and organizations; financial institutions (FIs); DNFBPs, such as lawyers, notaries, and accountants; and virtual asset service providers (VASPs) (FATF 2022).

By law, designated persons and entities do not lose title to their funds (that is, they are not confiscated). Rather, they lose the ability to *access or move* their funds without government authorization (that is, to access or move those funds at will, until such point as the sanctions are removed, a process known colloquially as delisting).⁶ The logic is straightforward: denying designated persons and entities access to their funds—and to financial services—hinders their use for nefarious purposes or in transactions that would benefit bad actors.

## When Are Targeted Financial Sanctions the Right Tool?

Governments have many tools for CFT and going after those who fund terrorism. Terrorist financiers may be targeted as part of intelligence or military operations, investigated and prosecuted by law enforcement, or subjected to targeted financial sanctions. Often, more than one of these tools is applied at the same time. It is, therefore, important to note that because targeted financial sanctions are almost always publicly announced—for reasons that include enabling universal implementation—their imposition makes clear to designated persons or entities, along with others in the same network, that authorities are aware of, and actively monitoring, their activities.⁷ As a result, governments should, and typically do, coordinate and consult internally⁸ to determine whether secret or sensitive operations could be compromised or otherwise damaged by the (imposition and) announcement of targeted financial sanctions. In such cases, governments may refrain from advancing certain new designations nationally or from proposing those same designations at the international (UN) level.

At the same time, in many cases the pursuit of a new designation at the national or international level is an option—assuming the established designation criteria are met—where, for whatever reason, prosecution or the use of other law enforcement tools at the national level is not. In some states, for example, a suspected terrorist may not be prosecuted if he or she cannot be brought to court.

---

⁵ The FATF Recommendations, including R.6 on the implementation of terrorism-related targeted financial sanctions, constitute international soft law obligations that are complemented by mechanisms for the monitoring and enforcement of national compliance.

⁶ Both the UN and national authorities compile lists of designated persons and entities, such that persons and entities no longer subject to sanctions are removed from those lists or delisted. Indeed, the term "delisting" is widely used across government and industry. The UN has a "Focal Point for De-listing" and procedures for the same.

⁷ The public announcement of targeted financial sanctions is a practical requirement of universal implementation and an international good practice. Nevertheless, some states choose not to publish their domestic designations, preferring only to circulate them to FIs, DNFBPs, and VASPs.

⁸ This is sometimes referred to as "equities checks."

In contrast, individuals may be designated regardless of where they live, whether they are within reach of law enforcement, or whether their immediate location is even known. Moreover, if domestic authorities believe the evidence against a particular person or entity is persuasive but not sufficient to meet the relevant criminal standard, designation may represent a potent alternative. This is because the standard for the imposition of targeted financial sanctions—the existence of reasonable grounds or a reasonable basis to suspect or believe that a given target meets the established designation criteria—was specifically designed to represent a lower standard or threshold for action than is applicable to prosecution on criminal charges. Finally, as a preventive measure, targeted financial sanctions may be imposed *as soon as* reasonable grounds are established to suspect or believe that a person finances or otherwise facilitates terrorism, rather than only *after* that person's guilt has been proven beyond a reasonable doubt.

As a result, targeted financial sanctions are best understood as an *alternative* or, in certain cases, a *complement* to prosecution,[9] rather than a mere *precursor* (that is, a temporary measure meant only to preserve assets and evidence in anticipation of an imminent prosecution that could ultimately result in confiscation). Those measures are generally referred to as seizures, but since they may also temporarily freeze assets, they can be confused with the independent and indefinite freezes that are part and parcel of targeted financial sanctions.[10]

## Objectives of Targeted Financial Sanctions

Knowing the circumstances in which targeted financial sanctions may be imposed is a critical first step; the second is to understand the objectives targeted financial sanctions are designed to achieve (that is, their intended added value) within the broader national and international effort to combat terrorist financing.

### *Disrupt Terrorist Cash Flows*

Targeted financial sanctions aim to prevent and suppress terrorist financing in several different ways. Successfully freezing the assets of designated persons and denying them access to financial services should prevent, or else hinder, persons and entities with the intention of financing terrorism from raising, storing, moving, or using funds. This is often referred to as terminating or disrupting terrorist

---

[9] Targeted financial sanctions may act as a complement or a measure taken in addition to prosecution where a government wishes (1) to take action against an active terrorist, a terrorist financier, or anyone else providing active support to a terrorist group before it has gathered enough evidence to bring criminal charges; or (2) to prevent a convicted terrorist or terrorist financier from accessing or transferring hitherto unknown or unlocated funds.

[10] Indeed, States Parties to the International Convention for the Suppression of the Financing of Terrorism are obligated to pursue such seizures or temporary freezing measures per Article 8, Paragraph 1 of that convention, which reads, "Each State Party shall take appropriate measures, in accordance with its domestic legal principles, for the identification, detection and freezing or seizure of any funds used or allocated for the purpose of committing the offences set forth in Article 2 as well as the proceeds derived from such offences, for purposes of possible forfeiture."

cash flows. Although comprehensive statistics are generally unavailable at the national (let alone global) level, the millions of dollars in funds frozen worldwide, along with the substantial number of attempted transactions rejected by FIs and DNFBPs, demonstrate that targeted financial sanctions have a real impact. To cite one relevant example, the United States reported that over $6 million in Al-Qaida assets were frozen under its jurisdiction as of 2018 (United States Department of the Treasury, Office of Foreign Assets Control 2018).

## Prevent Abuse of the Regulated Financial System

However significant the total amount of funds frozen worldwide, they represent only a fraction of those available to designated terrorists and terrorist groups.[11] Terrorists tend to fund their activities in cash and operate outside the regulated financial system because of sanctions themselves, a desire to avoid detection, and fear of law enforcement action (among other factors).[12] This dynamic is sometimes used as a critique or cited as a weakness of targeted financial sanctions, given that the informal collection, storage, movement, and/or disbursement of terrorist funds makes it difficult for authorities to track them, electronically or otherwise. Yet a broader objective is at stake. When targeted financial sanctions are successfully implemented, terrorists are forced to use higher-cost, higher-risk alternatives to raise, store, move, and use their funds. For example, storing large amounts of cash in caves or warehouses exposes it to degradation, theft, or military destruction;[13] moving cash using individual couriers is slow, expensive, and uncertain, given the very real possibility of interception.[14]

## Change the Behavior of Terrorists and of Terrorist Financiers and Sympathizers

In addition to complicating and disrupting ongoing efforts to finance terrorism, targeted financial sanctions may prompt designated persons and entities (and their supporters) to abandon those efforts altogether. This dynamic relies on the fact that targeted financial sanctions apply to *all* the assets and transactions of

---

[11] UN Analytical Support and Sanctions Monitoring Team 2019. (See https://undocs.org/S/2020/53.)

[12] Note that although targeted financial sanctions must be applied by all persons and entities under the jurisdiction of a given state—meaning by licensed banks and money remitters as well as by unlicensed FIs and ordinary individuals—terrorists looking to evade sanctions often work with the latter, which tend to be less sophisticated and more permissive than the former. Alternatively (or in addition), terrorists may work with purely criminal networks to move and store funds or procure arms and supplies (Global Counterterrorism Forum and United Nations Interregional Crime and Justice Research Institute 2019). See https://www.thegctf.org/LinkClick.aspx?fileticket=GZAXnYJWfuQ%3d&portalid=1.

[13] Note the well-reported bombing of Islamic State of Iraq and the Levant (ISIL) cash storage facilities in Iraq and Syria from 2016 onward. See, for example, Eric Schmitt, "U.S. Says Its Strikes Are Hitting More Significant ISIS Targets," *New York Times*, May 25, 2016. (See https://www.nytimes.com/2016/05/26/us/politics/us-strikes-isis-targets.html.)

[14] FATF 2010. (See https://www.fatf-gafi.org/content/fatf-gafi/en/publications/Methodsandtrends/Ml-through-physical-transportation-of-cash.html)

designated persons, not just to those demonstrably linked to terrorist groups or activities. This means that designated persons and entities, along with those who provide them any sort of material assistance, are strongly incentivized to cease their support of terrorism and then pursue delisting in order to regain access to their assets and engage freely in legitimate economic activity. Indeed, according to the UN Office of the Ombudsperson, as of June 2020, of the 83 delisting cases it concluded, 62 petitions were granted and 21 were denied. Most of the petitions were ultimately granted on the basis that the designated individual or entity had ceased the activities that led to their designation.

### Deter Would-Be Terrorists and Their Financiers

Ideally, the consequences of being subject to targeted financial sanctions—including public identification, freezing of assets, loss of access to financial services, and, under certain circumstances, a travel ban—are so onerous that already designated persons and entities are prompted to change their behavior while others are deterred from engaging in (or supporting) similar behavior in the first place. In other words, a related objective of targeted financial sanctions is to dissuade would-be terrorists and terrorist financiers from acting, or attempting to act, on their rhetoric or intentions. This dissuasive element may be particularly relevant when terrorist sympathizers are based in low-capacity states; though they may regard their own governments as incapable of detecting or countering their activities through traditional means/ law enforcement tools, they cannot count on impunity since the UN and/or governments other than their own may be able to levy sanctions to greater effect.

### Uncover and Map Terrorist Financing Networks

In parallel, and regardless of any impact on the mindset of terrorists or terrorist sympathizers, the implementation of targeted financial sanctions supports national intelligence and law enforcement agencies in their efforts to map terrorist financing networks or money trails. The FATF requires that states obligate their FIs, DNFBPs, and VASPs to report frozen funds—along with the attempted transactions of designated persons and entities—to competent authorities (FATF 2022). Those reports constitute a valuable source of financial intelligence that may ultimately be used to identify previously unknown terrorist financiers or facilitators, locate terrorist assets, and gain insight into how (and when) such assets are moved.[15] The value of this form of financial intelligence is often directly related to how widely it is shared within a given government. Enabling only officials responsible for the administration of targeted financial sanctions to view reports of frozen assets and attempted transactions may limit

---

[15] For a comprehensive discussion of the use of financial intelligence in combating terrorist financing, see Chapter 3 of this book.

their value. Making those reports available to other competent authorities—including, but not limited to, the financial intelligence unit (FIU), financial supervisors, intelligence agencies, and law enforcement bodies—will maximize their value.

### Disrupt and Dismantle Terrorist Financing Networks

Targeted financial sanctions can also play an important role in disrupting and dismantling terrorist financing networks. To the extent that designated persons or entities fulfill critical functions within a particular terrorist financing network (for example, as introducers, intermediaries, fundraisers, or fronts), their public identification and loss of access to financial services could cause that network to weaken, fracture, or collapse. Moreover, the designation of any member of a terrorist financing network—even a little-known individual without a prominent role—can be sufficiently disruptive, dissuasive, or discomfiting to compromise its ability to function.

### Foster International Cooperation

Finally, the process of imposing targeted financial sanctions itself may have value regardless of the impact of any given designation. UN listings typically involve inputs from multiple member states, as well as sufficient cooperation and consensus building to clear any temporary holds on a proposed listing and avoid vetoes; third-party designation requests almost always require sensitive information to be shared among national authorities. As such, generating and finalizing designations fosters international cooperation while helping to establish specific channels for exchanging insights, information, and intelligence.

## GLOBAL VERSUS NATIONAL TARGETED FINANCIAL SANCTIONS

### Implementing UNSCR 1267 (1999)

Although targeted financial sanctions all around the world take roughly the same form—and pursue roughly the same objectives—their applicability varies widely. Targeted financial sanctions may be wielded by the international community to respond to global terrorist threats, or by individual states or groups of states to respond to national or regional terrorist threats. At the UN, the Security Council is responsible for imposing, amending, or lifting binding international sanctions (meaning sanctions that all member states are obligated to implement). The legal basis for such sanctions is contained in chapter VII, Article 41 of the UN Charter, which states as follows:

> The Security Council may decide what measures not involving the use of armed force are to be employed to give effect to its decisions, and it may call upon the Members of

the United Nations to apply such measures.[16] These may include complete or partial interruption of economic relations and of rail, sea, air, postal, telegraphic, radio, and other means of communication, and the severance of diplomatic relations.

UN sanctions are a widely accepted tool of the international community, functioning as an alternative to military force or as a step that may be taken before force is considered.

## Generating and Submitting UN Listing Requests

Member States are primarily responsible for identifying and proposing additions to the ISIL (Da'esh) and Al-Qaida Sanctions List.[17] Maintaining the List through regular amendments, additions, and delistings is vital to keeping pace with the evolving nature of the threat and to demonstrating the continuing resolve of the international community to counter these groups and their affiliates. The criteria for adding a name to the ISIL (Da'esh) and Al-Qaida Sanctions List are set forth in paragraphs 2 through 4 of UNSCR 2610 (2021). These include, among others, individuals, groups, or entities who are (1) financing, planning, facilitating, preparing, or perpetrating acts in support of ISIL (Da'esh) or Al-Qaida; (2) supplying, selling, or transferring arms and related materiel to such groups or their affiliates; or (3) recruiting for; or otherwise supporting acts or activities of Al-Qaida, ISIL (Da'esh), or any cell, affiliate, splinter group, or derivative thereof.[18]

Listings related to ISIL (Da'esh) and Al-Qaida are the responsibility of the "Security Council Committee pursuant to resolutions 1267 (1999), 1989 (2011), and 2253 (2015) concerning ISIL (Da'esh), Al-Qaida, and associated individuals, groups, undertakings, and entities." The committee, also known as the 1267 Committee, comprises all 15 Security Council members and makes its designation decisions by consensus. Sanctions seek to target the leaders of these groups as well as the individuals and organizations that support or enable their activities, including human traffickers and those involved in the smuggling or sale of antiquities, cultural property, or petroleum.

---

[16] It should be noted that a Security Council Resolution that decides or, similarly, one that requires or demands, would generally be considered legally binding upon member states. Debate surrounds whether a resolution adopted under chapter VII of the UN Charter that simply "calls upon" is similarly binding (Churchill 2008).

[17] Such additions are generally referred to as "listings" or "designations."

[18] The procedures for submitting listing requests by member states are detailed here: https://www.un.org/securitycouncil/sanctions/1267#listing_criteria. In brief, member states are advised to provide a detailed statement in support of the proposed listing, including findings demonstrating that the listing criteria are met; information regarding connections to currently listed parties and/or other relevant actions by the person or entity; and supporting documents or evidence. This information is submitted using forms provided for proposed listings to the 1267 and 1989 Committee: SC-1267-Committee@un.org.

## Implementing UN Listings Without Delay, Levying and Enforcing an Ongoing Prohibition

Regardless of their role in generating or proposing new listings, all member states are obligated to implement Security Council sanctions. Consistent implementation across all jurisdictions "without delay" closes potential gaps and helps to achieve the objective of the sanctions themselves, including by avoiding asset flight (meaning the dissipation of funds subject to an asset freeze).[19] The Interpretive Note to FATF R.6 on the implementation of targeted financial sanctions related to terrorist financing provides further details on states' obligations, requiring that they establish the necessary legal authorities to ensure the implementation of UN sanctions without delay and identify the domestic agencies responsible for enforcement. In addition, states should maintain a mechanism for communicating sanctions listings to their FIs, DNFBPs, and VASPs, and require them to report sanctions-related actions to the relevant domestic authority. As a matter of good practice, member states and the private sector are encouraged to subscribe to an electronic distribution list that provides notice of updates to UN sanctions lists.[20]

## Exemptions

As asset freeze provisions apply to all funds or other assets of designated individuals, including those that may be necessary for their (or their dependents') sustenance and those held jointly with a bona fide third party, there is a process for seeking exemptions. This allows the Security Council to distinguish between legitimate and illegitimate expenses—as well as between jointly held assets of bona fide third parties and comingled funds of possible coconspirators—and to promote transparency and accountability when a member state implements the asset freeze. There are exemptions to the assets freeze for basic and for extraordinary expenses. Basic expenses are food, rent or mortgage, medical costs, taxes, and insurance and utility charges, as well as professional fees associated with the provision of legal services. Extraordinary expense exemptions are simply for those expenses that are not basic expenses.[21] Both must be requested of the committee in a written application, even if they are subject to different approval

---

[19] The issue of implementing UN listings without delay is discussed in more detail as a key challenge for the effectiveness of targeted financial sanctions in combating terrorist financing.

[20] Updates to the UN Security Council Consolidated Sanctions List can be obtained electronically by subscribing to the mailing list maintained by the UN's Security Council Affairs Division: https://www.un.org/securitycouncil/content/un-sc-consolidated-list#Mailinglist.

[21] Different types of exemptions may be used to achieve seemingly similar objectives, depending on the specific circumstances. For instance, a basic expenses exemption may be requested to provide for the sustenance of a designated individual's spouse or minor children/dependents, whereas an extraordinary expenses exemption may be requested to permit the unfreezing of certain funds held jointly by that spouse or by adult children, to the extent that they are confirmed to be bona fide third parties acting in good faith.

procedures.²² In cases where exemptions are granted, the requesting member states are encouraged "to report in a timely way on the use of such funds, with a view to preventing such funds from being used to conduct any of the acts described in the Listing Criteria." Requests for both types of exemptions are submitted to the chair of the 1267 Sanctions Committee at SC-1267-Committee@un.org.

## Delisting

Sanctions measures are intended to be in place so long as a designated person or entity continues to meet one or more of the designation criteria. There may be cases where a designated person or entity is determined to no longer pose a threat or otherwise meet the criteria for listing. Listings under the ISIL (Da'esh) and Al-Qaida Sanctions Committee can be challenged, amended, and removed in a process that is initiated either by a member state or by a designated person or entity submitting a request to the Ombudsperson.²³ Member states seeking to remove a listing must explain why the designee no longer meets the listing criteria and present details about the designee's current occupation and/or activities, along with other relevant information such as the assets available to the designee. Where individuals have died, member states should provide a death certificate or similar documentation whenever possible, along with information about whether any legal beneficiary of the deceased's estate or any joint owner of their assets is on the sanctions lists.²⁴

The Ombudsperson to the ISIL (Da'esh) and Al-Qaida Sanctions Committee is appointed by the UN Secretary General. Their mandate is to review requests from "individuals, groups, undertakings or entities seeking to be removed from the ISIL (*Da'esh*) and Al-Qaida Sanctions List of the Security Council's ISIL (*Da'esh*) and Al-Qaida Sanctions Committee." The Ombudsperson is further mandated as follows:

> [to] gather information and to interact with the petitioner, relevant States and organizations with regard to the request. Within an established timeframe, the Ombudsperson will then present a comprehensive report to the Security Council's ISIL (*Da'esh*) and Al-Qaida Sanctions Committee. Based on an analysis of all available information and the Ombudsperson's observations, the report will set out for the Committee the principal arguments concerning the specific delisting request. The report will also contain a recommendation from the Ombudsperson to the Committee on the delisting request.²⁵

---

²² The process for seeking exemptions to asset freezing measures is detailed here: https://www.un.org/securitycouncil/sanctions/1267/travel-ban/assetsfreeze.

²³ For UN sanctions that are not related to UNSCR 1267 (1999), there is a Focal Point for De-listing.

²⁴ Procedures for delisting requests can be found here: https://www.un.org/securitycouncil/ombudsperson/application.

²⁵ Further information regarding the Ombudsperson and mandate can be found here: https://www.un.org/securitycouncil/ombudsperson.

## Implementing UNSCR 1373 (2001)

Terrorist threats may be global in nature or scale, but they may also be national or regional. The overall objective of UNSCR 1373 (2001) is for member states to have a mechanism for depriving those who represent a terrorist and security threat to their jurisdictions of access to funds, other assets, and economic resources. These persons or entities may not necessarily have any connection with those listed by the Security Council. States remain sovereign to determine which entities qualify as terrorist groups, meaning that a threat in one state may not be seen the same way in another. However, given that terrorists do not respect national borders—and, indeed, may cross borders specifically to take advantage of different national laws or capabilities—submitting and receiving designation requests to/from other states is integral to the 1373 mechanism. States may also decide to introduce a regional designation mechanism.

### Generating and Considering Domestic Designations

Paragraphs 1(c) and 1(d) of UNSCR 1373 (2001) set out an obligation for member states to introduce a domestic freezing mechanism with adequate due process safeguards and protections for the rights of bona fide third parties. As a complementary tool to the targeted financial sanctions established by UNSCRs 1267 (1999), 1988 (2011), 1989 (2011), and 2253 (2015), the provisions included in Resolution 1373 require each member state to establish its own domestic designation and asset freezing mechanism. This is to include an ongoing and inclusive prohibition on the provision of funds, financial or economic resources, and financial or other related services to designated persons and entities. Once persons or entities are designated, all related funds and other assets or economic resources are frozen without prior notice to the target(s) and it is prohibited to make any funds, economic resources, and financial or other related services available to them.[26]

The designation criteria included in UNSCR 1373 (2001) cover the following:

- any person who commits, or attempts to commit, terrorist acts or participates in or facilitates the commission of terrorist acts
- any entity owned or controlled directly or indirectly by such persons
- any person or entity acting on behalf of, or at the direction of, such persons and entities

Within this general framework, each member state may add its own domestic designation criteria to those set out in UNSCR 1373 (2001). As an example, some member states have established incitement to commit a terrorist act as grounds for designation, whereas others have not.

Domestic asset freezing measures must not be conditional upon (the existence of) criminal proceedings but may be implemented in parallel with a criminal

---

[26] A "designation target" is a person or entity being actively considered for designation.

investigation to prevent funds being dissipated (FATF 2022).[27] Procedures for issuing domestic designations may be administrative, executive, or judicial in nature, depending on the specific legal and institutional framework of each state.

## Implementing Domestic Designations Without Delay and Levying and Enforcing an Ongoing Prohibition

As with UN listings pursuant to UNSCR 1267 (1999), domestic designations in line with UNSCR 1373 (2001) must be issued without prior notice to the designation target and implemented without delay to avoid asset flight. In the context of UNSCR 1373 (2001), however, "without delay" means "upon having reasonable grounds, or a reasonable basis, to suspect or believe that a person or entity is a terrorist, one who finances terrorism or a terrorist organization" (FATF 2022).

Publication of domestic designations is an option, not a requirement. However, as all persons and entities under the jurisdiction of a state imposing sanctions are required to apply them—and to do so within a legally prescribed time frame—it is impossible to ensure effective implementation if the names of designees are not made public in a timely manner, whether in the official gazette, nationally circulated newspapers, or the website of a relevant authority. This also means that traditional law enforcement watch lists cannot implement or substitute for targeted financial sanctions, even if lists that are not publicly available are shared occasionally with trusted FIs.

## Exemptions

As noted, targeted financial sanctions regimes must include the possibility of exemptions, as an asset freeze pertains to all funds and property owned or controlled by a designated person, including those that may be necessary for individuals' sustenance. Specifically, paragraph 19 of UNSCR 2253 (2015) stresses that the prohibition in paragraph 1(d) of that resolution should be strict and inclusive. No funds may be provided to a designated person or entity, even if not intended for a terrorist purpose. This provision was further reinforced in paragraph 6 of UNSCR 2322 (2016) and reaffirmed in paragraph 20 of UNSCR 2368 (2017), paragraph 3 of UNSCR 2462 (2019), and paragraph 84 of UNSCR 2610 (2021).[28]

In compliance with UNSCR 1452 (2002), persons and entities designated in line with UNSCR 1373 (2001) may request from the designating state partial access to frozen funds or economic resources for basic and extraordinary expenses. Member states must, therefore, establish an administrative or judicial authority responsible for receiving and considering exemption requests submitted by or on behalf of designated persons or entities as well as bona fide third parties. They

---

[27] Domestic authorities should also work to ensure that the implementation and announcement of targeted financial sanctions do not unduly compromise any related military, intelligence, or law enforcement operations.

[28] UN Security Council Counter-Terrorism Committee Executive Directorate 2017.

must also ensure that the procedure to submit an exemption request is publicly available or that the designated person or entity has been notified personally.

## Delisting

To ensure that designated persons and entities do not remain subject to sanctions in error—or beyond the period during which they meet the applicable criteria—member states must ensure that domestic designations can be adequately challenged.[29] Affected persons or entities must be able to appeal their designation before an independent administrative or judicial body and should be able to request periodic review of their designation. The ultimate decision of that body should be public, even if it decides not to publish aspects that could raise privacy or security concerns. In a similar vein, the procedures for challenging a designation must be publicly available and notified to all designees.

Given that the domestic competent authority may have used sensitive, confidential, or classified information in making its initial determination that a person or entity has met the designation criteria, that authority will have to determine what information (for example, the full designation dossier or a sanitized version thereof) may be passed on to the independent body. That body must then review the original determination in line with applicable procedures to decide whether to sustain or cancel a designation.

## Submitting and Receiving Third-Party Designation Requests

Persons or entities designated in one state may still maintain assets or conduct financial transactions in other states. As such, UNSCR 1373 (2001)

> **Box 5.1. Widening the Designation**
>
> The use of third-party designation requests is a good practice, as terrorists rarely conduct operations or transactions only within a single state. Moreover, depending on the proximity of the states in which certain terrorists or terrorist groups are active, governments should consider going a step further by pursuing regional designations.
>
> In some parts of the world, regional designations are essentially well-coordinated and simultaneously announced domestic designations that have their origins in identical third-party requests made to several states at the same time. In others, like the European Union, regional designations are a formalized mechanism whose implementation is mandatory for all member states upon the decision of the competent intergovernmental body.
>
> Precisely because targeted financial sanctions may be applied at the global, national, or regional levels, governments should map the geographical extent of existing and emerging terrorist (financing) networks and respond accordingly.

---

[29] Even absent a legal challenge or formal request, member states should work quickly to delist persons and entities that do not or no longer meet the designation criteria. This means that governments should reevaluate designations when they receive credible new information indicating that a designation is no longer appropriate or that a person or entity may have been designated in error.

requires member states to make a prompt determination when they receive third-party designation requests. In practice, the use of third-party designation requests affords member states the possibility of extending the scope of their freezing measures beyond their own jurisdiction (Box 5.1). An effective domestic designation regime should include specific provisions to submit, receive, and examine such requests.

Nevertheless, member states remain sovereign; each receiving state determines for itself whether a given third-party request meets the reasonable basis evidentiary threshold in its own domestic legislation and whether the grounds for designation in the requesting state correspond to grounds for designation in the receiving state. When approved, third-party requests come into effect—and, under many national legal frameworks, gain instant legal recognition—as national designations, such that the affected persons and entities are then subject to sanctions under the jurisdiction of the receiving state.

When submitting a third-party request, domestic authorities should provide as much information on the designation target and supporting evidence as possible, along with the specific reasons for designation and the details of any identified funds or other assets in the receiving state.

## Obligation of IMF Members to Notify the Imposition of Sanctions

Whereas so far this chapter has focused on terrorism-related targeted financial sanctions and the complexities associated with implementation, many forms of financial sanctions could be described as "restrictions on the making of payments and transfers for current international transactions" or, more colloquially, "exchange restrictions." For the 190 members of the IMF, Article VIII, Section 2(a) of the Articles of Agreement prohibits the imposition of exchange restrictions without IMF approval. In that context, a desire among the membership to employ exchange restrictions for reasons of national or international security, coupled with a recognition that the IMF is not a suitable forum for discussion of the political, military, or security considerations underlying such actions, led the Executive Board to an August 14, 1952, decision (Decision No. 144) on procedures for approving such exchange restrictions that would avoid IMF involvement in national security issues.

Decision No. 144 requires all members to notify the IMF *before* imposing any exchange restrictions solely for the preservation of national or international security, a category that includes terrorism-related targeted financial sanctions pursuant to UN listings or domestic designations, regardless of whether the target is an individual, a group, an entity, or a government. If circumstances prevent prior notification, then notification should be made "as promptly as circumstances permit, but ordinarily not later than 30 days after imposing such restrictions."[30] Having fulfilled this requirement, the member may then assume that the IMF has

---

[30] International Monetary Fund, "Payments Restrictions for Security Reasons: Fund Jurisdiction," Decision No. 144-(52/51), adopted August 14, 1952, https://www.imf.org/external/SelectedDecisions/Description.aspx?decision=144-(52/51).

no objection to the imposition of the notified restrictions, "[u]nless the Fund informs the member within 30 days after receiving notice from the member that it is not satisfied that such restrictions are proposed solely to preserve [national or international] [...] security."[31]

In the nearly seven decades since Decision No. 144 was issued, the Executive Board has never objected to the imposition of targeted financial sanctions. As such, members of the IMF have employed targeted financial sanctions to combat terrorism while upholding their broader commitment to a stable and well-functioning international monetary system.

## Status of Implementation of FATF R.6

Although notifications under Decision No. 144 could be compiled into a history of the imposition of terrorism-related targeted financial sanctions, a more thorough and rigorous analysis would track states' compliance with FATF R.6, which captures legal and procedural requirements in relation to UNSCRs 1267 (1999) and 1373 (2001), along with their performance on FATF IO.10, which captures the effectiveness of states' *use* of targeted financial sanctions in mitigating their terrorist financing risks.[32] In other words, states' ratings on R.6 and IO.10—as determined through peer-driven mutual evaluations—provide valuable insight into whether adequate legal and regulatory frameworks to implement terrorism-related targeted financial sanctions are both in place and in use around the world.

### *Historically Poor Technical Compliance*

The FATF *Third Round of AML/CFT Mutual Evaluations* from 2004-2014 assessed states' legal and regulatory frameworks for implementing terrorism-related targeted financial sanctions as a function of their technical compliance with Special Recommendation III (SR.III), the predecessor to R.6. The results were poor: of 192 assessed jurisdictions, only 27 were sufficiently compliant, while 165 were insufficiently compliant.[33] Indeed, at the time of their mutual evaluations, just 2 out of 192 jurisdictions were deemed to have no deficiencies in their legal and regulatory frameworks for implementing terrorism-related targeted financial sanctions. A full breakdown of the third round of technical compliance ratings is provided in Table 5.1.

---

[31] Ibid.

[32] Note, however, that IO.10 also reflects the effectiveness of states' efforts to prevent nonprofit organizations from being used to finance terrorism. This issue, combined with the fact that states are not required to report frozen assets to the UN, makes gauging the worldwide implementation of targeted financial sanctions a particularly tricky task.

[33] Technical compliance with the FATF Recommendations is rated on a four-point scale. From highest to lowest, the available ratings are "compliant," "largely compliant," "partially compliant," and "non-compliant." Jurisdictions rated "compliant" and "largely compliant" may be considered "sufficiently compliant," whereas jurisdictions rated "partially compliant" and "non-compliant" may be considered "insufficiently compliant."

**TABLE 5.1.**

| Third and Fourth Round Ratings: Terrorism-Related Targeted Financial Sanctions | | |
|---|---|---|
| Rating | Third Round[1] | Fourth Round[2] |
| **Technical Compliance[3]** | | |
| Compliant (C) | 1% (2) | 15% (19) |
| Largely Compliant (LC) | 13% (25) | 46% (58) |
| Partially Compliant (PC) | 40% (77) | 31% (40) |
| Non-Compliant (NC) | 46% (88) | 8% (10) |
| **Effectiveness[4]** | | |
| High Effectiveness (HE) | N/A | 2% (2) |
| Substantial Effectiveness (SE) | N/A | 13% (17) |
| Moderate Effectiveness (ME) | N/A | 45% (57) |
| Low Effectiveness (LE) | N/A | 40% (51) |

Source: Financial Action Task Force (FATF).
[1] Percentage (and corresponding number) of jurisdictions of the 192 assessed.
[2] Percentage (and corresponding number) of jurisdictions of the 127 assessed as of May 2022.
[3] The ratings presented are for SR.III in the third round and R.6 in the fourth round.
[4] The ratings presented are for IO.10 in the fourth round (through May 2022); jurisdictions were not specifically assessed for their effectiveness in mitigating money laundering/terrorist financing risks in the third round.

## Improving Technical Compliance, but Lacking Effectiveness

Fortunately, it appears that since the third round, states' technical compliance has improved markedly, in part due to pressure from the FATF and other assessing bodies and in part owing to technical assistance from the IMF, the World Bank, the UN (for example, the 1267 Monitoring Team, the Counter-Terrorism Committee Executive Directorate, and the UN Office on Drugs and Crime), and other providers, including national bodies.

Of the 127 jurisdictions that had undergone a fourth round of AML/CFT mutual evaluations as of May 2022, 77 were sufficiently compliant, meaning that only 50 remained insufficiently compliant. By contrast, of those same 127 jurisdictions, only 19 were deemed sufficiently effective, while 108 were deemed insufficiently effective.[34] A full breakdown of the fourth round of technical compliance and effectiveness ratings is provided in Table 5.1.

While it is true that many of the states with low or moderate effectiveness in this area have taken other important steps to counter terrorist financing, the results from the fourth round of mutual evaluations clearly suggest that targeted financial sanctions are an underused—or, at any rate, poorly used—part of the broader CFT toolkit.

## Inherent Limits of Targeted Financial Sanctions in Combating Terrorist Financing

Although the impact of this tool is most often limited by factors such as lack of use or poor implementation (see the key challenges elaborated in this chapter),

---

[34] Effectiveness in mitigating money laundering/terrorist financing risks is rated on a four-point scale. From highest to lowest, the available ratings are: "high," "substantial," "moderate," and "low." Jurisdictions rated "high" and "substantial" may be considered "sufficiently effective," whereas jurisdictions rated "moderate" and "low" may be considered "insufficiently effective."

inherent limits also hamper its effectiveness. Even well-resourced governments can find it difficult to identify and compile sufficiently specific information regarding terrorists and their supporters to make frequent use of targeted financial sanctions. Moreover, terrorists may take advantage of criminal financing networks that, by their nature, do not comply with national laws and regulations. Terrorists and their supporters also tend to operate in cash or use unregistered money services businesses, knowing that transactions are more difficult to identify outside the banking system. Finally, savvy operators making use of electronic financial services, including mobile banking, crowdfunding platforms, or virtual assets, are sometimes able to withdraw, move, or conceal funds immediately after discovering that they have been designated, counting on governments, FIs, DNFBPs, and VASPs to react too slowly to prevent certain forms of asset flight.

One other potential limit to the effectiveness of this tool relates to the lack of transparency regarding the beneficial ownership of legal persons.[35] As targeted financial sanctions are normally name-based (that is, applied to all the assets and transactions of specifically designated persons and entities), effective implementation is hindered to the extent that FIs, DNFBPs, and VASPs fail to accurately identify the (designated) beneficial owners of legal persons. Such failures may come about because legal requirements are absent or else totally insufficient; corporate or government records are inadequate; the private sector lacks awareness, training, commitment, or perseverance, including with respect to verification; and/or designated persons and entities make concerted efforts to maintain bank accounts and conduct transactions in the names of firms or nongovernmental organizations that have (purposefully) obscure ownership and control structures.

Therefore, as a starting point, all states should implement the full range of international requirements regarding beneficial ownership,[36] including by obliging FIs, DNFBPs, and VASPs to identify, and take reasonable measures to verify, the beneficial owners of their legal person customers, in line with FATF Recommendations 10, 15, and 22.[37] Such obligations are necessary but not sufficient for avoiding the sorts of failures described in this chapter. For example, a survey of the fourth round of mutual evaluations conducted by the FATF-Style Regional Bodies (FSRBs), the IMF, and the World Bank makes clear that in many states public registries are critical to the timely and effective identification of beneficial owners by members of the private sector. Beneficial ownership registries help FIs, DNFBPs, and VASPs in conducting customer due diligence and provide valuable information to civil society organizations working to counter terrorism or corruption. Similarly, the establishment of nonpublic registries of all the bank accounts in a given jurisdiction may be critical to the effectiveness of intelligence

---

[35] The FATF defines "beneficial owner" as "the natural person(s) who ultimately owns or controls a customer and/or the natural person on whose behalf a transaction is being conducted. It also includes those persons who exercise ultimate effective control over a legal person or arrangement" (FATF 2022).

[36] For a detailed account of those requirements, along with an analysis of the key challenges and best practices involved in their implementation, see *Unmasking Control: A Guide to Beneficial Ownership Transparency* (Berkout and Fernando 2022), recently published by the IMF.

[37] Per FATF R.22, this obligation only applies to DNFBPs under certain circumstances (FATF 2022).

and law enforcement agencies charged with tracking terrorism-related financial flows or investigating terrorist groups, including in the context of mutual legal assistance.[38]

This chapter does not claim to have simple solutions for pushing past these longstanding limits. Instead, it aims at a more practical and achievable goal: identifying the key challenges that can—and must—be overcome to maximize the effectiveness of targeted financial sanctions in combating terrorist financing.

## LACK OF AWARENESS AND USE OF THE DESIGNATION TOOL AT THE UN AND NATIONAL LEVELS

### Key Challenges

A persistent lack of awareness of targeted financial sanctions, which causes them to be underused, is a key challenge. Since the Security Council adopted UNSCR 1267 (1999), only about 25 percent of the UN's 193 member states have submitted or cosponsored a listing request to the 1267/1989 or 1988 committees. Similarly, in its ongoing dialogue with member states on the implementation of UNSCR 1373 (2001), the UN's Counter-Terrorism Committee Executive Directorate has noted that even as more states have introduced legal provisions *establishing* domestic designation regimes over the past two decades, their *use* of those regimes continues to be limited.

Lack of awareness and/or use of targeted financial sanctions represents both a missed opportunity and a challenge to the broader effectiveness of national and international efforts to combat terrorist financing. The reason is straightforward: if domestic law enforcement authorities or security and intelligence services are either unfamiliar with or wary of the designation option, they may take action only with respect to those persons or entities that they can reach with more familiar tools. But UN listings and domestic designations may be an option where prosecution or other repressive approaches are not. For example, they can be useful in cases where domestic authorities cannot locate suspected terrorists to bring them to justice[39] or believe the available evidence of terrorist activity to be persuasive if insufficient to meet the applicable criminal standard. The same applies to the use of targeted financial sanctions against terrorists' material support networks. In many states, certain types of sanctions violations constitute criminal offenses, such that levying targeted financial sanctions against known members of terrorist networks may open the door to prosecuting other, previously unknown members for conducting transactions with their designated associates.

---

[38] Indeed, in paragraph 19(d) of UNSCR 2462 (2019), the Security Council called upon member states to consider "the establishment of a mechanism by which competent authorities can obtain relevant information, including but not limited to bank accounts, to facilitate the detection of terrorist assets, in compliance with international law, including international human rights law."

[39] And do not have the ability to prosecute them *in absentia*.

## Insufficient Awareness or Understanding of the Potential of Targeted Financial Sanctions

Anecdotal evidence suggests that the lack of use of targeted financial sanctions—both at the UN and domestic levels—is closely related to a lack of awareness of the tool, along with an insufficient appreciation of its potential.

As sanctions have become increasingly prominent, certain national authorities—particularly those focusing on CFT—are now well aware of this tool and its potential to help tackle national and international security threats. Other counterterrorism authorities, including some in the intelligence and law enforcement communities, appear not to have been adequately sensitized to the existence of targeted financial sanctions, their unique properties (including the ways in which they differ from existing mechanisms for the temporary seizure of funds as part of an active investigation), or the ways in which they may complement other, more traditional tools. Since both UN listings and domestic designations tend to stem from leads and information generated by national authorities, lack of awareness or enthusiasm translates into inaction.

Moreover, even fully sensitized authorities may fail to exploit the full potential of targeted financial sanctions. They may regard the freezing or seizure of assets as provisional measures ancillary to criminal proceedings rather than as powerful tools in their own right. Indeed, most domestic designations appear to be of persons or entities already convicted of terrorist offenses (including terrorist financing). While such designations are not inconsistent with the objectives of UNSCR 1373 (2001), they may have only modest impact, particularly since many of the individuals concerned will have been detained or imprisoned, and so are already cut off from direct access to funds and financial services.

## Practical Impediments

States frequently encounter practical challenges when identifying possible targets for UN listing or domestic designation. For example, some states struggle to generate sufficient derogatory information on their own because their independent intelligence collection resources are modest.[40] Moreover, institutional or legal barriers to sharing the interagency information and intelligence necessary to identify persons or entities who might meet the applicable criteria hamper national authorities' ability to propose names for consideration or assemble coherent designation files.[41]

---

[40] Officials in such states may not be aware of the procedure for processing listing requests at the UN level, which includes review by the Analytical Support and Sanctions Monitoring Team and circulation to the Security Council, whose members are requested to provide additional information (UN Security Council 1267 Committee 2018).

[41] Such files, also known as dossiers or packages, are effectively compilations of all the information a government has amassed about a particular designation target. That information is then reviewed by a national competent authority to determine whether the associated target should be put forward for UN listing or, alternatively, whether the target meets the standard for domestic designation.

Similar, if more acute, challenges may also arise when submitting a third-party request. When the requesting authority is unable to transmit all the information in its possession—whether due to the absence of intelligence-sharing agreements, secure communications channels, or relationships among key individuals or institutions—the receiving authority is likely to have a more difficult time establishing that the reasonable basis standard has been met.

Even with full information at their disposal, some governments still hesitate to propose a given target for UN listing or to proceed with a domestic designation because there is confusion or ambiguity about what constitutes the reasonable basis standard. National competent authorities rarely define that standard for their own internal purposes—or clarify how it differs from the standard used in criminal proceedings. For practical purposes, the resultant uncertainty about whether a target meets the applicable criteria may lead to delays, the substitution of another (generally higher) standard as found in criminal law, or, in a worst-case scenario, the complete paralysis of the decision-making process that would otherwise give rise to UN listing proposals or domestic designations.

## International Good Practices[42]

Targeted financial sanctions can only be effective when actively used, particularly in circumstances where the use of more traditional tools would be inefficient, if not impossible.

### Conduct Domestic Awareness-Raising Campaigns

One foundational good practice to further the use of targeted financial sanctions in combating terrorist financing is to conduct comprehensive domestic awareness-raising campaigns. These are typically led by the competent authority responsible for generating new UN listings and considering and administering domestic designations. Conducting in-person sensitization meetings with the relevant law enforcement, security, and intelligence agencies is a common good practice, as is crafting and distributing an interagency memorandum of understanding, process map, protocol, manual, or set of guidelines.

Regardless of the form that domestic awareness-raising campaigns may take, the content should be comprehensive and include the following:

- A general description of targeted financial sanctions and their implications
- A discussion of the possibility of both UN listings and domestic designations
- An explanation of the procedure for generating, developing, and proposing designation targets
- A list of key points of contact

---

[42] As noted in the introduction to this book, the good practices identified in each chapter draw on practices identified in the References and Resources at the end of the chapter, the wide range of practices currently applied by IMF members, and the professional experiences of the authors.

The goal is straightforward: to ensure that all relevant domestic authorities are aware of targeted financial sanctions as a tool for combating terrorist financing and are prepared to help generate and develop designation targets (when the designation criteria appear to be met and designation appears to be the most appropriate tool for dealing with a particular threat).

## Focus on Persons and Entities beyond the Reach of Traditional Tools

A related good practice is to emphasize the unique properties of targeted financial sanctions as part of a campaign to raise awareness. The most successful campaigns highlight those circumstances in which targeted financial sanctions can be employed when traditional tools (such as those available to military, intelligence, or law enforcement agencies) can not. Here, the goal is also straightforward: to avoid situations where relevant authorities take no action in response to a potential designation target simply because more familiar tools are unavailable or of no help. For example, intelligence agencies should understand that classified information may be included in a designation file, even if a clandestine operation based on that information would be too risky to carry out. Similarly, law enforcement agencies should be clear that the standard of proof required to sanction an individual at the UN or domestic level is lower than what is required for criminal proceedings—and that targets need not be located in the national territory, let alone in the custody of national authorities—such that designation may be feasible in cases where prosecution is not.

In general, targeted financial sanctions should be considered in the context of a state's broader counterterrorism and CFT strategies and used alongside (or, if helpful and appropriate, in place of) other relevant tools. Based on specific risks identified in each state, national authorities may decide to use targeted financial sanctions against a range of persons or entities, including fundraisers, sympathizers, and foreign terrorist fighters.

## Facilitate the Generation and Sharing of Sensitive or Classified Information

However desirable for combating terrorist financing, developing robust intelligence-gathering and analysis capabilities is an expensive, long-term proposition beyond the immediate reach of many states. By contrast, even states with low capacity should be able to implement the following good practices to facilitate the intelligence-driven preparation of viable designation files.

The first is to eliminate barriers to domestic intelligence sharing when generating and developing designation targets. Many states achieve this by requiring the members of an interagency committee charged with considering possible UN listing proposals or domestic designations to circulate any information their home departments or agencies may have on a given person or entity. Such a requirement helps prepare viable designation files without threatening long-established divisions of responsibility or tearing down barriers to broader information sharing that may serve a legitimate purpose.

The second good practice is for states facing a common terrorist or terrorist financing threat to conclude agreements for intelligence sharing in the specific context of making and receiving third-party requests or considering joint designations.[43] Another approach, often favored by states that already maintain robust intelligence-gathering capabilities, is to provide downgraded intelligence as part of third-party requests (that is, to transmit national intelligence products that have been redacted or otherwise modified to remove especially sensitive content while still conveying critical, nonpublic information). Such downgrading must generally be done on a case-by-case basis, depending on the nature and source of the original information and the closeness of the relevant states' relationship.

Relatedly, the sharing of sufficient identifiers (information unique to the designation target, such as the full name, address, date of birth, and passport number) is a FATF requirement and a critical part of any successful UN listing or third-party request. As such, it is a good practice to avoid classifying or withholding identifiers whenever possible. Indeed, under certain circumstances, the only information a requesting state might be able to give a receiving state (or the Security Council) is the name and set of identifiers of a target it wishes to see designated (or listed). This is not ideal, but is not necessarily fatal: the third-party designation and UN listing processes are collaborative by nature and by design, such that receiving states, or else the Analytical Support and Sanctions Monitoring Team and members of the Security Council, will be able to contribute whatever information they may have to a proposed target's file prior to final consideration.

## Facilitate Public Access to Existing National or Regional Lists

Another good practice to promote the robust use of targeted financial sanctions is to provide easy public access to existing lists of persons and entities designated at the national or regional levels. Public access is normally achieved by the posting of such lists online.

Indeed, the publication of such lists could be considered an essential—rather than merely a good—practice, as it is otherwise nearly impossible to expect, let alone ensure and enforce, the implementation of targeted financial sanctions by the general public.[44] Beyond that, the advantages of providing easy public access are twofold. First, making national and regional lists fully public raises global awareness of terrorist and terrorist financing threats and so may prompt private sector actors in one state to pay particularly close attention to the transactions of persons and entities designated in another, even if they are under no legal obligation to do so. Second, the published national list of any given state might be scrutinized by others to determine whether initiating a third-party request would be appropriate (for instance, if a person designated in one state is known

---

[43] "Joint designations" may be understood as coordinated and simultaneously announced domestic designations.

[44] Some states choose to announce designations through press releases and/or publication in newspapers or the official gazette but do not maintain comprehensive, public lists of the designations in force.

to conduct financial transactions involving a neighboring state in which that person is not yet designated).[45]

Indeed, in UNSCR 2462 (2019), the Security Council called upon states to "consider making publicly available their national or regional asset freezing lists." This provision is aimed at enhancing bilateral, regional, and international cooperation in combating terrorist financing and ensuring the effectiveness of targeted financial sanctions adopted pursuant to UNSCR 1373 (2001), in particular. As compatible with regional obligations, where applicable, states remain sovereign in their determinations about whether—and to what extent—to incorporate these lists domestically, should they determine that persons and entities sanctioned by others meet their own designation criteria, in line with their own legal and regulatory frameworks.

### *Develop a Working Definition of Reasonable Grounds*

A final good practice to facilitate the robust use of targeted financial sanctions is for national authorities to develop a working definition, or else a common understanding, of the reasonable basis or reasonable grounds standard to be applied when proposing UN listings and considering domestic designations. This would help the responsible officials to make a prompt determination as to whether a target meets the applicable designation criteria. There is no universal (UN) or standard (FATF) definition of "reasonable basis" or "reasonable grounds," but sanctions practitioners around the world tend to look at similar elements when making a determination. Broadly speaking, those elements capture the extent to which the derogatory information available is (1) credible, (2) sufficiently detailed, (3) from more than one source, and (4) generally coherent (meaning that it tells a largely consistent story and is not contradicted by equally credible and detailed information also available to the authorities).

## LACK OF IMPLEMENTATION WITHOUT DELAY

### Key Challenges

A second set of key challenges for targeted financial sanctions revolves around the lack of consistent implementation without delay on the part of individual states.

This challenge relates specifically to the implementation without delay of new UN listings, rather than of new domestic designations, as the former generally become public (through a UN press release) before individual states implement

---

[45] When considering whether to submit a third-party request, and to which jurisdiction(s), states should make full use of financial intelligence, as well as any other information on the subject person or entity that may be available to law enforcement agencies, intelligence services, or other relevant institutions. The nationality of the individual in question, any known previous state(s) of residence or of employment, and the presence of close relatives or family members are all important elements to consider when assessing whether they are likely to be holding any funds, assets, or property abroad, or else conducting transactions that would touch more than one state.

them, whereas national governments control the timing of the latter's announcement. When used in this section, the "implementation" of sanctions in an individual state should be understood as the coming into force of a legal obligation to freeze terrorist assets in accordance with a new UN listing. UN actions bind its member states, and so, in most cases, are not directly binding on private persons or entities until specifically transposed into national law.

As defined in the FATF glossary, "without delay" means "ideally, within a matter of hours of a designation by the UN Security Council or its relevant Sanctions Committee (e.g., the 1267 Committee, the 1988 Committee, the 1718 Sanctions Committee)."[46] In this context, the word "hours" is key; experts generally view the "without delay" standard as requiring new UN listings to be implemented within 24 hours of issuance, as implementation outside of that time frame would represent "a matter of *days*" rather than "a matter of *hours*."[47] For practical purposes (for example, determining the extent to which jurisdictions are in compliance with FATF R.6), FATF assessors sometimes consider a jurisdiction to have implemented a UN listing without delay if it does so on the same day the listing is issued or on the next business day. The logic is that such an approach accounts for challenges associated with the existence of different time zones around the world, the occasional issuance of new listings just before (or during) the weekend in a substantial number of states, and officials' frequent inability to specify the exact time of day a given listing was implemented. Regardless of the test one applies to determine whether the implementation of terrorism-related UN targeted financial sanctions has taken place without delay, many states fail to achieve a passing grade on a consistent basis.

Consistent implementation of targeted financial sanctions without delay is not merely desirable; it is necessary to maximize the effectiveness of targeted financial sanctions in combating terrorist financing. The glossary to the FATF Recommendations gives the following explanation, as part of the requirements:

> the phrase without delay should be interpreted in the context of the need to prevent the flight or dissipation of funds or other assets which are linked to terrorists, terrorist organisations, [and] those who finance terrorism [...] and the need for global, concerted action to interdict and disrupt their flow swiftly. (FATF 2022)

In lay terms, implementation without delay is key to preventing asset flight (the successful withdrawal, transfer, or concealment of assets subject to a freeze, often within the first few days of the issuance of a new UN listing). Put simply, the effectiveness of targeted financial sanctions is compromised to the extent that the delay between the issuance of a new UN listing and its implementation on the part of individual member states is long enough that a newly designated person

---

[46] FATF 2022.

[47] The effectiveness of targeted financial sanctions is directly affected by the speed of their implementation, such that even a 24-hour standard is somewhat arbitrary. At the same time, a standard of immediate, simultaneous implementation, while ideal for maximizing effectiveness, could not currently be observed by most UN member states.

or entity has time to withdraw[48], transfer[49], or conceal[50] assets, such that they remain available to support terrorism rather than being frozen.

Moreover, such delays postpone the implementation of the ongoing prohibition component of targeted financial sanctions, along with the requirement for FIs, DNFBPs, and VASPs to report attempted transactions. This means that any implementation delay risks depriving national authorities of pertinent financial intelligence in the critical few days following the issuance of a new UN listing—days in which a designated person or entity with assets in the regulated financial system is most likely to try to evade sanctions by withdrawing, transferring, or concealing those assets.

## The Time Factor

As mentioned, some of the delay in individual states' implementation of new UN listings is due to mundane impediments. For many member states, the announcement of new listings often falls outside of working hours (for example, a new listing announced between 9:00 a.m. and 5:00 p.m. in New York would be received in much of Asia between 9:00 p.m. that same day and 5:00 a.m. the following day). For others, the announcement of new listings often falls over the weekend (for example, a new listing announced at 5:00 p.m. on a Friday in New York would be received over the weekend in much of the Middle East, where weekends typically run from Friday to Saturday, and on a Saturday in Asia). This means that states requiring government action to transpose new UN listings into national law—a process often referred to as domestication—may face a particular challenge, as key personnel may not be at work when those listings come through.

## The Domestication Factor

Some of the delay in individual states' implementation of new UN listings is also a result of specific procedures they have put in place, often as part of the domestication process. By and large, those procedures fall into three categories: (1) procedures for receiving (that is, becoming aware of) new UN listings, (2) procedures for transposing new listings into national law, and (3) procedures for communicating those listings to FIs, DNFBPs, and VASPs.

Many states require that new UN listings be communicated to the authorities responsible for domestication through diplomatic channels or their foreign affairs ministries. Typically, this means that New York-based diplomatic personnel must communicate new listings to headquarters-based officials in their national capital using a (secure) system—and that those officials must then notify the relevant authorities, who may be attached to a different office, department, or ministry (for example, the Office of the Attorney General or the Ministry of Finance). While such requirements may address legitimate bureaucratic or organizational

---

[48] Generally, in cash.
[49] To nondesignated persons or entities.
[50] For example, through their placement with shell companies.

concerns, they may also unduly delay the "official" receipt of new listings that are otherwise publicly announced, freely available on the UN's website, and simultaneously shared with subscribers to the relevant Security Council mailing list. This *does not* mean that states' permanent missions to the UN have no role in the broader effort. On the contrary, they often make valuable contributions, including by helping the competent authorities get answers to technical questions or contact the relevant UN committees and experts. However, it *does* mean that governments should be aware of and mitigate delays from unduly formalizing the process of communicating new listings from the UN headquarters in New York to national capitals.

Once competent authorities receive new listings, the prescribed procedures for transposing UN obligations into national law become key to determining the speed and efficiency of domestication. In some states, domestication is a quasi-automatic process completed by civil servants pursuant to standing ministerial orders. This represents an efficient form of domestication but still does not guarantee implementation without delay. In other states, however, domestication may be officious, cumbersome, and/or vulnerable to a single node of failure. For example, some states require the input or consent of multiple lower-level officials before the responsible minister may sign the orders necessary to transpose into national law UN listings that, in principle at least, are subject to neither rejection nor modification. For some member states, a previous order—or else, the annex to a previous order—may simply be updated; for others, a stand-alone ministerial decision must be issued with respect to each new listing. Lastly, in some states, only one official (for example, the Attorney General, Minister of Finance, or Director of the FIU) may sign the order, decision, or other paperwork necessary for domestication, such that that official's absence—whether owing to a transition of power, travel, schedule conflicts, illness, or other factors—effectively precludes implementation without delay.

Finally, in some cases, national law specifies that the trigger for the obligation to implement domesticated designations is not the *issuance* of a ministerial order, but its *circulation* to FIs, DNFBPs, and VASPs. This means, for example, that banks in a given state would not be required to implement a domesticated designation until their supervisor specifically informs them of the corresponding government decision or action. The result may be substantial delay, as ministries communicate the names of newly sanctioned persons or entities to supervisors and self-regulatory bodies, which then circulate the same to FIs, DNFBPs, and VASPs through secure portals or email distribution lists.

The immediate practical impact of delay may range from severe (asset flight) to negligible (implementation is unaffected because banks' sophisticated monitoring software alerts them to new UN listings immediately after they are announced), but the longer-term impact is worse. Terrorists and terrorist sympathizers may attempt to safeguard their assets by migrating them to lower-capacity FIs and/or lower-capacity states, counting on a delay in the implementation of targeted financial sanctions to help them avoid the attendant consequences.

As a rule of thumb, the greater the number of actors involved in transmitting, domesticating, or circulating new UN listings, the longer the time frame for implementation and the higher the likelihood of asset flight and other undesirable consequences of failing to comply with UN and FATF requirements.

## International Good Practices

States use a range of models to implement UN listings. At one end of the spectrum is the National List Only model, whereby a state maintains a single list of the persons and entities sanctioned under its jurisdiction and dutifully duplicates UN listings as domestic designations.[51] That model maximizes national control over designations, but it is so resource- and time-intensive that the barriers to implementation without delay are high.

In the middle of the spectrum is the Mandatory Domestication model, whereby national law *requires* a competent authority to take the action necessary to domesticate new listings (for example, "the Minister shall issue an order" or "the Committee shall post on its website"), leaving no room for those listings to be modified or rejected. That model greatly reduces national control over UN listings but remains somewhat resource-intensive, such that the barriers to implementation without delay are moderate.

At the other end of the spectrum is the Direct Incorporation model, whereby a state directly incorporates UN Security Council decisions taken under chapter VII of the UN Charter into national law—or else obliges FIs, DNFBPs, VASPs, and all other persons and entities under its jurisdiction to consult the relevant UN list(s) regularly and implement new listings automatically (without intervention by domestic authorities). That model allows for absolutely no control over UN listings, such that there are effectively no barriers to implementation without delay.

The key point is that all three models can, in principle at least, yield compliance with states' UN obligations and with the FATF Recommendations, but each model involves trade-offs, the most important of which are the time and resources required to ensure implementation without delay.

### Choose the Right Model for the Implementation of New UN Listings, Given Relevant Domestic Considerations

This discussion has highlighted a foundational good practice for implementing new UN listings without delay: governments should anticipate the volume of UN and domestic designations, delistings, and listing modifications that they will have to implement and then evaluate the available models in light of resource constraints, domestic legal considerations, and other relevant factors before selecting the one that best suits their circumstances. While the Mandatory Domestication

---

[51] In one part of the world, which is characterized by the presence of a strong and active intergovernmental organization, this could be called the Regional List model, in that UN listings are individually evaluated and transposed into regionwide designations that must then be implemented in each member state.

model is by far the most common, it might not be ideal for resource-constrained states or those whose financial sectors are particularly adept technologically. Almost all states have already established the laws and regulations necessary to implement UN listings (that is, targeted financial sanctions regimes). Also, definite costs are associated with changing models, including when drafting and enacting new legislation; crafting new guidelines for FIs, DNFBPs, and VASPs; or conducting public outreach. Still, some states may decide the costs are worth absorbing to streamline or eliminate the domestication process so that UN listings may be more easily and reliably implemented without delay.

States that elect (or elect to continue using) the National List Only or Mandatory Domestication models may wish to consider a set of good practices for streamlining the domestication process. For example, one good practice for addressing challenges in receiving or becoming aware of new UN listings is to ensure that officials based in the national capital register for automatic updates from the UN 1267/1989 and 1988 committees and regularly consult the relevant UN websites. Doing so might not eliminate the need to receive formal notification through diplomatic channels, but it typically enables competent authorities to begin—or even complete—the domestication process far more quickly. States that implement this good practice with the greatest success generally assign the task to officials working in the offices, departments, or ministries responsible for domestication to eliminate the "game of telephone" that would otherwise be necessary to forward the relevant names and details.

## *Streamline the Domestication Process*

A second good practice is to review and streamline all of the steps involved in domestication, as and when consistent with national law. For example, some competent authorities issue standing orders for new UN listings to be transposed automatically into national law based on actions taken at the technical (versus political) level. Such orders may take different forms or use different language, but all eliminate the need for ministers or other high-ranking officials to take action in response to new listings. For cases in which standing orders or similar documents cannot be issued (for example, because of domestic legal constraints), ministers or other high-ranking officials sometimes delegate authority to one or more deputies or senior administrators to clear the bottlenecks in the domestication process that might result from their unavailability.

## *Use Efficient Mechanisms to Trigger Private Sector Action*

A final good practice is to change existing laws, regulations, and/or practices to establish the posting of UN listings on a government website as the trigger for the application of sanctions on the part of FIs, DNFBPs, and VASPs (as opposed to slower dissemination through sectoral supervisors or publication in the official gazette). It is certainly possible to envision other alternatives, such as automatic notification using a secure portal, but the goal is the same: to reduce or eliminate delays related to the action that, by law, triggers the formal obligation to freeze assets and implement an ongoing prohibition. In this context, a practical distinction can and should be made between actions that have a triggering function and those that have different but still important functions: for example, the dissemination of listings by sectoral supervisors to facilitate compliance or publication in the official gazette to ensure that sanctions are reflected in the public record.

## INCONSISTENT IMPLEMENTATION BY THE PRIVATE SECTOR

### Key Challenges

A third set of key challenges for targeted financial sanctions involves their inconsistent implementation by the private sector. This inconsistency is largely a function of two factors: resource limitations and insufficient commitment, the latter of which may result from a lack of supervision or other regulatory oversight.

For example, some private sector actors, such as large banking groups or international money remitters, have the human resources, technological infrastructure, and regulatory sophistication needed to implement sanctions quickly and comprehensively on a consistent basis.[52] Others, such as small FIs, DNFBPs in remote areas, or recently established VASPs may not. Many private sector actors fall somewhere in between these two poles.

Moreover, private sector actors demonstrate different degrees of commitment to implementing targeted financial sanctions. Some calculate their risk of terrorist financing abuse to be so low—and the cost of full compliance with their legal obligations to be so high—that they cannot justify the investment needed for ongoing monitoring of all accounts and transactions.

A similar dynamic may also affect the quality of supervision. When AML/CFT supervisors lack resources or are so heavily focused on other risks that they cannot or, at any rate, do not adequately monitor and enforce the implementation of targeted financial sanctions, private sector actors may slacken their commitment, or, at the very least, become complacent.

As a result, the speed, quality, and reliability of private sector implementation of targeted financial sanctions varies a great deal, both within and across states. This has a clear impact on the effectiveness of the tool in combating terrorist financing. Just as a chain is only as strong as its weakest link, a targeted financial sanctions regime is only as strong as its weakest implementer. If designated persons and entities can avoid having their assets frozen and their access to financial

---

[52] This means they are able to assure the continual screening of customers and transactions, to identify in real-time those potentially subject to targeted financial sanctions, and to react appropriately, for example by freezing and reporting relevant assets within the legally prescribed time frame or by seeking immediate assistance from the government in deconflicting any possible false positives.

services blocked simply by avoiding large, international banks, then sanctions may function primarily as an irritant rather than an impediment.

Moreover, inconsistent private sector implementation represents something of a vicious cycle. To the extent that it is easier for smaller, less resourced, or more remote FIs to be used for nefarious purposes, terrorists and other criminals will seek them out, thereby widening the existing gulf between the sophisticated FIs that terrorist financiers avoid and the less sophisticated ones that they come to rely on.

## Differences in Resources and Technology

Much of the responsibility for implementing targeted financial sanctions lies with the private sector—the FIs, DNFBPs, and VASPs that take deposits and provide financial and related services.[53] As noted, some are large, well-resourced firms that use either commercial or proprietary monitoring software/screening systems to learn of new or amended UN listings and domestic designations shortly after they are announced and ensure that all customers and transactions are automatically scrutinized for sanctions compliance. Other relevant, obligated actors are stand-alone professionals or private citizens who take deposits or provide financial services on an informal basis. Actors fitting that description tend to lack resources and technology and so are forced to rely on information provided by the authorities or communicated to the general public (for their awareness of new or amended UN listings and domestic designations) and on manual processes (to comply with their legal obligations).

These pronounced differences in resources and technology yield equally pronounced differences in the implementation of targeted financial sanctions, including the speed at which assets are frozen and the likelihood that attempted transactions are detected, rejected, and reported.

## Differences in Supervision

Differences in the quality of sanctions implementation across the private sector may also reflect differences in commitment. In an ideal world, all FIs, DNFBPs, and VASPs would be committed to implementing targeted financial sanctions because of an intrinsic desire to combat terrorism. In practice, the mitigation of supervisory and reputational risks, including a fear of being fined for failing to respect legal obligations related to targeted financial sanctions, is also a strong driver. The result is that private sector actors in higher-risk jurisdictions or those who are subject to more frequent and/or rigorous supervision may be more committed to implementing targeted financial sanctions quickly and comprehensively than private sector actors operating in lower-risk jurisdictions or those who are subject to less intense supervision—if they are subject to any AML/CFT supervision at all.

In some states, AML/CFT supervision is conducted primarily, if not exclusively, by government regulators, typically some combination of central banks, supervisory

---

[53] State-owned banks are a notable exception.

commissions, or FIUs. In other states, the AML/CFT supervision of many, most, or all DNFBPs is the responsibility of self-regulatory bodies, such as bar associations for lawyers, that may also function as professional associations. Regardless, FIs, DNFBPs, and VASPs appear to be heavily influenced by the actions of their supervisors, which may (or may not) issue comprehensive guidance, carry out thorough on-site inspections to determine the actual extent of implementation, and impose proportionate and dissuasive penalties for noncompliance.

## Differences in the Extent of Official Guidance

Authorities from state to state make different investments in the provision of guidance to FIs, DNFBPs, and VASPs on their obligations related to targeted financial sanctions. FATF, FSRB, and other AML/CFT assessors frequently find that key private sector actors, including many outside the financial sector, lack the understanding needed to adequately implement new or amended UN listings and domestic designations—let alone delistings at either level. In other words, it is one thing to be aware that a particular person or entity is subject to targeted financial sanctions and quite another to understand (and execute) the full range of obligations that this entails. For example, it is common for DNFBPs interviewed by AML/CFT assessors to have an incomplete understanding of their obligations related to targeted financial sanctions, including to report frozen assets and attempted transactions.

## The Challenging Case of Virtual Assets

A number of studies (such as Dion-Schwarz, Manheim, and Johnston 2019) indicate that terrorists and their sympathizers could become increasingly attracted to virtual assets (VAs)[54] to raise, transfer, and store funds. To date, the key drivers of that attraction have been the efficiency—meaning ease and low cost—of the transfer of VAs and the level of anonymity afforded their users. Going forward, the expansion of VA networks as their popularity grows, along with the stability of their value,[55] are likely to become additional drivers. Of these, the level of anonymity afforded to users is particularly salient, both for the present and prospective use of VAs to finance terrorism. Indeed, once a natural or legal person has used fiat currency to purchase a virtual asset, their holdings and transfers of that asset may be linked to an online account or public key[56] with no clear connection to, or accurate record of, their actual identity, particularly if the asset is

---

[54] The FATF defines "virtual assets" as "a digital representation of value that can be digitally traded, or transferred, and can be used for payment or investment purposes. Virtual assets do not include digital representations of fiat currencies, securities and other financial assets that are already covered elsewhere in the FATF Recommendations" (FATF 2022).

[55] The stability of the value of VAs is likely to increase with the continuing development of so-called global stablecoins.

[56] In the case of the most prominent virtual asset, Bitcoin, a public key is a unique string of random numbers.

held outside a regulated VASP. The multitiered challenge this represents for the implementation of terrorism-related targeted financial sanctions is evident.

First, and as already noted, VAs may be held in, or transferred between, what are effectively anonymous accounts. If users choose to hold funds outside the confines of regulated VASPs subject to robust customer due diligence obligations or to patronize VASPs located in jurisdictions without adequate regulation and supervision, they may be able to secure a level of anonymity that exceeds what is typically available in the banking system. While the challenge of anonymity is not unique to VAs, it is certainly more pronounced in that context. This is because the regulation of VAs and VASPs is only at an advanced stage in a few parts of the world, whereas most states already maintain longstanding obligations related to the conduct of customer due diligence by FIs and DNFBPs—as well as longstanding prohibitions on the maintenance of numbered or otherwise anonymous bank accounts.

Second, the transfer of VAs may be nearly instantaneous, including between users in different states, and is often completed on a purely peer-to-peer basis, such that it does not involve a (registered or licensed) VASP or an FI providing relevant services. Consider the possible involvement of intermediaries or other facilitators who are unknown to, or unsuspected by, national or international authorities and the elevated terrorist financing risks presented by VAs come into focus. Within a matter of days, if not hours, a terrorist or terrorist group could receive in VAs or in local currency the equivalent of substantial sums of money raised overseas without their names or other identifying information ever being formally associated with the relevant transactions. In principle, terrorists and their sympathizers could achieve a similar result through some combination of traditional financial products and cash couriers, though not nearly as quickly or with such a low likelihood of detection.

Finally, there are certainly differences in the resources and levels of commitment with which VASPs implement terrorism-related targeted financial sanctions, just as there are among FIs and DNFBPs. Those, along with differences in the quality of the AML/CFT supervision of VASPs—if such supervision is even conducted—easily translate to unevenness in the quality of implementation of sanctions-related obligations. Compounding this challenge is a fact already alluded to: that the governments of many states are still at the initial stages of identifying and registering (or licensing) the VASPs serving their citizens and other persons subject to their jurisdiction.

## International Good Practices

Full compliance with targeted financial sanctions by the private sector is critical to the effectiveness of these measures and to achieving the broader objectives of denying designated persons and entities access to funds and financial services. As noted, global FIs, by virtue of the resources available to them—as well as the products and services they offer, which include cross-border payments—tend to have well-developed procedures for ensuring that any amendments to UN or national sanctions lists are quickly captured by their (commercial or proprietary) screening systems. Smaller institutions that may or may not engage as frequently in cross-border financial transactions often lack such systems, relying more heavily on manual processes that may be highly prone to human error.

The following good practices are aimed at closing the gap between larger FIs and other private sector actors (for example, smaller FIs, DNFBPs, and VASPs), while ensuring that both general and specific guidance is available to any person or entity looking to implement targeted financial sanctions.

## Purchase or Develop Tools for Automated Account and Transaction Monitoring

The first good practice applies throughout the private sector. It is to purchase or develop monitoring software that updates automatically as UN listings and domestic designations are announced, modified, or terminated, and screens every customer and transaction accordingly. In some states, private sector actors have reduced costs through joint purchases of commercial software. In others, industry or professional associations have developed their own software, designed to suit specific national conditions or requirements. Most governments encourage the use of monitoring software and some require it. The objective, however, is universal. That is to strengthen the effective implementation of targeted financial sanctions by automating account and transaction screening.[57] Automation increases speed and efficiency while decreasing the scope for human error. That said, governments and the private sector alike must understand that no form of automation can or should replace the human analysis and judgment required by the FATF, including when individual customers or transactions are flagged by monitoring software.

Related to this, governments can establish searchable and printable databases of persons and entities subject to targeted financial sanctions, whether pursuant to UN listings or domestic designations. Such databases may be fed into monitoring software or consulted directly, including by private individuals who, like FIs, DNFBPs, and VASPs, must also fully apply targeted financial sanctions. Indeed, the implementation of targeted financial sanctions is a universal obligation, but one relevant primarily to FIs, DNFBPs, VASPs, and those unlicensed persons and entities who nevertheless hold assets or deposits, make loans, or provide other financial services.[58] The UN maintains a consolidated sanctions list in multiple file formats for ease of downloading—and, where useful, printing—by governments, commercial vendors, industry and professional associations, and/or members of the public.

---

[57] Note that the implementation of targeted financial sanctions is rule-based rather than risk-based, meaning, effectively, that all (not only certain higher-risk categories of) customers and transactions must be screened against the applicable sanctions lists, whether through manual or automated checks.

[58] It is generally illegal for persons or entities without a license or other official authorization to hold assets or deposits, make loans, or provide other financial services on a for-profit basis, but this does not absolve such persons or entities of their obligations related to targeted financial sanctions.

## Conduct Robust Supervision

The second good practice is to ensure that the relevant supervisors consistently monitor and enforce the compliance of FIs, DNFBPs, and VASPs with laws and regulations related to targeted financial sanctions.

At an operational level, many supervisors—whether government authorities or self-regulatory bodies—will test the screening systems of FIs, DNFBPs, and VASPs during on-site inspections. These may include checks on UN-listed persons and entities, domestically designated persons and entities, people who are *not* subject to targeted financial sanctions, and fictitious persons, as legally permissible. Effective supervisors will also focus on the quality and efficiency of the procedures to respond to (potential) hits along with the supervised entity's compliance monitoring and assurance testing programs. In so doing, supervisors may assess the extent to which the internal controls of each FI, DNFBP, and VASP ensure that the relevant systems function as described. To inform their on-site work, supervisors should have complete information on any steps previously taken by an FI, DNFBP, or VASP to implement targeted financial sanctions (for example, evidence of consistent screening and data regarding any asset freezing measures in place, along with the related reports that were transmitted to the appropriate authority). Faced with an FI, DNFBP, or VASP that has yet to make any positive matches, supervisors should seek to interview frontline staff to determine what they *would* do if they were to encounter a transaction involving a designated person or entity.

Effective supervisors will likewise examine corporate policies, along with decision-making and reporting processes, to ensure that internal oversight is sufficient to mitigate the risk of compliance failures. Upon identifying a violation, supervisors should prescribe remedial action and consider imposing penalties, as appropriate.[59] And when remedial actions are prescribed or penalties are imposed, supervisors should conduct rigorous follow-up to ensure that the necessary reforms have been fully and faithfully implemented.

## Provide Comprehensive Guidance

The third good practice is for governments to provide comprehensive guidance to FIs, DNFBPs, and VASPs on their obligations in implementing UN listings and domestic designations—as required by the FATF—and post that guidance, along with case studies, frequently asked questions, and other practical information, online by means of a secure or publicly accessible website, as appropriate (FATF 2019). Especially for FIs, the consistent and effective implementation of targeted financial sanctions involves many steps, including monitoring accounts and transactions, freezing assets (and reporting them to a competent authority),

---

[59] A broader discussion of the importance of effective supervision in preventing and detecting terrorist financing through FIs, DNFBPs, and VASPs is presented in Chapter 2 of this compendium.

denying financial and other related services (and reporting attempted transactions), and administering authorized exemptions. Governments should, therefore, prioritize the provision of guidance, considering specific elements of national law, such as any requirement to transfer frozen funds to a centralized asset management authority.

As an additional good practice, governments should consider issuing guidance to address common questions, misconceptions, or mistakes that may arise. For example, private sector actors often believe that they must reject incoming funds transfers involving a designated person or entity, effectively returning them to the sender. Guidance could be used to address this misconception, specifying that the subject funds should instead be frozen by the recipient and reported to the appropriate authority, which would then conduct an analysis and provide any necessary feedback.

These good practices are closely linked to the implementation of an effective communications strategy with the private sector, to include awareness-raising or sensitization before new or expanded requirements come into force. Sensitization has several positive effects, including the development of the interpersonal relationships and lines of communication that can facilitate close coordination between the government and the private sector when particularly difficult or unusual cases come about.

## Establish Mechanisms to Provide Case-Specific Guidance at Short Notice

A final, related good practice for facilitating consistent and effective private sector implementation is to establish hotlines or other mechanisms for FIs, DNFBPs, and VASPs to obtain tailored guidance—effectively, timely answers to pressing operational questions. The availability of such (case-specific) guidance may be the difference between success or failure in implementing targeted financial sanctions under challenging circumstances. For example, when hotlines are staffed by knowledgeable officials with access to the relevant government databases, they may help an FI, a DNFBP, or a VASP to distinguish between designated and nondesignated persons with similar names—or, under the circumstances described elsewhere in this section, to take the correct action in response to an incoming transfer.[60] The UN provides email contact information for staff who can assist member states seeking guidance regarding the listing process, and this mechanism is used on a regular basis.

---

[60] Distinguishing between designated and nondesignated persons with similar names is sometimes referred to as "deconflicting false positives." To facilitate the deconflicting of false positives—which is necessary to avoid freezing assets in error and/or incentivizing FIs, DNFBPs, and VASPs to drop whole categories of customers assessed to present elevated risks—designations should include robust identifiers, leveraging biometrics when permitted and available.

# LACK OF CLARITY AND ACCESSIBILITY IN DELISTING

## Key Challenges

The fourth and final set of key challenges presented here concerns a lack of clarity or accessibility in delisting, meaning the process of terminating targeted financial sanctions with respect to a particular person or entity. Governments may neglect to provide designated persons or entities with sufficient information on the delisting processes at the UN or domestic levels, or they may maintain unnecessarily limiting, cumbersome, or opaque domestic procedures.

At first glance, challenges involving delisting may not seem particularly relevant to the effectiveness of targeted financial sanctions in combating terrorist financing. It is worth recalling, therefore, that a central objective of targeted financial sanctions is to motivate designated persons and entities to change their behavior so as to obtain their delisting—and thus regain both access to their assets and the ability to engage freely in legitimate economic activity. Delisting processes[61] must be readily available, clear, and efficient if they are to help fulfil this objective, as individuals who believe they will never be delisted—or will never see the benefits of their delisting[62]—have a reduced incentive to change their behavior.

More broadly, the most potent legal and political objections to the use of targeted financial sanctions tend to revolve around due process concerns, specifically the lack of transparency around designations (especially as compared to the greater transparency typically afforded by criminal trials) and the perception that affected persons and entities lack sufficient recourse to challenge or reverse their status. The surest way to tackle such objections, and so ensure that targeted financial sanctions are generally accepted as both fair and rigorous, is to maximize the visibility and transparency of the delisting process at every level.

### Unclear Processes

Designated persons and entities often find the process of appealing their designation or requesting their delisting to be unnecessarily opaque, especially without help from an attorney. This is most often caused by a lack of accessibility of information about the UN and domestic delisting processes—or, when applicable, about the generic steps for challenging administrative actions—sometimes stemming from insufficient outreach on the part of domestic authorities. The FATF is unambiguous: "States should provide for a mechanism through which a designated person or entity can challenge [a domestic] designation, with a view to having it reviewed by a competent authority or a court. With respect to designations on the Al-Qaida Sanctions List, states should inform designated persons

---

[61] Delisting processes include application, consideration, the rendering of a final decision or judgment, and, ultimately, the rapid implementation of that decision or judgment on the part of both the relevant authorities and the private sector.

[62] For example, cases in which no right to a bank account or to financial services exists and FIs have a history of closing the accounts of recently delisted persons or refusing to do business with them.

and entities of the availability of the UN Office of the Ombudsperson, pursuant to resolution 1904 (2009), to accept de-listing petitions" (FATF 2022).

Still, some governments have yet to provide this information publicly or to do so in an accessible way (such as through a prominent official website). Others provide only minimal information, noting that delisting requests should be submitted to the UN Office of the Ombudsperson or that domestic designations may be appealed to a competent court, but not specifying the relevant points of contact, applicable time frames (for cases in which there is a limited window to petition for removal from a national list), or types of documentation that would be accepted or required. Still others provide comprehensive public information, but only in a passive way, posting guidelines on the internet while making little or no effort to communicate them directly to designated persons or entities with known addresses.

## Limited Options

Neither the FATF nor the UNSCRs on which the relevant FATF Recommendations are based prescribes the way states should handle domestic delistings, specifying only that they are to establish "procedures […] to allow, upon request, review of the designation decision before a court or other independent competent authority" (FATF 2022). In practice, this means that the options for domestic delisting vary widely in scope and convenience.

In some states, persons or entities may submit what is commonly known as an "administrative delisting request" to the competent authority responsible for their designation while preserving the option to file a petition in court. That option is not available everywhere. Some states allow courts located throughout the national territory to hear petitions or appeals; others reserve that competency for only one court, which is generally located in the capital.

The implications are obvious: the more limited the options for the submission of a delisting request, the more daunting it becomes for designated persons or entities to consider the sorts of behavioral changes that targeted financial sanctions are designed, in part, to bring about.

## International Good Practices

As has been stressed in this chapter, a key goal of targeted financial sanctions is to incentivize designated terrorists and terrorist financiers to change their behavior in the hope and expectation of delisting, thereby allowing them to regain access to financial services and any funds that may have been frozen. To maintain that incentive, states should proactively review designations, consider establishing an administrative delisting option, and ensure that information about both the domestic and UN delisting processes is publicly available.

### Make Information on Delisting Processes Readily Available to the Public

One good practice is to make information on the applicable UN and domestic delisting processes readily available to the public (for example, on the website of the competent authority or its parent department or agency). This should include the following: (1) relevant contact information, (2) the standard(s) for delisting (that is, the grounds on which a person or entity may seek delisting/be delisted), and (3) examples of the types of information or documentation that could or should be submitted as part of a court challenge, petition for independent review, or administrative delisting request (where possible). The rationale is straightforward, as it is the availability of comprehensive delisting processes and detailed information about those processes that establishes the necessary incentive for designated persons and entities to consider abandoning their support for terrorism.

### Include Information about Delisting When Providing Initial Notice of Designation

The second good practice supplements the first. When providing a person or entity with initial notification of their UN listing or domestic designation, the relevant authorities should include information about the option(s) for requesting delisting or challenging a designation. These would include petitioning the Office of the Ombudsperson, submitting an administrative delisting request where possible, or applying to a competent court or other independent body. The FATF does not require that specific, personal notice be provided to newly designated persons or entities, but many states do so. Such notice represents an additional opportunity to convey information about the applicable delisting process(es).

### Review Designations Proactively, Whether on a Regular Basis or Upon Receipt of Pertinent New Information

A third good practice relevant to delisting is to ensure, on an ongoing basis, that UN listings and domestic designations remain appropriate, meaning that the persons and entities subject to targeted financial sanctions continue to meet the established designation criteria. Governments should review existing UN listings and domestic designations both *reactively* (for example, upon the filing of a court challenge or the receipt of a delisting request) and *proactively* (for example, on a regular basis or upon the receipt of pertinent new information). Some states provide, in law, for annual or biannual reviews of all domestic designations, obligating the competent authority to revisit its past decisions according to a set schedule, including by seeking out any new information regarding each person or entity on the national list. Those reviews could be extended to cover any citizen, resident, or locally based person or entity subject to terrorism-related UN sanctions. Other states maintain a policy or practice of reviewing any listing or designation about which they should otherwise uncover or receive new information, whether through domestic sources, as part of routine intelligence or law enforcement activity, or foreign sources, as part of standing or specific exchanges. Either way, the goal is the same: to be continually satisfied that the persons and entities whose assets have been frozen still represent an active or potential terrorist threat.

### Consider Establishing an Administrative Delisting Process

A final good practice is to consider establishing an administrative delisting mechanism as an option/initial option for domestically designated persons or entities seeking to challenge their status. As noted, the FATF requires states to maintain a mechanism for a designated person or entity to challenge their status and specifies that the reviewing body, if not a court, should be independent.[63] It does *not* require the original designating authority to establish a supplemental process for persons or entities on the national list to force that same authority to revisit, reevaluate, or otherwise review its original decision. However, that is something governments should consider in designing or redesigning their terrorism-related targeted financial sanctions regimes. The advantages are threefold. Administrative delisting mechanisms (1) may allow governments to avoid long, costly, and, under certain circumstances, embarrassing legal challenges, (2) enable classified information considered as part of the designation process to remain strictly controlled (rather than exposed to review by judges and, potentially, attorneys—whether for the designating authority or for the designated person or entity), and (3) generally represent the most efficient form of resolution, as the officials most familiar with the case may be tapped to help evaluate any new information provided or uncovered. In sum, administrative delisting mechanisms *may usefully supplement but not replace* designated persons and entities' recourse to a court or other independent body.

## CONCLUSION

Targeted financial sanctions can be a powerful tool for combating terrorist financing, but their effectiveness depends very much on the design and implementation of national laws, regulations, and processes, and the form and resourcing of the range of relevant authorities. The extent of outreach to the public, as well as to the private sector firms on the frontlines, is also critical. This much is evident in the challenges and good practices discussed in this chapter, which reflect the diversity of approaches taken by states all over the world in pursuing the same objective: depriving terrorists of the resources needed to attract and pay new recruits, obtain weapons and supplies, and carry out deadly attacks.

## REFERENCES

Churchill, R. 2008. "Conflicts between United Nations Security Council Resolutions and the 1982 United Nations Convention on the Law of the Sea, and Their Possible Resolution." *International Law Studies* 8: 146.

Berkhout, Richard, and Fernando, Francisca, eds. 2022. *Unmasking Control: A Guide to Beneficial Ownership Transparency*. Washington, DC: International Monetary Fund.

Dion-Schwarz C., D. Manheim, and P. Johnston. 2019. *Terrorist Use of Cryptocurrencies: Technical and Organizational Barriers and Future Threats*. RAND National Security Research Division Report, RAND Corporation. Santa Monica.

Financial Action Task Force (FATF). 2010. *International Best Practices: Detecting and Preventing the Illicit Cross-Border Transportation of Cash and Bearer Negotiable Instruments*. Paris: FATF.

---

[63] FATF 2022.

Financial Action Task Force (FATF). 2022. *International Standards on Combating Money Laundering and the Financing of Terrorism & Proliferation: The FATF Recommendations*. Paris: FATF.

Global Counterterrorism Forum and UN Interregional Crime and Justice Research Institute. 2019. *Policy Toolkit on the Hague Good Practices on the Nexus between Transnational Organized Crime and Terrorism*. The Hague.

UN Analytical Support and Sanctions Monitoring Team. 2019. *Twenty-Fifth Report of the Analytical Support and Sanctions Monitoring Team Submitted Pursuant to Resolution 2368 (2017) Concerning ISIL (Da'esh), Al-Qaida and Associated Individuals and Entities*. New York.

UN Security Council. 1999. *Resolution 1267*. New York.

UN Security Council. 2001. *Resolution 1373*. New York.

UN Security Council. 2002. *Resolution 1452*. New York.

UN Security Council. 2011a. *Resolution 1988*. New York.

UN Security Council. 2011b. *Resolution 1999*. New York.

UN Security Council. 2015. *Resolution 2253*. New York.

UN Security Council. 2016. *Resolution 2322*. New York.

UN Security Council. 2017. *Resolution 2368*. New York.

UN Security Council. 2019. *Resolution 2462*. New York.

UN Security Council. 2021. *Resolution 2610*. New York.

UN Security Council Committee Pursuant to Resolutions 1267 (1999), 1989 (2011), and 2253 (2015) Concerning ISIL (Da'esh), Al-Qaida, and Associated Individuals, Groups, Undertakings, and Entities. 2018. *Guidelines of the Committee for the Conduct of Its Work*. New York.

UN Security Council Counter-Terrorism Committee Executive Directorate. 2017. *Technical Guide to the Implementation of Security Council Resolution 1373 (2001) and Other Relevant Resolutions*. New York.

United States Department of the Treasury, Office of Foreign Assets Control. 2018. *Terrorist Assets Report: Calendar Year 2018 Twenty-Seventh Annual Report to the Congress on Assets in the United States Relating to Terrorist States and Organizations Engaged in International Terrorism*. Washington, DC.

## RESOURCES

Financial Action Task Force (FATF). 2013. *International Best Practices: Targeted Financial Sanctions Related to Terrorism and Terrorist Financing (R.6)*. Paris: FATF.

Financial Action Task Force (FATF). 2021. *Methodology for Assessing Technical Compliance with the FATF Recommendations and the Effectiveness of AML/CFT Systems*. Paris: FATF.

# CHAPTER 6

# International Cooperation in Combating the Financing of Terrorism

Kathleen Kao, Jean-Paul Laborde, Paul Riordan,
Dermot Brauders, Hyung Keun Yoon,
Miguel Angel Garcia, and Nedko Krumov

## CHAPTER IN BRIEF

### The Challenge

Terrorism incidents inflicted on societies almost always feature an international element, including in the context of terrorist financing. Consequently, international cooperation among countries is an indispensable tool for combatting terrorist financing. The challenges vary for each jurisdiction but the most common are (1) capacity limitations, (2) inadequate information sharing and prioritization at the domestic and international level, (3) lack of trust among partners, and (4) underdeveloped legal regimes.

### Why It Happens

A lack of agreement exists among international partners on the application of counter-terrorism tools. Often, security classifications hinder the information-sharing process and limit Combating the Financing of Terrorism (CFT) efforts. The contrasting application of terrorist financing-combating measures among countries impedes the formation of successful international partnerships. Further, terrorist financing typologies are constantly evolving, and the nature of information identified by a certain type of agency (such as intelligence agencies) differs from that identified by supervisory authorities. However, communication between the two types of agencies is not always optimal, a situation that creates blackholes in global CFT efforts. As a result, even if bilateral cooperation were established among international counterparts, terrorist financing-related information would remain lacking.

### The Solution

This chapter discusses countries efforts in forming a comprehensive information-sharing framework at the domestic level. These frameworks may have a potential multiplier effect on other countries. As a next step, countries should identify the most important international partners with a view toward entering into bilateral/multilateral information-sharing agreements to facilitate CTF efforts. To be effective, such practices must start and be promoted at the domestic level.

# THE CHANGING GLOBAL CHALLENGE

> *Even as a host of treaties lay the ground to bridge gaps in tackling the increasing sophistication of cross-border funding for terrorism, lack of consensus, distrust, and conflicting priorities create barriers to cooperation between jurisdictions. A focus on good practices, including secure sharing of classified information, can facilitate effective action while sustaining sovereignty and respecting human rights.*

The methods of terrorist financing are evolving. The growing linkages between terrorist activity and other financial crimes (for example, organized crime, drug trafficking, and corruption) and the increasingly cross-border nature of the financing, organization, and execution of attacks have changed the methods and means of terrorist financing. Technology and globalization provide terrorist groups ever-changing means for seeking funding and undertaking financial activities. Due to the complex and frequently transnational nature of terrorist financing, a single authority or even a single country seldom alone has visibility into the entire network of terrorism operations, including revenue generation and financial services. As with other financial crimes, a significant proportion of evidence and information (including financial intelligence held by financial intelligence units [FIUs]) that is necessary to further criminal proceedings is often held abroad or in multiple jurisdictions. International cooperation is, therefore, essential to counterterrorism and for CFT, both nationally and globally.

This chapter addresses some of the most significant challenges to international cooperation in global CFT efforts by proposing good practices to improve the effectiveness of international cooperation and identifying common challenges. The challenges and good practices described herein are based on the experience of international organizations and their member countries in cases and the development of national policies and global standards. That noted, many of the difficulties described when cooperating with foreign authorities are not unique to efforts to suppress terrorist financing.

---

**Box 6.1. International Conventions, Treaties, and Resolutions for Cooperation**

Extensive international consultations and negotiations over the past two decades have produced several international conventions and treaties to impel, facilitate, and govern collaboration between and among signatory countries in relation to terrorism and terrorist financing as well as to money laundering. These include the following:

- **The International Convention for the Suppression of the Financing of Terrorism (UN CFT Convention 1999):** The UN CFT Convention is the primary instrument articulating standards, including on criminalization, for international

### Box 6.1. *(continued)*

cooperation in terrorist financing matters. The UN CFT Convention has been ratified by 188 countries. All parties to the UN CFT Convention are required to define the financing of terrorism in a manner consistent with theefinetion contained in the convention.

- **The UN Convention against Transnational Organized Crime (UNTOC 2000):** The UNTOC, also called the Palermo Convention, requires signatories to provide the widest possible range of mutual legal assistance (MLA) for its covered offenses, which can include terrorism related to money laundering and financing in some circumstances.
- **The Vienna Convention:** Applies only to drug-related offenses and sets some general principles for interpretation of specific treaty terms.

Other instruments that can serve as a minimum basis for international cooperation in terrorist financing cases include the Scheme Relating to Mutual Legal Assistance in Criminal Matters within the Commonwealth (Harare Scheme); the Inter-American Convention Against Terrorism; ASEAN Convention on Counter Terrorism; Council of Europe Convention on the Prevention of Terrorism; the Council of Europe Convention on Laundering, Search, Seizure and Confiscation of the Proceeds from Crime and on the Financing of Terrorism; and African Union regional instruments (such as the African Union Convention on the prevention and combating terrorism) or subregional instruments. Several multilateral treaties also provide a basis for extradition and MLA in terrorist financing matters: the UN CFT Convention, the UNTOC, and the Merida Conventions.

Some UNSCRs—notably, 1373 and 2322—also contain specific obligations related to international cooperation in CFT matters (especially when adopted under chapter VII of the UN Charter). UNSCR 2322 explicitly calls upon states to exchange information and enhance cooperation in counterterrorism matters, and to use all applicable international instruments to which they are a party as a basis for MLA and extradition. UNSCR 2462, adopted under chapter VII, is devoted to preventing and suppressing terrorist financing and includes special provisions on international cooperation, namely on extradition and MLA.

This framework of conventions, treaties, and resolutions, if fully implemented, provides authorities with the tools needed to combat the financing of terrorism, including mechanisms to facilitate international cooperation. However, not all signatories of these instruments have fully implemented them, or have done so in ways that make the cooperation mechanisms cumbersome and time consuming to use.

Source: Authors, based on the United Nations Treaty Collection. https://treaties.un.org/.
Note: ASEAN = Association of Southeast Asian Nations; CFT = combating the financing of terrorism; MLA = mutual legal assistance; UNSCR = UN Security Council Resolution; UNTOC = UN Convention against Transnational Organized Crime.

The Financial Action Task Force (FATF) standards include principles for international cooperation in both money laundering and terrorist financing matters. FATF Recommendations 36–40 focus on technical compliance, the legal and institutional framework of member countries, and the effective implementation of IO.2 relating to international cooperation.

IO.2 requires FATF and FATF-Style Regional Body (FSRB) members to provide constructive and timely assistance when requested by other countries. Such assistance includes locating and extraditing criminals; identifying, freezing, seizing, confiscating, and sharing assets; and providing information related to money laundering and terrorist financing (including financial intelligence, supervisory information, and information on beneficial ownership). The technical compliance requirements related to international cooperation are contained in Recommendations 36–40 of the FATF standard and do not differentiate between money laundering and terrorist financing. Countries are required to have proper legal basis and domestic mechanisms to seek and provide mutual legal assistance (MLA) for terrorist financing investigations, prosecutions, and related proceedings. These mechanisms should empower a country to identify, freeze, seize, confiscate, or recover funds and other assets associated with terrorist financing, as well as to execute extradition requests. Competent authorities (such as FIUs and law enforcement) should cooperate with foreign counterparts in terrorist financing investigations both upon request and spontaneously. As featured later in this analysis, these requirements also provide instruments that can increase the effective implementation of international cooperation on terrorist financing matters.

Other international organizations are engaged in anti-money laundering/combating the financing of terrorism (AML/CFT) measures to strengthen international cooperation through technical assistance training, the identification of weaknesses, and the development of best practices. Such organizations include the Egmont Group, the United Nations Office on Drugs and Crime (UNODC), the IMF and the World Bank, INTERPOL and the Council of Europe.

## FORMS OF INTERNATIONAL COOPERATION

International cooperation has both "nonjudicial" and "judicial" aspects (Bassiouni 2008).[1] Nonjudicial cooperation refer to the exchange of information between competent authorities, including law enforcement, FIUs, and intelligence agencies, while the judicial components of international cooperation are aimed at sharing information or gathering evidence in the context of a judicial proceeding involving MLA and extradition requests. The spectrum of authorities relevant for CFT efforts can be quite broad and include customs, intelligence services, FIUs, supervisory authorities, and the judiciary, depending on the particular procedural aspects of each jurisdiction. A significant amount of cooperation on takes place through global and regional law enforcement channels. Cooperation also occurs

---

[1] The principles underpinning cooperation with foreign authorities in terrorist financing judicial proceedings are the same as those generally applied to international cooperation in other matters, including respect for sovereignty, specialty, dual criminality, reciprocity, and *ne bis in idem* (no legal action can be instituted twice for the same cause of action). For a more comprehensive discussion, see Cherif Bassiouni, International Criminal Law, Second Edition, volume II, Extradition issues feature on pages 229–54 (for the United States) and 227–301 for the European approach; and for judicial assistance and mutual cooperation refer to Cherif Bassiouni, International Criminal Law, Third Edition, volume II, For chapters on MLA and Cooperation in Criminal Matters, see pages 388–402 for the United States, 413–436 for the Commonwealth, and 455–465 for Europe and 504 for the EU.

between FIUs through the Egmont Group. An important aspect of international cooperation occurs between intelligence agencies, but information on the nature, extent, and amount of such cooperation has not been collected for the purpose of this publication. In this chapter, competent authorities refer to FIUs and law enforcement in the context of information sharing and to investigators and prosecutors in the context of judicial cooperation.

This chapter also looks at the practical aspects of procedures in requests for MLA and extradition, considering the diversity of legal systems and other procedural requirements in each state. This text should be treated as a guide rather than providing prescriptive measures as to how such requests should be dealt with. Generally, states have their own internal procedures/legislation on the applicable structure and format for forwarding requests to foreign counterparts. It would be nearly impossible to provide a set of universal guidelines applicable to requests for MLA and extradition as differences will exist in the legal systems of each state (for instance, common versus civil/continental law). The good practices contained in this chapter should, therefore, be regarded as guidelines that can be tailored to meet the specific legal and other requirements of each state.

## Nonjudicial Forms of Cooperation

Nonjudicial forms of cooperation occur mostly at the operational/administrative level and encompass the many ways states cooperate regarding terrorist financing. FIU-to-FIU exchanges allows the sharing of financial intelligence on a bilateral and multilateral basis. Cooperation between FIUs can be facilitated by the Egmont Group's platform for the secure exchange of expertise and financial intelligence. Security agencies are also critical partners in the detection of terrorist financing at both national and international levels. They, too, exchange information with counterpart organizations in other states on a discretionary basis and generally through reciprocal liaison officers.[2] Law enforcement cooperation can involve joint investigations by the agencies of two or more jurisdictions. For example, the EU Agency for Criminal Justice Cooperation (Eurojust) promotes and facilitates the creation of joint investigation teams between EU member states to bridge or overcome MLA difficulties. They can also include non-EU members (an example being the investigation into the shooting down of Malaysian Airlines flight MH17 in 2014, where Ukraine and Australia were included). Such operational cooperation tends to be on a "like-to-like" basis (such as police-to-police or FIU-to-FIU); however, in recent years, attempts have been made to improve indirect[3] cooperation, which is also envisaged by the FATF standard.

---

[2] The nature and extent to which security intelligence agencies share information/intelligence with each other and other agencies is not fully known outside of such agencies, and no such agencies were consulted for this book.

[3] According to the FATF Methodology, indirect exchange of information refers to information that passes from the requested authority through one or more domestic or foreign authorities before being received by the requesting authority. Such an exchange of information and its use may be subject to the authorization of one or more competent authorities of the requested country.

### Legal/Judicial Forms of Cooperation

Legal/judicial cooperation in operational matters is generally undertaken to acquire evidence across national boundaries, secure material evidence, seize assets, or seek the detention and extradition of suspects through judicial proceedings. In this regard, authorities in one jurisdiction may seek MLA from the investigative or prosecutorial authorities[4] in another, in line with an MLA convention or treaty. Authorities generally seek MLA when conducting or facilitating an investigation or collecting evidence for use in judicial proceedings in the requesting state. A country may also seek assistance in locating suspects or witnesses bilaterally or may request other states, through INTERPOL communications, to arrest or detain a suspect pending initiation of extradition proceedings. Assistance specific to terrorist financing cases may also include locating and freezing suspected terrorist assets in another country under UN conventions or UN Security Council Resolutions (UNSCRs).

## CHALLENGES AND GOOD PRACTICES

Many of the enforcement and financial intelligence challenges discussed in earlier chapters have a cascading effect on international cooperation. For example, issues noted in Chapter 4 on the lack of a comprehensive approach in the criminalization of the terrorist financing offense and on what can be deemed a "terrorist organization" may affect international cooperation if, for example, dual criminality[5] is applied in an excessively formalistic manner. Where poor cooperation makes the domestic exchange of information difficult, that may affect international cooperation and the timely provision of requested information (if the requested domestic authority cannot obtain it in a timely manner because cooperation with another domestic authority is inadequate).

It should be noted that in the articulation of challenges and good practices related to judicial forms of cooperation, the principles and rights governing extradition and MLA should always be respected. These are among internationally accepted norms enshrined in many treaties, whether global, regional, or subregional. These principles also appear in bilateral treaties and when implementing the principle of reciprocity under UNSCR 2322. Procedural solutions must be identified within that international legal framework, which encompasses the universal fundamental values of human rights and rule of law; otherwise, states might rely on extrajudicial measures that have no due process considerations or protections. In that respect, it is imperative to find the right balance between the

---

[4] In some cases, MLA may be sought and/or provided in the context of administrative or other proceedings, which may involve other authorities (such as supervisory authorities). However, this form of international cooperation is less relevant in the context of terrorist financing.

[5] Dual criminality is a condition to provide international legal assistance in criminal matters, and it requires that the alleged criminal conduct should be considered criminal under the laws of both the requesting and the requested state.

importance of respecting international values and states' interests while implementing treaties on extradition and MLA.

## Trust and Confidence

Distrust between states and counterparts can significantly impede open and willing exchanges of information. While structural issues may have to be dealt with in a way that corresponds with how commitments are formalized in each jurisdiction, issues of political will and prioritization can frustrate international cooperation.

### *Challenges*

Insufficient trust among states may be one of the most critical factors hampering robust information sharing. Lack of trust has various origins, among them poor rule of law and corruption, state capture, political instability, human rights concerns, insecure communication channels, lack of protections and safeguards for confidential or sensitive information, and different interpretations of key concepts. Lack of trust may also arise from legal and institutional weakness (actual or perceived) in states that would otherwise be critical partners in counterterrorism and CFT efforts. Whatever the cause, where trust is deficient, countries or agencies may be reluctant to share information that may be critical for their counterparts.

Governance and rule of law weaknesses may also prevent some countries from fully participating in all international forums. Bodies such as the Egmont Group have strict requirements for member states, such as the obligation to have adequate mechanisms and protections in their legal and institutional frameworks to protect information shared within the group against security breaches and misuse. While these entry requirements foster and facilitate international cooperation, some relevant counterparts from countries with shortcomings in their frameworks may not be integrated into the global network of information sharing. Governance and rule of law weaknesses directly impact MLA. Challenges related to MLA generally have an even greater impact on extradition. Given the nature of the request and the deprivation of liberty involved, refusal of extradition is more frequent than for other types of requests for international assistance (not only in terrorist financing cases but also in general). Refusals for human rights or humanitarian reasons should not be considered impediments, as they are necessary for the protection of freedoms; rather they should be considered as preconditions for the effective provision of international cooperation.

Despite the numerous international legal instruments against terrorism and terrorist financing, a discrepancy remains between the almost universal ratification of the UN CFT Convention and the degree that its provisions are incorporated domestically. This discrepancy is demonstrated by the many objections raised by countries in the context of domestic implementation (see Chapter 4 for more detailed information).

Furthermore, despite all the treaties mentioned in this chapter, experience shows that while the obligation to extradite or prosecute (*aut dedere aut judicare*) has been applied in some criminal sectors, this principle presents more of a challenge for investigations into terrorism and terrorist financing. Terrorist attacks and the financing of those attacks and/or of terrorist organizations are considered direct attacks on a country's sovereignty and carry grave social weight. Victims (and the wider populace) may not understand the reasons why such cases would be tried outside of the territory where the attack occurred. These attributes of terrorist attacks (and affiliated offenses) often lead to resistance in transferring cases to another jurisdiction. However, reluctance can undermine effective enforcement when obstacles to domestic enforcement (as described in Chapter 4) are not overcome.

### Good Practices

International bodies often support their members by directly assisting with information sharing or facilitating discussion among counterparts. In the technical aspect, international entities such as INTERPOL and the Egmont Group are constantly seeking to improve their established information-sharing mechanisms to assure member states that the information they contribute is managed securely and used only for legitimate purposes.

The fundamental and internationally accepted principles and rights governing extradition and mutual assistance should always be respected. As noted above, the social cost of refusing cooperation in terrorist financing cases is significant. Accordingly, countries should avoid a blanket policy of outright refusal and instead seek ways to incorporate protection of human rights in their engagements with each other. In such a context, and as an example of the implementation of *aut dedere aut judicare*, the UNODC Digest of Terrorist Cases featured the mutual agreement between the United States and Germany as one that captured this principle well.[6]

### Conflicting Legal Regimes and Procedural Hurdles

Cooperation in judicial matters is essential to ensure that terrorist financiers are held accountable in at least one jurisdiction. As with other types of cases requiring international assistance, the speedy execution of judicial cooperation (through MLA and extradition requests) is a determining factor of success in terrorist financing cases, especially as it is important to preserve evidence that could be lost or otherwise unavailable after the passage of too much time. Experience shows that law enforcement officials engaged in transnational

---

[6] Under the terms of the Germany-United States bilateral extradition treaty, Germany is obligated to either extradite the accused or submit the case for prosecution in the same manner as a serious domestic offense. In the 1985 hijacking of a Trans World Airlines flight shot down in Germany, Mohammed Hamadei was convicted and sentenced to life imprisonment. American authorities, while expressing a preference to have prosecuted the case in the United States (due to the death of an American citizen), publicly expressed understanding of the German position, cooperated with the German prosecution by supplying necessary witnesses, and complimented German authorities for solving the case.

investigations often feel that judicial cooperation, although a powerful and important tool, in practice operates so slowly and in such cumbersome ways that it can impede investigations. Given that international cooperation is often unavoidable, the identification of key challenges and good practices is useful for streamlining and optimizing it.

Procedural requirements and compliance with international principles are more stringent for extradition than for MLA, since extradition can infringe human rights (through deportation, detention, and so on). For example, the principle of dual criminality may not be necessary for MLA in all cases but is always required for extradition.

## *Challenges*

Many of the challenges described in this chapter stem from poor or incomplete implementation of conventions and international standards (Box 6.2). Many countries have not ratified treaties other than the UN CFT Convention or have done so with reservations. In some countries, there are still no laws or regulations outlining special procedures for achieving full compliance with UNSCR 1373, and legislation is often inadequate.

---

**Box 6.2. The Parliamentary Assembly of the Mediterranean Example**

All states attending a workshop organized by the Parliamentary Assembly of the Mediterranean[1] had ratified the UN CFT Convention, but many had criminalized the offenses of the Convention in different ways. The inconsistencies in national legislation made proper cooperation not possible. In some cases, inconsistencies with the UN CFT Convention were also identified.

These differences show it is imperative for international prosecutorial and judicial cooperation that a strong connection is made in the national criminalization of terrorist acts between those crimes and ones defined in the UN CFT Convention. Otherwise, judicial authorities will not be able to adequately respond to mutual legal agreements, requests for extradition, or the freezing and confiscation of assets.

Source: Authors, based on the Parliamentary Assembly of the Mediterranean. https://www.pam.int/en..
Note: UN CFT Convention = The International Convention for the Suppression of the Financing of Terrorism.

[1] Members of Parliaments from 34 countries of the region and more were represented in the workshop, which took place in Rome in the premises of the Senate on April 4, 2017.

---

Several legal issues related to the criminalization of terrorist financing (see Chapter 4) also affect international cooperation, particularly judicial cooperation. The UN CFT Convention is the only instrument that contains a general definition of "terrorism" but allows for reservations; however, many countries still do not adhere to its comprehensive definition of "terrorism." Few countries have fully implemented the convention, and, most importantly, there is no universal agreement on the definition of "terrorist organizations."[7]

Another challenge stems from the overly stringent application of the principle of dual criminality. Dual criminality is a precondition to providing international legal assistance in criminal matters. It requires the alleged criminal conduct to be considered criminal under the laws of both the requesting and the requested state. Dual criminality is applied in the basic mechanisms of international criminal law, primarily extradition, but also when providing assistance that requires the transfer of proceedings and the execution of foreign penal judgments. Overapplication of the principle to noncoercive actions is a major source of delay. Overly stringent application also impedes the fast and efficient procedures necessary to trace terrorist financing. Delays can endanger the outcome of judicial proceedings.

The application of dual criminality for coercive actions, such as freezing, seizure, and confiscation of assets, can be even more difficult as exemptions from dual criminality are not permitted. While exceptions can be made for noncompulsory measures, the principle of dual criminality is almost always required for requests to freeze, seize, and confiscate assets. As countries have had varying degrees of success in capturing the elements necessary to criminalize terrorist offenses under the UN CFT Convention, it can be a challenge to satisfy dual criminality requirements in cases where coercive actions are required.

Similarly, with respect to freezing, seizing, and confiscating assets, poor formulation and documentation of requests can be a barrier to receiving the necessary assistance. Due to the complexity of these types of operations, requests must be accompanied by sufficient documentation (for example, identifying seized property) to proceed efficiently with the requested measures. Failure to provide required documentation is a common source of delay in delivering the requested assistance.

### Good Practices

One of the key good practices for expediting implementation of MLA requests is, to the extent possible, requiring the application of the principle of dual criminality only when actions are coercive, as coercive actions most strongly affect fundamental human rights. The FATF standard espouses this approach as it requires countries not to make dual criminality a condition for giving assistance where MLA requests do not involve coercive actions. The UN Convention against Corruption follows the same approach.

Solutions can also be found in international instruments providing legal mechanisms to interpret dual criminality in the broadest sense possible, particularly where noncoercive actions are sought. Examples would be requests for testimony,

---

[7] Except during war time, an international crime, neither Geneva and The Hague Conventions of the International Humanitarian Law nor the Rome Statute would apply to most of terrorist offenses. As such, terrorism can be considered a national offense with several transnational elements. It means that terrorist offenses are criminalized in national legislation and that all the principles of international cooperation will be applied to them whenever transnational elements occur.

witness videoconferences, or banking statements. Overall flexibility should be established as a principle, provided international human rights law and international humanitarian law are respected. An example can be seen in the latest US mutual legal assistance treaties, which provide flexibility for information sharing, such as allowing for video testimonials (Box 6.3). Another example is the voluntary Harare Scheme, applicable for Common Law countries, which lays out specific recommendations and commentaries that can be helpful when preparing or responding to MLA requests. Under paragraph 15 of the Scheme, "a request may seek assistance in facilitating the personal attendance of a person for the purposes of an investigation or to appear as a witness before a court exercising jurisdiction in the requesting country." In addition to the information required, the request needs to specify the following: (1) the subject matter relevant to the person's attendance and (2) the reasons why the personal attendance of the person is required.

---

**Box 6.3. Limiting Dual Criminality Requirements in MLA Treaties: The US Experience**

Recent US mutual legal assistance treaties do not make dual criminality a prerequisite for cooperation. As a result, a requested state must render assistance, even for acts that are not criminalized in that state. In some cases, a mutual legal assistance treaty may impose a dual criminality requirement for certain types of assistance. For example, the mutual legal assistance treaty between Switzerland and the United States imposes dual criminality when a request is made to obtain evidence through the use of compulsory measures (Bassiouni 2008).

Source: Bassiouni 2008.

---

Similar methods to those already described can be adopted for compulsory measures. While enforcement of the principle of dual criminality is understandable for confiscation requests (since they are almost always nonreversible), more flexibility should be considered for freezing and seizure (as they are reversible measures). Bilateral treaties or arrangements are strengthened when they adopt provisions from the UN Convention against Transnational Organized Crime or the UN Convention against Corruption, which have more recent and more efficient mechanisms related to MLA and freezing, seizure, and confiscation.

Where possible, assistance should be provided in the manner defined by the requesting member state. To maximize the chances of evidence gathered abroad being admissible, the 2000 EU MLA Convention provides a new approach—the *forum regit actum* principle (Article 4 of the 2000 Convention). According to this principle, a requested member state must comply with the formalities and procedures indicated by the requesting member state. The reason for this provision is to allow information gathered by mutual assistance to be used as evidence in subsequent legal proceedings in the requesting member state. The terms "formalities" and "procedures" should be interpreted in a broad sense and may include, for example, a situation where a request indicates that a representative of the judicial authorities of the requesting member state or a defense representative must be permitted to attend when evidence is taken from a witness. Because this type of request might burden the requested member state, the requesting member state should set out only formalities and procedures that are indispensable for its investigations. The requested member state can only refuse to give effect to such formalities and procedures where they conflict with its fundamental principles of law or where the Convention itself expressly states that execution of requests is governed by the law of the requested member state.

Transfer of criminal proceedings is an alternative in cases where an authority cannot, for whatever reason, extradite or provide MLA. Still, this mode is rarely used in pursuing terrorist financing since these cases invoke intense national interest and victims of an attack understandably wish to see suspects prosecuted and sentenced in the jurisdiction where the attack was committed. Application of that mechanism between the United States and Scotland can be seen in one of the most important cases to come from the Lockerbie Disaster (Bassiouni 2008). Execution of foreign sentences is needed when a country wishes to repatriate its national(s) after a judgment issued abroad, which provides a sense of ownership in the criminal justice process. Recognition of foreign penal judgments is also key for confiscation of assets located outside of the country in which the judgment was issued.

## Capacity and Mandates

Successful international cooperation depends on all counterparts having the capacity needed to make a request for assistance and to carry out requested assistance. Authorities should be well versed in the elements necessary for a successful request, in both substance and procedure. Authorities also need to have the requisite authority and legal basis to make and fulfill such requests.

### Challenges

Many countries lack either sufficient or dedicated resources (for example, professional staff, case management systems) to seek and reply to international requests for information. Although this weakness has a big impact on a state's ability to respond to requests for assistance, it can also often impede proactiveness and the capacity to seek information from abroad for terrorist financing cases that have cross-border elements. A general lack of awareness and low prioritization of international assistance among law enforcement agencies can also contribute. Specialized staff can help to resolve these issues by promoting available cooperation tools and channels.

Experience shows that linkages between terrorists and criminals are strongest in fragile and conflict-affected states. As conflict is a main driver of governance failures, jurisdictions with rule of law weaknesses often provide "ideal conditions for the blending of criminal and terrorist activities."[8] Weaknesses in rule of law

---

[8] "Enhancing International Cooperation in the Fight Against the Financing of Terrorism," *Journal of Global Change and Governance* 1, no. 3 (2008).

can contribute to both legal and capacity issues, making those jurisdictions the weakest link in the information chain.

## Good Practices

Establishing and using central authorities is key to overcoming difficulties in international judicial cooperation. Special units should be resourced with well-trained specialists who have knowledge of human rights and rule of law issues and who are trained to use the UNODC's MLA Tool to facilitate and reinforce international cooperation in criminal matters. Central authorities will be in a position to support bilateral treaties, agreements, and arrangements whenever necessary to promote MLA and/or extradition in CFT matters. Additionally, they will be able to prioritize requests in accordance with the UNODC Manual on CFT MLA and Extradition—another important tool for the prevention of terrorist attacks.

Central authorities also have an essential role in building trust among prosecutorial and judicial authorities of many countries at international, regional, and bilateral levels. They know how to use informal channels, such as Eurojust or other regional forums, to speak informally with colleagues in other countries to prepare a proper MLA or extradition request. That new form of international cooperation in judicial cooperation is among the most important tools to develop, according to all the main actors in the UN CFT Sector, and it is recommended by the FATF in *FATF President's Paper: Anti-Money Laundering and Counter Terrorist Financing for Judges and Prosecutors*.[9]

Besides establishing and using formal channels, states can pave the way for international cooperation by raising the visibility of procedural requirements and fostering overall cooperation between counterparts. States can publicize information on the requirements for MLA and extradition so that an authority making a request is able to use them. Where capacity and resourcing allow, requested states should offer assistance in reviewing draft requests prior to formal submission to ensure they meet procedural requirements. Authorities should make use of avenues of cooperation outside the formal MLA process (such as contact points or liaison officers) prior to submitting the formal request.

Case management systems are also essential to effectively deal with incoming and ongoing requests in a timely manner. Such systems allow information to be managed in one repository while communicating with internal and external stakeholders.

Finally, international organizations and bodies can be leveraged for technical assistance and capacity building. As an example, the Organization of American States has tasked its Inter-American Committee against Terrorism (CICTE) with overcoming challenges related to the lack of dedicated terrorist financing resources and experience with managing international requests. The CICTE promotes cooperation and dialog among member states to prevent and combat terrorism and acts as a focal point to exchange experiences and good practices. The CICTE

---

[9] See http://www.fatf-gafi.org/publications/methodsandtrends/documents/jem-judges-2019.html.

circulates details on national points of contact in the Americas and on particular patterns related to terrorist financing and counterterrorism.

## Confidentiality and Privacy Protections—Overreliance and Overclassification of Intelligence

Due to the inherent link to national security information on individuals and groups involved in terrorism, terrorist financing cases are often subject to stringent confidentiality rules and/or security classifications. While confidentiality provisions and security restrictions should not be considered impediments (as they serve legitimate purposes), they can be obstructions if improperly applied or if exemptions are not permitted where justified. Habitual overly stringent application of secrecy and security measures can hamper terrorist financing enforcement efforts. Countries should be cognizant of ways to facilitate cooperation under these circumstances. Efforts are also needed to improve the utility of intelligence for criminal proceedings.

### *Challenges*

Confidentiality and privacy protections can impede or restrict cooperation and information sharing between and among jurisdictions. States will always reserve the right of discretion in sharing information about their own citizens with foreign countries. Some states have constitutional privacy protections that affect the extent and manner of information disclosure about their citizens. States cannot be reasonably expected to set aside such constitutional anchors. In other instances, protections and restrictions pertaining to banking secrecy or legal privileges also could impact the exchange of information domestically and across jurisdictions.

Furthermore, national security considerations sometimes prevent classified information from being shared—not only with foreign counterparts, but even with the defendant. Anecdotally, numerous reports show such provisions impeding investigations, but relatively little verified information is available about the frequency and extent of those impediments in CFT cases.

Elaborating on security classifications, countries and agencies seeking to obtain or share information with foreign counterparts are likely to encounter difficulties due to the national security implications of terrorism and counterterrorism efforts. Although information is shared internationally among intelligence agencies, the classified nature of such operations and relationships means little information is available on the quantity and use of such cooperation, or on the main modalities through which it occurs. Experience shows, however, that collaboration and information sharing between intelligence agencies and other bodies is limited, both domestically and internationally. Despite the importance of the relationship between law enforcement and intelligence agencies, this channel is often blocked for national security and confidentiality reasons. As a result, information relevant to a terrorist financing investigation may not be available or able to be shared with law enforcement and other competent authorities abroad. Even when intelligence can be shared, an additional challenge arises in identifying the appropriate secure transmission channel. In the experience of the Egmont Group, although diagonal information exchange through FIUs has proven effective and has been provided in a timely manner, intelligence services may not be fully aware of FIU capabilities for rapid international information exchange or protections FIUs can afford.

Intelligence sharing between and among intelligence agencies appears extensive. It is almost always carried out on a reciprocal bilateral basis, governed by exchange agreements that circumscribe the use and dissemination of such information. For such information to be disclosed or used in judicial proceedings, consent of the originating intelligence agency is required. Permission may be granted on a case-by-case basis, depending on the sensitivity of the information and whether the national interest of its release outweighs the potential harm from its disclosure.

Apart from the sensitivity of intelligence information and the sources from which it is derived, another impediment to its use in judicial proceedings arises from the fact that intelligence information is frequently obtained by means and from sources that may not meet procedural requirements law enforcement agencies would be obliged to follow when acquiring such information. In many, if not most states, lack of adherence to the necessary procedures would render such information inadmissible in judicial proceedings, even if the intelligence provider is willing to consent to its release.

## Good Practices

As per the FATF standard, a country's domestic authorities should cooperate to ensure AML/CFT requirements are compatible with data protection and privacy rules and other similar provisions (such as data security/localization). Where information is shared internationally, countries should not prohibit or place unduly restrictive conditions on the exchange of information or assistance in relation to laws that require reporting entities to maintain secrecy or confidentiality. Several countries have developed mechanisms that allow classified information to be accessed and shared (Box 6.4). Notably, the EU has developed legislation for intelligence agencies and law enforcement agencies in member states precisely for this purpose.

---

### Box 6.4. Sharing Intelligence Information—Country Examples

**United States:** The Patriot Act was amended in October 2001 to allow classified information to be shared when "a significant purpose" was to collect foreign intelligence. This amendment relaxed a requirement that the government had to reveal when its primary purpose was for reasons other than criminal prosecution. The Foreign Intelligence Surveillance Court of Review found that the 2001 statutory change made it clear that cooperative management of intelligence operations, considering both

### Box 6.4. *(continued)*

intelligence collection goals and criminal evidentiary purposes, was legitimate. Furthermore, the United States can rely on the Classified Information Procedures Act (CIPA), a statutory regime that allows for the protection of intelligence information in court proceedings. As a procedural statute, CIPA does not change the substantive rights of a defendant or the discovery obligations of the government, but rather it ensures protection of classified information after a criminal indictment becomes public. Such a regime is critical to the successful use of intelligence information in terrorist financing matters.

*France:* The system in place has the advantage of permitting pertinent facts resulting from intelligence activities to be admitted in criminal judicial proceedings when it meets certain conditions. Evidence collected through intelligence operations can be summarized and included in judicial investigative proceedings without having to specify the sources or methods of collection. It is the task of the professional magistrate to decide whether to consider the intelligence information as admissible evidence. Nevertheless, this information, standing alone, is not sufficient to justify a charge and must be supported by other elements.

Source: Authors.
Note: CIPA = Classified Information Procedures Act.

---

The use of intelligence information in cross-border judicial proceedings is a troublesome issue in national and international security investigations, particularly for terrorist financing investigations and prosecutions. Domestic authorities and the international community should expand efforts to find more ways to resolve these issues and to establish the admissibility of intelligence information domestically and across borders in certain narrowly defined cases while respecting due process as much as possible (see Box 6.5 for an example).

To the extent possible, countries should leverage secure platforms for the secure exchange of intelligence and information with foreign counterparts. INTERPOL's I-24/7, Europol's Secure Information Exchange Network Application (SIENA), and the Egmont Secure Web are useful information and intelligence exchange platforms that can handle restricted content on counterterrorism and terrorist financing.

### Box 6.5. Terrorist Finance Tracking Program

Following the 9/11 attacks, the US Department of the Treasury initiated the Terrorist Finance Tracking Program (TFTP), a powerful system used to identify, track, and pursue terrorists and their networks. The program essentially consists of the US Treasury issuing subpoenas to the Society for Worldwide Interbank Financial Telecommunication (SWIFT) to seek information on suspected international terrorists or their networks. Under the terms of the subpoenas, the government may only review information as

### Box 6.5. *(continued)*

part of specific terrorism investigations. Recognizing the importance of the TFTP in preventing terrorism and its financing in the EU and elsewhere, in 2016 the United States and the EU expanded the program through an agreement to facilitate direct exchange of information between Europol and financial intelligence units (FIUs) on requests for information by an FIU for a TFTP check.

The TFTP has provided valuable leads to EU member states, that have aided in the investigation of many of the most visible and violent terrorist attacks and attempted attacks of the past decade. As a recipient of information spontaneously disseminated by the US Treasury, Europol will inform member states of financial intelligence leads based upon an agreed procedure. The US Treasury, as the original owner of the intelligence data, must consent to sharing this data with the member states concerned. Europol facilitates an integrated response between Europol and relevant member states (and Eurojust when appropriate). Under this agreement, Europol cross-checks all financial intelligence against other databases to find or trigger hits with other investigations. The program includes controls and safeguards on the use and dissemination of data, as well as physical security arrangements for handling, to ensure the strict confidentiality of the data.

From 2016 to 2019, there were 14 requests for TFTP checks from 6 different EU FIUs. The low number of requests may be due to FIUs generally working directly with counterterrorism law enforcement agencies. TFTP checks led to almost 3,500 potential leads being shared with FIUs. In 2019, more than 3,200 potential leads were received and processed.

Source: Authors, based on the Terrorist Finance Tracking Program. https://home.treasury.gov/policy-issues/terrorism-and-illicit-finance/terrorist-finance-tracking-program-tftp

Note: EU = European Union; FIU = financial intelligence unit; SWIFT = Society for Worldwide Interbank Financial Telecommunication; TFTP = Terrorist Finance Tracking Program.

Securing and protecting intelligence information is essential to bolstering trust among counterparts and enhancing information exchange. Countries should make all the necessary efforts to protect national security data (Box 6.6). Operational measures should be in place to ensure that appropriate safeguards are applied, requests are handled in a confidential manner to protect the integrity of the process, and intelligence information is exchanged only for authorized purposes.

### Box 6.6. Data Protections in Global Initiatives

INTERPOL has a robust data protection mechanism in place, especially in the counterterrorism area. The Counterterrorism Intelligence Analysis File is INTERPOL's analytical tool that is employed to improve participating member states' capacity to identify terrorists, including foreign terrorist fighters. To ensure its data processing is secure and to encourage participating member states to provide high-value or sensitive information, INTERPOL maintains its stand-alone structure, with no connection to other databases, restricts access to authorized General Secretariat staff only, and gives member states substantial control over data they contribute.

### Box 6.6. *(continued)*

> Egmont Group members exchange financial intelligence using a secure network called the Egmont Secure Web (ESW). European Egmont members within the EU (and some third-party FIUs) can also exchange financial intelligence with EU FIUs via FIU.Net. FIU.Net allows for the exchange and sharing of joint case files and the pseudonymized matching of data in real time (using Match3 technology), and it provides a channel for cross-border reporting of suspicious transactions.
>
> Source: Authors.
> Note: ESW = Egmont Secure Web; EU = European Union; FIU = financial intelligence unit.

## Fragmentation of Information across Different Jurisdictions

The increasingly global nature of terrorism and the financing thereof makes understanding the full picture of any one terrorist organization and its activities, terrorist act, or terrorist financing scheme extremely challenging. Putting together the pieces of the entire story necessitates communication and cooperation with foreign counterparts who may possess information not available to other authorities. Only strong international cooperation can ensure that relevant authorities receive all of the information they need, and in the manner and form required, to successfully pursue criminal cases.

### *Challenges*

One of the main challenges in criminal investigations into terrorist financing relates to the difficulty of pursuing investigations and charges in other countries. For example, the November 2015 Paris attack required a terrorist financing investigation across several jurisdictions, including analysis of transactions the attackers had attempted to make while traveling from Syria to France through Turkey (before entering the EU in Greece) and Italy. Successful terrorist financing disruption and enforcement requires timely collection and analysis of intelligence and information which may be scattered across different countries and among different national agencies. Fragmentation of information across different jurisdictions remains a significant challenge.

The transnational nature of terrorism and terrorist financing and the fragmentation of information among domestic authorities limit the visibility of the entirety of the evidence or intelligence for any given agency (or jurisdiction). Even when the activities of a terrorist group are confined to one jurisdiction or territory, its financial infrastructure could be global. To complicate matters further, the intensification of the nexus between organized crime and terrorism implicates agencies that may not traditionally have a CFT mandate. Linkages and insights from disparate pieces can be forged only with the aid of other national agencies and foreign counterparts. This limitation is amplified at the international level, where agencies need to cooperate not only with their foreign counterparts but also with foreign agencies of a different nature. Data restriction and privacy rules can present additional barriers that if not overcome can prevent terrorist financing intelligence from being shared with national and international partners.

Challenges also exist regarding the type of information needed for terrorist financing cases (intelligence, bank records, information on companies), which may be held by different agencies. Although nonjudicial types of international cooperation typically occur between two counterparts of the same nature (for example, police-to-police), for judicial forms of assistance, the request usually goes through a national contact point, which then needs to obtain the information or an action from some other agency. Even for nonjudicial forms of cooperation, the requested peer agency may not hold or have direct access to the requested information. As such, issues of poor domestic cooperation or difficulties that the requested agency faces in obtaining information in a timely manner may also affect international cooperation and efforts to disrupt and sanction terrorist activities.

Fragmentation of terrorist financing intelligence dissemination is also apparent among specialized international bodies. Despite proactive attempts by the international community to improve information exchanges (for example, INTERPOL for law enforcement, World Customs Organization for customs, and the Egmont Group for FIUs), cooperation between international bodies is also limited because the respective organizations have different roles, mandates, priorities, and governance structures. In addition, the exponential growth of data managed by the private sector, along with technical innovations, have driven further fragmentation of financial information across the world.

## Good Practices

Given the scattered nature of terrorist financing intelligence across regions, it is crucial that law enforcement authorities can access all available sources. Accordingly, they should use international cooperation channels to deliver appropriate information, financial intelligence, and evidence needed to facilitate action against terrorist financiers. In some countries (for example, the United States), the solution to fragmentation of information has been the creation of fusion centers between law enforcement agencies to share resources, expertise, and information for detecting criminal and terrorist activity. The goal is to integrate the information held by each agency to prevent security gaps due to lack of communication.

Bilateral agreements between law enforcement agencies can provide the legal basis for cooperation on joint operations, information sharing, and cross-border police measures such as surveillance, controlled delivery, and hot pursuit (that guarantees a police measure in one jurisdiction has legitimacy in another). Although most of these agreements are executed between neighboring states for better control of shared borders, geographically remote states enter into such agreements for different purposes. These agreements provide a means for institutional cooperation, and they form a foundation for cooperation between responsible competent authorities. Some law enforcement agencies will also communicate on a reciprocal or voluntary basis to expedite the exchange of information and evidence (Box 6.7).

> **Box 6.7. Good Practice in Enhancing Bilateral Cooperation—Specialized Liaison Officers**
>
> In some jurisdictions, law enforcement can establish a *standing* or *ad hoc* body composed of international police *attachés* deployed to the host state to build bilateral trust and share information. Such initiatives can also facilitate robust multilateral interactions among police attachés.
>
> *Liaison officers* deployed to partner organizations or police attachés in foreign missions can also be used as a standing channel to share information or to facilitate investigations and other police measures, including the extradition of fugitives. The scope of cooperation and the role of these officers vary depending on the legal framework, priorities, and relations of the countries involved. Some countries deploy several officers with different areas of expertise to the same destination, including counterterrorism and organized crime. After the 2016 Brussels attacks, for example, officers in Belgium conducted robust intelligence exchange and liaison work, which led to the detection, prosecution, and conviction of terrorist financiers.
>
> Source: Authors.

Bilateral cooperation on an investigation offers only a small piece of the total picture, given the global nature of modern terrorism. Bilateral cooperation does not capture the actual size and reach of a possible network, and it misses crucial aspects, such as the interconnectedness of individual activities. Multilateral international cooperation is often necessary and can be facilitated by regional and global platforms like INTERPOL, Europol (the EU's law enforcement agency), and the Egmont Group (for finance intelligence units).

International and regional forums provide platforms for the exchange and dissemination of information as well as analytical and operational support by identifying links between related cases, coordinating investigations and the provision of technical and forensic expertise. The INTERPOL I-24/7 network enables authorized users to send and receive messages with counterparts across the globe (Box 6.8). Delivering messages on pending cases in real time across an organization with near-universal membership is particularly beneficial given the characteristics of terrorist financing. Europol also hosts the secure SIENA platform for members to exchange information. The G7 24/7 Cybercrime Network also enables the exchange of cyber information in emergency situations or when delays in sharing evidence would compromise an investigation.

> **Box 6.8. INTERPOL and Europol Initiatives**
>
> **I-24/7**
>
> INTERPOL operates a secure global communication system known as I-24/7. Each member country hosts an INTERPOL National Central Bureau, which connects their national law enforcement with counterparts in other countries and with the INTERPOL Secretariat through I-24/7. INTERPOL is working closely with its member states to extend the access rights of I-24/7 beyond national central bureaus to not only border

### Box 6.8. *(continued)*

checkpoints or seaports but also specialized investigation units and government authorities, including FIUs. This I-24/7 extension initiative can help the beneficiary entity access selected INTERPOL databases on a real-time basis. In the context of terrorist financing, I-24/7 access at border checkpoints or in airports can help detect fund flows in the informal sector, including cross-border cash smuggling for terrorist financing or money laundering.

### Databases

INTERPOL also allows its members to cross-check intelligence against its 17 databases in seven areas (notices, individuals, forensics, travel and official documents, stolen property, firearms, and organized crime networks). Law enforcement of member states have real-time access to these databases as part of their investigations using I-24/7. In terrorist financing cases, information contained in these databases may help develop or trigger investigations by connecting fragmented leads. For example, the Stolen and Lost Travel Documents database, containing around 89 million records contributed by member states, can improve the detection of terrorist financing and other financial crimes involving transactions with stolen or lost travel documents.

Europol also hosts several databases relevant to terrorist financing matters, one on counterterrorism and another on serious organized crime. Both databases contain intelligence provided by Europol partners (collected through SIENA, the Secure Information Exchange Network Application) and treated by analysts and specialists. Although the Europol membership is mostly law enforcement, some other competent authorities (such as FIUs and customs) can also exchange information through Europol's secure platform.

### INTERPOL Notices

INTERPOL also disseminates information through international alerts to law enforcement agencies across the globe through its color-coded Notice system. Notices are generated by National Central Bureaus (NCBs) or authorized international entities and disseminated to all 194 INTERPOL member states. Notices can also be used by the UNSC to warn that certain individuals and entities face UN Sanctions. The most relevant Notices in the terrorist financing context are Red Notices (to seek wanted persons), Purple Notices (to share modus operandi), and Orange Notices (to warn of an imminent threat). Member countries or authorized international entities may also disseminate information directly to a country or countries of their choice by means of another alert mechanism (Diffusion).

### Europol SIENA

SIENA has a special application (CT SIENA) developed to connect exclusively counterterrorism units to exchange counterterrorism information between member states as well as third parties. By the end of 2016, 90 percent of all member states and 46 counterterrorism authorities were connected to a dedicated SIENA counterterrorism environment.

### Europol Financial Intelligence Public Private Partnership (EFIPPP)

The EFIPPP was set up in December 2017. It brings together 21 international financial institutions with an international footprint. The first goal of the EFIPPP is to build a

## Box 6.8. *(continued)*

common intelligence picture and understanding of threats and risks, notably through the definition of risk indicators. Where Europol cannot directly share tactical information with financial institutions, information sharing between all participants in this transnational public–private partnership is possible when no personal data are involved.

The EFIPPP has issued detailed typologies based on recent investigations carried out by Europol and competent authorities to improve the detection of suspicious transactions.

Source: Authors.

Note: EFIPPP = Europol Financial Intelligence Public Private Partnership; FIU = financial intelligence unit; NCB = National Central Bureau; SIENA = Secure Information Exchange Network Application; UNSC = UN Security Council.

FIUs can exchange information through reciprocity or mutual agreement, either upon request or spontaneously. The global platform with the widest membership base is the Egmont Group, comprising 166 FIUs. Members exchange expertise and financial intelligence using the ESW, a secure electronic communication system that allows encrypted sharing of emails and financial intelligence, as well as other information of interest (see also Box 6.6).

Financial intelligence can also feed into international investigative efforts. FIUs are investing effort to establish more direct/electronic ways to share information with law enforcement agencies. Persons of interest for an FIU in terrorist financing can be placed in an anonymized list. These lists are matched on a daily basis with new suspicious transaction reports, circulated by the participating FIUs in the EU. In this way, EU-based FIUs can monitor the financial activities of relevant persons in other member states (when these are reported). The Egmont Group FIUs also invest significant effort to improve their analytical IT tools to identify and connect payments and networks related to terrorist financing (Box 6.9). Some are experimenting with new technologies such as graph analytics to identify missing links in already existing networks. These innovations can fill information gaps in specific cases, and their successful implementation will enhance the ability of FIUs to analyze terrorist financing networks and risks.

## Box 6.9. Egmont Group ISIL Projects

In February 2015, the Egmont Group launched Phase I of the Egmont ISIL Project to develop financial profiles, indicators, and typologies of suspected foreign terrorist fighters associated with the Islamic State of Iraq and the Levant (ISIL), Al-Nusra Front, and other affiliates or splinter groups of ISIL and Al-Qaida.

A year later, project members used the recommendations from Phase I to launch a second phase with the same goals but with improved collaboration practices and a focus on facilitation networks. Among the main objectives was to identify and share CFT-related financial intelligence multilaterally. In addition, the operational information and analysis have contributed to several urgent investigations and the addition of ISIL financial facilitators on national or international asset-freezing lists.

### Box 6.9. *(continued)*

> In July 2019, the Egmont Group finalized its project dedicated to small cells and lone-actor terrorism and terrorist financing activities. Its Public Summary is available on the Egmont Group public website: https://egmontgroup.org/en/content/new-publication-counter-terrorist-financing-project-lone-actors-and-small-cells-public.
>
> Source: Authors, based on the Egmont Group website: https://egmontgroup.org/.
> Note: CFT = combating the financing of terrorism; ISIL = the Islamic State of Iraq and the Levant.

Global platforms can also facilitate global indirect cooperation. In 2018, INTERPOL and a member state pioneered a proof of concept for an information-sharing operation called FIN-LEX (finance to law enforcement exchange) to cross-check data in the context of CFT. The initiative was conducted as a test phase for developing a sustainable model for "diagonal" information sharing between INTERPOL and its noncounterpart, an FIU. INTERPOL received a list of over 30,000 nominal data points on individuals suspected of terrorism-related activities from the participating country's FIU. INTERPOL cross-checks against its database on Notices and stolen and lost travel documents generated a substantial number of hits related to 24 member states. INTERPOL Operation CAPTIVE is a CFT project on global data-sharing among law enforcement and noncounterparts: the FIU in the United Kingdom and two financial institutions. This operation is designed to allow INTERPOL to screen historical transaction data from the private sector against the organization's databases on travel documents, including stolen documents and those associated with Notices. The cross-check results are shared with the participating financial institutions so that they can file suspicious activity reports to the UK FIU, completing the flow of sanitized information from INTERPOL to the FIU via the private sector.

Countries have also collaborated on their own multilateral initiatives to address threats specific to a particular region or related to a specific group (6.10). These initiatives can be platforms for information sharing, joint disruption, or enforcement efforts, or they can be an avenue for providing technical assistance.

### Box 6.10. Multilateral CFT-Related Initiatives

**Southeast Asia Counter-Terrorism Financing Working Group (SEA CTFWG)**

The SEA CTFWG, composed of the ASEAN countries, coordinates information sharing among FIUs and other regional agencies that have a role in CFT. Collectively, intelligence generated through this initiative provides regional authorities and partners with greater insights into the movement and tracking of funds suspected to be linked to terrorist financing.

Box 6.10. *(continued)*

> **Terrorist Financing Targeting Center (TFTC)**
>
> The TFTC is a multilateral partnership between the United States and six Gulf Cooperation Council countries in combating the financing of terrorism. Engagements include (1) identifying, tracking, and sharing information about terrorist financing networks; (2) coordinating joint disruptive actions; and (3) offering capacity-building assistance. Since its inception in May 2017, TFTC has issued five rounds of designations, sanctioning a total of 67 individuals and entities. These tranches have targeted key members of ISIL in Yemen, AQAP, IRGC-QF, the Taliban, Hizballah, and the Basij Resistance Force (Basij).
>
> Source: Authors.
> Note: ASEAN = Association of Southeast Asian Nations; AQAP = Al-Qaida in the Arabian Peninsula; CFT = combating the financing of terrorism; FIU = financial intelligence unit; IRGC-QF = Iran's Islamic Revolutionary Guard Corps Quds Force; ISIL = Islamic State of Iraq and the Levant; SEA CTFWG = Southeast Asia Counter-Terrorism Financing Working Group; TFTC = Terrorist Financing Targeting Center.

Similarly, judicial authorities have developed initiatives to support and facilitate cooperation with foreign counterparts. Although MLA is generally a bilateral process, for terrorist financing cases, the need to trace and track financial transactions or cash-courier operations across multiple countries requires MLA to be taken not only on a bilateral basis but also on a multilateral basis.

In this respect, the EU has dedicated significant effort to increase simultaneous MLA actions among countries. Eurojust (composed of representatives from all the prosecution services of EU countries) aims to improve the efficiency of MLA by enhancing coordination and information sharing among its members. Even though it is a voluntary instrument that does not create binding obligations, the Harare Scheme provides a framework for the provision of MLA among members. The Scheme lays out specific recommendations and commentaries, which can be helpful in the preparation of or response to MLA requests. In addition, the new European Investigative Order (EIO), aimed at facilitating evidence gathering in the EU, is recognized as a major step forward in judicial cooperation within the EU. The EIO has no dual criminality requirement and has become the main legal tool to gather transborder evidence. However, even the EIO could be further improved through rules that would allow the mutual admissibility of evidence gathered using the EIO.

# CONCLUSION

International cooperation is critical to the success of domestic counterterrorism and CFT efforts. However, in the context of terrorist financing, it can be extremely challenging for myriad reasons, including lack of trust among partners, conflicting legal regimes, rule-of-law weaknesses, capacity constraints, and insufficient information sharing and prioritization (both on a domestic and international level). Despite a comprehensive international framework underpinning international cooperation in terrorist financing and counterterrorism matters, a lack of consensus on critical issues and inconsistent national application continue to create obstacles in practice. Furthermore, understanding or insight into terrorist financing schemes can be fragmented due to insufficient "diagonal" cooperation between non-like counterparts. Security classifications of relevant information can impede the ability of authorities to cooperate both domestically and with foreign counterparts. These obstacles can be overcome with effective communication and coordination. Good domestic and international practices generally tend to promote information sharing and cooperation—for instance, through bilateral and multilateral agreements and secure platforms, along with respect for fundamental human rights. To be effective, such practices also must start and be promoted at the domestic level.

## REFERENCES

Bassiouni, Cherif. 2008. *International Criminal Law, Volume II*. 3rd edition. Martinus Nijhoff Publishers.
The International Convention for the Suppression of the Financing of Terrorism (UN CFT Convention). 1999.
The United Nations Convention against Transnational Organized Crime (UNTOC). 2000.

## RESOURCES

Acharya, Arabinda. 2009. *Targeting Terrorist Financing: International Cooperation and New Regimes*. New York: Routledge.
Argomaniz, Javier, Oldrich Bures, and Christian Kaunert. 2015. "A Decade of EU Counter-Terrorism and Intelligence: A Critical Assessment." *Intelligence and National Security* 30, nos. 2–3: 191–206.
Brzoska, Michael. 2011. "The Role of Effectiveness and Efficiency in the European Union's Counterterrorism Policy: The Case of Terrorist Financing." Economics of Security Working Paper, No. 51.
Deflem, Mathieu, 2007. "International Police Cooperation against Terrorism: INTERPOL and Europol in Comparison." *Understanding and Responding to Terrorism* 19.
Financial Action Task Force (FATF). 2015. *Emerging Terrorist Financing Risks*. Paris.
Financial Action Task Force (FATF). 2018. *Terrorist Financing Disruption Strategies*. Paris.
Stephens, Tim. 2004. "International Criminal Law and the Response to International Terrorism." 27 U.N.S.W.L.J. 454.
Stojanovski, Sasho M., Metodija Dojchinovski, and Biljana M. Stefanova. "The Role of INTERPOL Dealing with Crime and Terrorism." *DANI ARČIBALDA RAJSA ARCHIBALD REISS DAYS*: 179.
Verdugo-Yepes, Concepcion. 2008. "Enhancing International Cooperation in the Fight Against the Financing of Terrorism." *Journal of Global Change and Governance* 1 (3).

# Index

*Boxes, figures, notes, and tables are indicated by b, f, n, and t following the page numbers.*

### A
administrative delisting requests. *See* delisting
Albania, mutual evaluation report of, 99*b*
Al-Qaida
    ISIL (Da'esh) and Al-Qaida Sanctions List, 120, 120*n*17, 122, 148–149
    Jemaah Islamiah network in Indonesia and, 102
    targeted financial sanctions against, 117
    UNSCR on, 95
Angel Garcia, Miguel, 153
anonymity of terrorist financers, 46, 47–48, 57, 144
artificial intelligence (AI), 57
assets. *See also* targeted financial sanctions; *specific asset types*
    asset flight after sanctions, 121, 124, 129, 136–137, 137*nn*48–50
    terrorist financing and, 24–28, 71, 91, 91*n*2, 114*n*2
Australia
    financial information-sharing partnerships, 76*b*
    mutual evaluation report of, 98–99
    public-private partnerships for information sharing, 56, 56*n*2
automated account and transaction monitoring, 145, 145*nn*57–58

### B
Bangladesh, disruption of terrorism financing in, 109*b*
Bartlett, Brent, 20, 21*f*
Belgium, Brussels attacks (2016), 172*b*
beneficial ownership identification, 48, 129–130, 129*nn*35–36
big data, 57
bilateral operational information, 85
biometrics, 57
Brauders, Dermot, 153
Brussels attacks (2016), 172*b*

### C
Canada
    financial information-sharing partnerships, 76*b*
    FINTRAC FIU in, 77*b*
cash. *See also* informal financial sector
    cultural preferences for, 51
    storing, risks of, 117, 117*n*13
    terrorist financing investigations and, 70
    terrorist financing prevention and, 41, 50
    terrorist financing risk assessments and, 16
charities. *See* nonprofit organizations
CICTE (Inter-American Committee against Terrorism), 165–166
circumstantial evidence, 101, 106, 107*b*
classified information
    barriers to information sharing and, 82–83
    delisting and, 125
    disseminating results of risk assessments and, 36
    facilitating generation and sharing of, 133–134
    international cooperation and, 166–167, 167–168*b*
    limitations on terrorist financing prevention and, 51
    PPPs and reclassified identification information use, 76
    protocols for use of, 35
    terrorist financing intelligence, sharing, 72
collaborations. *See also* information sharing; international cooperation to combat terrorist financing; public-private partnerships
    for financial intelligence analyses, 81
    international conventions and treaties for, 154–155*b*

collaborations (*continued*)
  multilateral and regional operational working groups, 85–86
  multilateral CFT-related initiatives, 175–176*b*
  shared learning and, 75
  targeted financial sanctions and, 119
collaborative analytics, 58
compliance officers and systems, 16–17, 16*n*22, 54, 56
confidentiality. *See* classified information; privacy rights and protections
Convention for the Suppression of Terrorism (Egypt, 1998), 95–96, 95*n*8, 96*n*9
corruption, 27, 82, 163
Counterterrorism Intelligence Analysis File of INTERPOL, 169*b*
criminal networks, 117*n*12. *See also* money laundering
cross-border declarations and disclosures, 26
cross-border information exchange, 44, 85
cross-border smuggling, 26–27
cross-border wire transfers, 73
crowdfunding platforms, 76, 77*b*
cryptocurrencies, 71, 143*n*56, 144
cryptography, 57
customer identification and profiling, 46, 48
customs and border agencies, 15–16, 26–27, 50, 85
Cybercrime Network of G-7, 172

## D

data collection. *See also* intelligence exchange platforms
  financial intelligence cycle and, 67–69, 68*f*
  interoperability among IT systems and, 70
  for use as evidence, 83
data for terrorist financing risk assessments
  challenges, 28
  scenario analyses and, 32–33, 32*b*, 34*b*
  sharing, 29, 29*t*
  speculative and "what if" methods, 30, 30–31*t*, 31*b*
  use perceptions and qualitative material, 29–30, 30*n*33
  using best available, 28
data mining, 57
data pooling, 58
data protection mechanisms, 169–170*b*
data quality issues, 72, 77
data restrictions, 171
Dawe, Steve, 1
deconflicting false positives, 147*n*60
delisting
  challenges, 148–149, 148*nn*61–62
  defined, 115, 115*n*6
  good practices for, 149–151
  requirements for, 118
  UNSCR 1267 and, 122
  UNSCR 1373 and, 125, 125*n*29
Denmark
  disruption of terrorism financing in, 109*b*
  mutual evaluation report of, 100
  proving intent in, 102, 104–105*b*
deportation of foreign terrorist fighters, 108, 108*b*
deradicalization, 108, 109*b*
designated nonfinancial businesses and professions (DNFBPs), 21–22, 21*n*27, 63
designated persons and entities. *See* targeted financial sanctions
Digest of Terrorist Cases (UNODC), 160
disruption of terrorism financing, 107–108, 108–109*b*
dissemination of information
  financial intelligence to counter terrorist financing and, 81–86
  fragmentation of, 171
  PPPs for, 36, 36*n*38
  terrorist financing risk assessments and, 35–36
distributed ledger technology, 57
domestic asset freezing measures, 123–126, 125*b*
domestication of sanctions, 137–140
domestic awareness-raising campaigns for sanctions, 132–133
domestic delisting, 149–150
Donovan, Terence, 41

dual criminality, 158, 158*n*5, 162–164, 163*b*, 176
due process, 123, 148, 158

## E

EFIPPP (Europol Financial Intelligence Public Private Partnership), 173–174*b*
Egmont Group
    Emergency Terrorist Financing Response Checklist of, 80
    FIU information sharing and, 174
    on information exchanges through FIUs, 167
    information-sharing platform of, 86, 157, 168, 170*b*
    international cooperation and, 156
    on lone actors and small cells, 74–75*b*
    member state requirements of, 159
    Principles for Information Exchange, 84
    role of, 66
Egmont Group ISIL Project, 174–175*b*
Egmont Information Exchange Working Group, 74–75*b*
Egmont Secure Web (ESW), 86, 157, 168, 170*b*
Egmont Tactical and Strategic Analysis Courses, 67
Egypt, Convention for the Suppression of Terrorism (1998), 95–96, 95*n*8, 96*n*9
EIO (European Investigative Order), 176
electronic money institutions, 45–46
El Khoury, Chady, 89
Emergency Terrorist Financing Response Checklist of Egmont Group, 80
emerging payment services, 50, 70
encryption, 86
enhanced monitoring, 49
equities checks, 115, 115*n*8
EU MLA Convention (2000), 163–164
Eurojust, 176
European Investigative Order (EIO), 176
European Union (EU). *See also specific countries*
    General Data Protection Regulation, 44
    simultaneous MLA actions in, 176
    Terrorist Finance Tracking Program and, 169*b*

Europol
    databases of, 173*b*
    initiatives of, 173–174*b*
    Secure Information Exchange Network Application, 86, 168, 172, 173*b*
    STRs, rates of use, 41, 54
    Terrorist Finance Tracking Program and, 169*b*
    terrorist financing reports, rates of use, 71
Europol Financial Intelligence Public Private Partnership (EFIPPP), 173–174*b*
Euskadi Ta Askatasuna in Spain, 100
evidence
    circumstantial, 101, 106, 107*b*
    financial intelligence as, 65, 83
    judicial forms of international cooperation and, 158
    lack of, 99, 101, 107
    proving intent and, 104–105*b*
    targeted financial sanctions and, 116, 130
exemptions for targeted financial sanctions, 121–122, 121*n*21, 124–125
explosives, 75*b*
extradition, 156–161, 160*n*6, 165

## F

FARC, 102
FATF (Financial Action Task Force). *See also* FATF Methodology; FATF Recommendations; mutual evaluation reports; terrorist financing risk assessments
    on beneficial owners, 129*n*35
    on dual criminality, 162
    funds or other assets, defined, 114*n*2
    *Guidance on AML/CFT Related Data and Statistics*, 33
    *Guidance on Criminalising Terrorist Financing*, 101
    on implementation without delay of sanctions, 136
    on international cooperation, 155
    *National ML and TF Risk Assessment*, 6
    nonprofit risk assessment and, 4*n*5

FATF (Financial Action Task Force)
  (*continued*)
  purpose of, 2
  *Stocktake on Data Pooling,
    Collaborative Analytics, and Data
    Protection,* 58
  targeted financial sanctions and, 115,
    115n5
  *Third Round of AML/CFT Mutual
    Evaluations,* 127, 127n33, 128t
FATF Methodology
  on FIUs and information sharing, 73,
    84, 157n3
  on FIUs and requisite authority, 80
  international norms and practices, 66
  purpose of, 5
*FATF President's Paper: Anti-Money
  Laundering and Counter
  Terrorist Financing for Judges and
  Prosecutors,* 165
FATF Recommendations
  on delisting process, 148–151
  FIU effectiveness and, 66, 66f
  on information sharing, 53, 73
  on international cooperation, 155–156
  MER comparative analysis on IO.9, 94
  on MVTS licensing, 74
  on reporting suspicious transactions, 66
  targeted financial sanctions and, 121,
    127–130, 127nn32–33, 128t
  terrorist act defined by, 92–93
  terrorist financing defined by, 90–92,
    91n1
  on understanding terrorist financing
    risk, 4
  on virtual assets, 114n2
FATF-Style Regional Bodies (FSRBs), 5,
  86, 129, 155–156
financial exclusion, 41, 51
financial information-sharing
  partnerships, 76b
Financial Intelligence Consultative
  Group, 86, 86n4
financial intelligence to counter terrorist
  financing, 63–88
  as added-value contribution, 64–65
  analyses of financial information and,
    77–81
  challenges, 69–72

dissemination and use of, 81–86
financial intelligence cycle, 67–69, 68f
good practices for, 72–77, 74–77b
international norms and practices,
  65–66, 67f
mapping terrorist financing networks
  with, 118–119
financial intelligence units (FIUs). *See also*
  Egmont Group
collaborations with CFT agencies, 81
dissemination of financial intelligence
  and, 81–82
establishment of, 66
financial intelligence cycle and, 67
information sharing with, 65, 70, 73,
  83–84, 157, 170b
international cooperation and, 156–
  157, 167, 174–175
limitations of, 78
mandate and authority of, 72, 80, 85
private sector expectations and, 44
resource allocation to, 79–80
targeted risk indicators of terrorist
  financing, provision of, 74–76
terrorist financing reports, rates of, 71
financial investigations, 64–65, 64n1
financial sector. *See also* private sector
  prevention of terrorist financing
abuse of, 4, 9–10, 10n13, 45–46
assessing terrorist use of, 19–24
complicit in terrorist financing
  activities, 70
international service providers, 44
reporting entities, enhancing
  effectiveness of, 42–46
targeted financial sanctions,
  inconsistent implementation of,
  141–147, 141n52
terrorist vulnerability analysis and,
  13, 15
Finland, proving intent in, 102–103,
  103–104b
FIN-LEX (finance to law enforcement
  exchange) of INTERPOL, 175
FINTRAC (FIU Canada), 77b
firearms, 75b
FIUNET, 86
FIUs. *See* financial intelligence units
Five Eyes, 86

foreign open-source information, 33
foreign terrorist fighters (FTFs)
  defined, 18n24
  deportation of, 108, 108b
  financing travel of, 23, 92, 99b
  information sources on, 33, 33n37
  investigative techniques for, 96–98, 100
  terrorist financing risk and, 18
*Forskningsinstitutt* (FFI), 96–97, 96n12
France
  international intelligence sharing and, 168b
  Paris attacks, 98, 170
frozen assets. *See* targeted financial sanctions
FSRBs (FATF-Style Regional Bodies), 5, 86, 129, 155–156
funds or other assets, 24–28, 71, 91, 91n2, 114n2. *See also* targeted financial sanctions

## G

G-5 (Group of 5) Sahel Joint Forces, 86
G-7 (Group of 7), 172
G-20 (Group of 20), 66
General Data Protection Regulation of EU, 44
Germany
  Germany-United States bilateral extradition treaty, 160, 160n6
  public-private partnerships for information sharing, 56, 56n2
Global FAFT, 5
Global Initiative Against Transnational Organized Crime, 97
globalization, 154
Global Terrorism Database, 33
Greece, disruption of terrorism financing in, 109b
*Guidance on AML/CFT Related Data and Statistics* (FATF), 33
*Guidance on Criminalising Terrorist Financing* (FATF), 101
Gulf Cooperation Council, 176b
guns, 75b

## H

Hamadei, Mohammed, 160n6
Hamas, 95
Harare Scheme (Scheme Relating to Mutual Legal Assistance in Criminal Matters within the Commonwealth), 163, 176
harmonization, 108, 109b
*hawala* arrangements, 50
Hizballah, 95
Hong Kong SAR, financial information-sharing partnerships, 76b
humanitarian project funding, 102, 103b
human rights, 44, 51, 73–74, 159, 161

## I

I-24/7 secure platform of INTERPOL, 168, 172, 172–173b
ICSFT (1999). *See* International Convention for the Suppression of the Financing of Terrorism
IMF (International Monetary Fund), 126–127, 129
immigration, 27, 27n31
implementation without delay of sanctions, 121, 135–141, 136n47
incitement to commit a terrorist act, 123
Indonesia, Jemaah Islamiah network in, 102
informal financial sector. *See also* cash; money or value transfer services
  avoiding targeted financial sanctions through, 117, 117n12
  information gap from, 73–74
  terrorist financing risk assessments and, 16
  terrorist financing risk associated with other assets and informality, 24–28
  terrorist organizations' use of, 97
information sharing. *See also* classified information; cross-border information exchange; intelligence exchange platforms; international cooperation to combat terrorist financing
  corruption and lack of trust, 82
  data for terrorist financing risk assessments, 29, 29n32, 29t
  financial information-sharing partnerships, 76b
  for financial intelligence, 65, 72–73, 81–86

information sharing (*continued*)
  with international counterparts, 83–84
  Operation CAPTIVE of INTERPOL and, 175
  platforms for, 85–86
  privacy protections and, 44
  private sector limitations on, 41, 52–54
  public-private partnerships for, 56
  structural barriers to, 51
  targeted financial sanctions and, 119, 131–132, 133–134
  targeted risk indicators of terrorist financing and, 74–76
  technological innovations for, 58
  terrorism risk assessments and, 29
  trust and, 56
information silos, 57, 82, 84–85
information sources
  diversity and accessibility of, 69–70
  facilitating access to, 72–73
  financial intelligence cycle and, 67–69, 68*f*
inherent risk, 11
integrated terrorism investigative teams, 84–85
intelligence community and law enforcement. *See also* information sharing
  financial intelligence use and, 65, 67–69, 83
  FIUs, coordination with, 66
  fusion centers for information sharing among, 171
  information silos and, 82
  international cooperation and, 156–157, 157*n*2, 167
  liaison officers, 172*b*
  mapping terrorist financing networks, 118–119
  public-private partnerships and, 56
  resource allocation to, 79–80
  secure communications technology and, 57
  targeted risk indicators of terrorist financing, provision of, 74
  terrorist financing risk assessments and, 15–16
intelligence exchange platforms, 86, 157, 168, 172, 172–173*b*

intent, proving, 89, 101–103, 103–105*b*
Inter-American Committee against Terrorism (CICTE), 165–166
International Convention for the Suppression of the Financing of Terrorism (ICSFT, 1999)
  domestic implementation of, 159, 161–162, 161*b*
  international norms and practices, 66
  overview, 154–155*b*
  targeted financial sanctions and, 116*n*10
  on terrorist financing offenses, 91–93, 91*n*4, 92*n*5, 96, 96*n*11
international cooperation to combat terrorist financing, 153–177
  capacity and mandates for, 164–166
  changing global challenge and, 154–156
  confidentiality and privacy protections, 166–169
  conflicting legal regimes and, 160–164
  conventions, treaties, and resolutions for, 154–155*b*
  data protection mechanisms and, 169–170*b*
  dual criminality requirements in MLA treaties, 163*b*
  Egmont Group ISIL Project, 174–175*b*
  exchanging information and, 83–84, 85, 167–168*b*
  fragmentation of information and, 170–176
  INTERPOL and Europol initiatives, 172–174*b*
  nonjudicial and judicial forms of, 156–158
  Parliamentary Assembly of the Mediterranean, 161*b*
  Southeast Asia Counter-Terrorism Financing Working Group, 175–176*b*
  specialized liaison officers and, 172*b*
  targeted financial sanctions and, 119
  Terrorist Finance Tracking Program and, 168–169*b*
  trust and confidence, 159–160

International Criminal Police
 Organization. *See* INTERPOL
International Monetary Fund (IMF),
 126–127, 129
international norms and standards, 65–
 66, 67*f*. *See also* FATF
International Organization for
 Standardization (ISO), 9, 9*n*11
international regulations, 90–93
international vs. national targeted
 financial sanctions, 119–130, 128*t*
INTERPOL (International Criminal
 Police Organization)
 databases of, 33*n*37, 173*b*
 data protection mechanisms of,
 169–170*b*
 FIN-LEX (finance to law enforcement
 exchange), 175
 I-24/7 secure platform, 86, 168, 172,
 172–173*b*
 judicial forms of international
 cooperation and, 158
 National Central Bureau of, 73
 Notice system, 173*b*
 Operation CAPTIVE, 175
 *World Atlas of Illicit Flows,* 97
investigation, prosecution, and sanction
 of terrorist financiers, 89–111. *See
 also* targeted financial sanctions
 defining terrorist financing and
 terrorism, 94–96
 disruption measures when conviction
 fails, 107–108, 108–109*b*
 financing travel to conflict zones, 99*b*
 implementation status, 93–94
 international regulation and, 90–93
 investigative techniques and, 96–101
 prosecution challenges, 101–106,
 103–105*b*, 107*b*
Ireland, PPPs for information sharing,
 56, 56*n*2
Islamic State of Iraq and the Levant (ISIL)
 cash storage facilities, bombing of,
 117*n*13
 Egmont ISIL Project and, 174–175*b*
 ISIL (Da'esh) and Al-Qaida Sanctions
 List, 120, 120*n*17, 122, 148–149
 strategic analysis of financing, 65
 UNSCR on, 95

ISO (International Organization for
 Standardization), 9, 9*n*11
Italy, deportation of foreign terrorist
 fighters from, 108*b*

**J**
Jemaah Islamiah, 102
jihadi terrorists, 96–97, 102
joint designations, 134, 134*n*42
joint investigations, 157
joint task forces, 56, 81
joint trainings, 75
judicial forms of international
 cooperation, 156–158, 160–164

**K**
Kao, Kathleen, 153
Know Your Customer utilities, 41, 46,
 48, 57
Krumov, Nedko, 153

**L**
Laborde, Jean-Paul, 153
Lando, Sabrina, 63
Landry, Marilyne, 63
law enforcement. *See* intelligence
 community and law enforcement
learning development opportunities, 75
Legal Entity Identifiers, 57
legal regimes and procedural hurdles,
 160–164
liaison officers, 172*b*
liberation movements, 95–96
Lockerbie Disaster (1988), 164
Lombardo, Giuseppe, 89
lone actor terrorists. *See* small cell and
 lone actor terrorists
low-value transfers, 24–28, 45

**M**
machine learning, 57
Malaysia
 disruption of terrorism financing
 in, 109*b*
 public support for technological
 innovations, 58
Manual on CFT MLA and Extradition
 (UNODC), 165
MERs. *See* mutual evaluation reports

metadata, 77–78, 77n3
money laundering
  financial system, use of, 10, 10n13
  smuggling and, 27
  terrorist financing risk assessments and, 1, 13–15, 13n17
  terrorist financing vulnerabilities similar to, 29n32
money or value transfer services (MVTS), 27–28, 50, 70, 73–74. *See also* informal financial sector
multilateral operational working groups, 85–86
Murr, Arz, 41
mutual evaluation reports (MERs)
  of Albania, 99b
  alternative measures used to disrupt terrorism financing, 107–108, 108–109b
  assessing risks prior to, 17–18
  of Australia, 98–99
  beneficial ownership registries, necessity for, 129–130
  comparative analysis of, 89, 94
  of Denmark, 100
  on intelligence use for counterterrorism, 66, 67f
  on-site visits, 16, 17
  study on terrorist financing risk assessments using, 5
  on supervisory practices, 50
  technical compliance rates and, 127–128, 127n33, 128t
  terrorist financing risk assessments and, 1, 17–18
  of United Kingdom, 100
mutual legal assistance (MLA)
  capacity and mandates, 165
  conflicting legal regimes and, 160–164
  expediting requests for, 162
  governance and rule of law weaknesses and, 159
  international conventions and treaties on, 154–155b
  judicial forms of cooperation and, 158, 158n4
  limiting dual criminality requirements in, 163–164, 163b

  requirements for, 156
  simultaneous actions among countries, 176
MVTS (money or value transfer services), 27–28, 50, 70, 73–74. *See also* informal financial sector

**N**

National Central Bureau of INTERPOL, 73
*National ML and TF Risk Assessment* (FATF), 6
National Risk Assessments (NRAs)
  dissemination of results, 35–36
  good practices for, 28–30
  meetings for, 29t
  mutual evaluations and, 17–18
  scenario exercises for, 32–33, 32b
  security and intelligence services and, 16
  terrorist financing risk assessments and, 1, 11
  work phases and objectives of, 8t
  world terrorism data for, 34
national security, 83, 126, 166, 169
national vs. global targeted financial sanctions, 119–130, 128t
Netherlands, public support for technological innovations, 58
net risk, 11
nonjudicial forms of international cooperation, 156–157
nonprofit organizations, 4, 4n5, 15, 49, 104b, 127n32
Norwegian Defence Research Establishment, 96–97, 96n12
notice of designation, 150
NRAs. *See* National Risk Assessments

**O**

offshore financial centers, 98
operational working groups, 85–86
Operation CAPTIVE of INTERPOL, 175
Organization of American States, 165–166

**P**

Palermo Convention (2000), 155b
Pan Am Flight 103 bombing (1988), 164

parallel financial investigations, 84, 97, 100
Paris attacks (2015), 98, 170
Parliamentary Assembly of the Mediterranean, 161*b*
peaceful or humanitarian project funding, 102, 103*b*
Popular Front for the Liberation of Palestine (PFLP), 102
post-attack investigations, 65
poverty alleviation, 108, 109*b*
PPPs. *See* public-private partnerships
prevention of terrorist acts, 107–108, 108–109*b*
prevention of terrorist financing. *See* private sector prevention of terrorist financing
privacy rights and protections
  access to relevant information and, 53
  CFT and, 44, 51
  dissemination of financial intelligence and, 82–83
  information sources for financial intelligence and, 70
  international cooperation and, 166–169, 171
  technological innovations for information sharing and, 58
private sector. *See also* public-private partnerships
  defined, 45
  disseminating results of risk assessments to, 36
  supervision of reporting entities, 45, 49–50, 72, 77, 141–143, 146
  targeted financial sanctions, inconsistent implementation of, 141–147, 141*n*52
  terrorist financing risk assessments and, 16–17, 16*n*22
private sector prevention of terrorist financing, 41–62
  challenges and solutions for, 52–54
  financial intelligence for, 70–72
  good practices for, 54–58
  impediments to understanding risk, 46–50
  implementation of sanctions and, 140–141

limitations of, 50–52
reporting entities, effectiveness of, 42–46
procedural requirements, 160–164
prosecution of terrorist financers. *See* investigation, prosecution, and sanction of terrorist financiers
public access to designated entities lists, 134–135, 134*n*44
public announcement of targeted financial sanctions, 115, 115*n*7, 124, 124*n*27
public keys, 143*n*56, 144
public-private partnerships (PPPs)
  for dissemination of risk assessment results, 36, 36*n*38
  Europol Financial Intelligence Public Private Partnership, 173–174*b*
  examples of, 55
  private sector prevention of terrorist financing and, 41, 56, 56*n*2
  targeted risk indicators shared with, 75–76
public sector, 56, 58
Purcell, Jay, 113

Q
qualitative information, 5, 29–30, 30*n*33

R
reasonable basis or reasonable grounds standard, 135
record keeping
  of nonfinancial businesses, 46
  technological innovations for, 57
recurring financial trends, 65
regional operational working groups, 85–86
regulatory sandboxes, 58
remittances, 27–28, 49, 74
reporting entities. *See* private sector prevention of terrorist financing
resistance movements, 95–96
resource allocation, 79–80
RHIPTO, 97
Riordan, Paul, 153
risk, defined, 9
risk assessments. *See* terrorist financing risk assessments
risk heatmap, 9, 10*f*

risk levels, defined, 10–11, 10n14
risk treatments, 9, 9n12
*The Role of Financial Information-Sharing Partnerships in the Disruption of Crime* (RUSI), 76b
Royal United Service Institute for Defense and Security Studies (RUSI), 76b
rule of law weaknesses, 159, 164–165, xvii

**S**

sanctions, 52–53. *See also* investigation, prosecution, and sanction of terrorist financiers; targeted financial sanctions
scenario analyses, 32–33, 32b, 34b
Schantz, Delphine, 113
Scheme Relating to Mutual Legal Assistance in Criminal Matters within the Commonwealth (Harare Scheme), 163, 176
SEA CTFWG (Southeast Asia Counter-Terrorism Financing Working Group), 175–176b, 175
secure communications technology, 57
Secure Information Exchange Network Application (SIENA) of Europol, 86, 168, 172, 173b
Secure Web of Egmont Group, 86, 157, 168, 170b
security clearances and designations, 16, 82. *See also* classified information
Shire, Jacqueline, 113
silos of information, 82, 84–85
Singapore
 financial information-sharing partnerships, 76b
 public support for technological innovations, 58
small cell and lone actor terrorists, 64–65, 74–75b, 106
smuggling, 26–27, 50
social media
 circumstantial evidence from, 107b
 emerging payment services through, 50
 financial data combined with, 57
 FIU monitoring of, 76
Society for Worldwide Interbank Financial Telecommunication (SWIFT), 168–169b
Soufan Group, 33

Southeast Asia Counter-Terrorism Financing Working Group (SEA CTFWG), 175–176b, 175b
sovereignty, 160
Spain, investigative techniques in, 100–101
specialized liaison officers, 172b
speculative methods to assess terrorist financing risk, 30, 30–31t, 31b
stakeholders
 data for terrorist financing risk assessments and, 29
 dissemination of risk assessment results to, 35–36
 terrorist financing risk assessments and, 15–17
*Stocktake on Data Pooling, Collaborative Analytics, and Data Protection* (FATF), 58
strategic analysis and intelligence, 65, 74–75b
supervision of reporting entities, 45, 49–50, 72, 77, 141–143, 146
suspicious transaction reports (STRs)
 barriers to use, 53
 comparing rates of use to investigations, 98
 informal financial sector and, 16, 26
 information sharing leading to, 77b
 lack of, 19, 19n25
 poor quality of, 71
 rates of use, 54
 on terrorist financing, rates of use, 41
Sweden
 circumstantial evidence, use of, 107b
 disruption of terrorism financing in, 109b
 investigative techniques in, 100–101
SWIFT (Society for Worldwide Interbank Financial Telecommunication), 168–169b
Syria, Albanian FTFs in, 99b

**T**

Taliban, 95
targeted financial sanctions (TFS), 113–152
 costs of monitoring, 54
 delisting, lack of clarity and accessibility in, 148–151

FATF R.6, implementation of, 127–130, 128*t*
IMF, notifying, 126–127
inconsistent implementation by private sector, 141–147
lack of awareness and use of, 130–135
lack of implementation without delay, 135–141
limits of, 128–130
terrorist financing risk assessments and, 15, 15*n*21
understanding, 114–119
UNSCR 1267/1999, 119–122
UNSCR 1373/2001, 123–126, 125*b*
targeted risk indicators and leads, 74–76
technology innovations
database interoperability and, 78
facilitating terrorist financing, 154
for financial information analyses, 80
for FIU information sharing, 174
intelligence exchange platforms, 86, 157, 168, 172, 172–173*b*
private sector prevention of terrorist financing and, 57–58
public sector investments in, 58
targeted financial sanctions, enforcement of, 142, 145
terrorism-related targeted financial sanctions. *See* targeted financial sanctions
terrorism risk vs. financing risk
challenges, 18
good practices for, 18
moving terrorist financing funds, 20–23, 21–22*t*, 21*f*
overview, 3
terrorist financing fundraising, 19–20, 20*t*
terrorist financing fund use, 23–24, 23–24*t*
terrorist, defined, 93, 95
terrorist act, defined, 93
terrorist attacks
as consequence of terrorist financing processes, 12
financial consequences of, xvii, xvii*n*4
intelligence community and avoiding, 16
misclassification or lack of, 18, 18*n*23
terrorist financing risk and, 18–19
use of funds for, 23–24, 23–24*t*
Terrorist Finance Tracking Program (TFTP) of United States, 168–169*b*
terrorist financing
defined, 90–93, 91*n*1
financial intelligence to counter, 63–88. *See also* financial intelligence to counter terrorist financing
international cooperation to combat, 153–177. *See also* international cooperation to combat terrorist financing
private sector disruption of, 41–62. *See also* private sector prevention of terrorist financing
prosecution and sanctions resulting from, 89–111. *See also* investigation, prosecution, and sanction of terrorist financiers
risk of, 1–40. *See also* terrorist financing risk
targeted financial sanctions and, 113–152. *See also* targeted financial sanctions
terrorist financing fundraising
assessment of, 19–20
information sharing and, 76, 77*b*
investigative techniques for, 97
risk assessment methodology and, 11–13
sources of, 4, 20*t*
terrorist financing lists, 71
terrorist financing risk, 1–40
assessments for, 6–18, 8*t*, 9–10*f*, 14*b*
associated with other assets and informality, 24–28
disseminating results of risk assessments, 35–36
lack of data and information for assessments, 28–35, 29–31*t*, 31–32*b*, 34*b*
terrorism risk vs. financing risk, 18–24, 20–24*t*, 21*f*
themes and standards for action, 2–5, 3*b*
terrorist financing risk assessments
challenges, 6
dissemination of results, 35–36

terrorist financing risk assessments (*continued*)
  good practices for, 6
  logical, structured process for, 6–7, 8*t*
  methodology for, 7–17, 9–10*f*
  money laundering risk assessments and, 1, 13–15, 13*n*17
  mutual evaluations and, 1, 17–18
  private sector prevention of terrorist financing and, 52–53
  vulnerability indicators, 14*b*
Terrorist Financing Targeting Center (TFTC) of United States, 176*b*
terrorist organizations. *See also* foreign terrorist fighters; small cell and lone actor terrorists; *specific organizations*
  defined, 93, 95, 162
  designation as, 4, 123–126, 125*b*, 132, 134
  intent, proving, 89, 101–103, 103–105*b*
  proving existence of, 105–106
  use of funds for, 23–24, 23–24*t*
TFS. *See* targeted financial sanctions
TFTC (Terrorist Financing Targeting Center) of United States, 176*b*
TFTP (Terrorist Finance Tracking Program) of United States, 168–169*b*
Thailand, public support for technological innovations in, 58
third-party designation requests, 125–126, 125*b*, 132, 134–135, 135*n*45
threshold monitoring, 75*b*
transfers of criminal proceedings, 164
travel of foreign terrorist fighters, financing of, 23, 92, 99*b*
trust, international cooperation and, 159–160, 169
TWA flight hijacking (1985), 160*n*6

**U**

United Arab Emirates, disruption of terrorism financing in, 108*b*
United Kingdom
  disruption of terrorism financing in, 108*b*
  financial information-sharing partnerships, 76*b*
  mutual evaluation report of, 100

public-private partnerships for information sharing, 56, 56*n*2
public support for technological innovations, 58
United States
  financial information-sharing partnerships, 76*b*
  Germany-United States bilateral extradition treaty, 160, 160*n*6
  international intelligence sharing, 167–168*b*
  mutual legal assistance treaties, 163
  proving intent in, 102, 102*n*15, 103*b*
  targeted financial sanctions of Al-Qaida, 117
  Terrorist Finance Tracking Program, 168–169*b*
  Terrorist Financing Targeting Center, 176*b*
UN Charter, 119–120, 120*n*16, 139
UN Convention against Corruption (2003), 163
UN Convention against Transnational Organized Crime (UNTOC, 2000), 155*b*, 163
UN Convention on the Suppression of Terrorist Financing (1999). *See* International Convention for the Suppression of the Financing of Terrorism
UN Counter-Terrorism Committee, 130
UN Office of the Ombudsperson, 118, 122, 149
UN Office on Drugs and Crime (UNODC)
  Digest of Terrorist Cases, 160
  Manual on CFT MLA and Extradition, 165
  MLA Tool, 165
UN Security Council Consolidated Sanctions List
  delisting, lack of clarity and accessibility in, 148–151
  implementation by private sector, 141–147
  implementation without delay, 121, 135–141, 136*n*47
  lack of awareness of, 130–132, 131*nn*40–41

Notice system of INTERPOL used by, 173*b*
updates to, 121*n*20
UN Security Council Resolutions (UNSCRs)
classification of terrorist organizations, 4
on international cooperation, 155*b*, 158
targeted financial sanctions and, 114, 114*n*4, 119–120, 120*n*16
UN Security Council Resolution (UNSCR)
1267/1999, 95, 119–122, 127, 130
1373/2001, 123–126, 127, 130–131, 155*b*
2178/2014, 92
2253/2015, 124
2322/2016, 155*b*, 158
2462/2019, 130*n*38, 135, 155*b*
2610/2021, 120
unregulated financial sector. *See* informal financial sector

**V**

Vienna Convention on the Law of Treaties (1969), 96, 155*b*
virtual assets, 71, 114*n*2, 143–144, 143*nn*54–56
virtual asset service providers (VASPs), 45–46, 63, 143–144
vulnerability analyses, 34*b*

**W**

weapons, 75*b*
"what if" methods to assess terrorist financing risk, 30, 30–31*t*, 31*b*
wire transfers, 73
working groups, 85–86
*World Atlas of Illicit Flows*, 97
World Bank, 129
world terrorism data, 33–34, 34*b*

**Y**

Yoon, Hyung Keun, 153
Yu, Yee Man, 41